The Old Testament:
A Bibliography

OLD TESTAMENT STUDIES

Volume 5

The Old Testament

A Bibliography

Arthur E. Zannoni

A Michael Glazier Book
THE LITURGICAL PRESS
Collegeville, Minnesota

A Michael Glazier Book published by The Liturgical Press

Cover design by David Manahan, O.S.B.

1   2   3   4   5   6   7   8   9

Library of Congress Cataloging-in-Publication Data

Zannoni, Arthur E., 1942–
    The Old Testament : a bibliography / Arthur E. Zannoni.
      p.   cm. — (Old Testament studies ; v. 5)
    "A Michael Glazier book."
    ISBN 0-8146-5658-7
    1. Bible. O.T.—Bibliography.   I. Title.   II. Series: Old
Testament studies (Wilmington, Del.) ; v. 5.
Z7772.A1Z36   1992
[BS1171.2]
016.221—dc20
                                    92-18820
                                    CIP

CONTENTS

INTRODUCTION

When attempting to compile a bibliography on the Old Testament I had to place some limitations on the research to make the task manageable. The material contained in the bibliographical lists is limited primarily to books with English-speakers in mind, though I have included some periodical articles and a few foreign language items. The lists are intended to be functional, not encyclopedic. No attempt was made to include bibliographical resources found on computerized data bases nor audio or video tape recordings.

The selections contained herein represent my interpretation of what should prove to be most useful for students, Christian educators, librarians, professional theologians, clergy, lay ministers and interested laity. Although some evangelical Christians may feel neglected and biblical fundamentalists excluded, I have attempted to be ecumenical in selecting authors and their publications. The entries include works published through 1989, with a moderate selection of 1990 titles.

My aim is to present both classic works in the field and an up-to-date representative sample of books and some articles available on a wide range of topics and disciplines utilized in the serious study of the Old Testament. The topics under the headings "Old Testament Theology and Themes" and "The World of the Old Testament" are quite vast and somewhat complicated so I have selected a wide variety of sources for the reader to consult. The section entitled "Excursus: Biblical Fundamentalism" may seem odd in a bibliography of this nature, but in my experience as a teacher of both undergraduate and graduate students I have discovered that many of my students are often looking for material to read in this area.

No publication is ever the product of any one individual. I consulted with my former colleagues at the University of St. Thomas, Dr. Gale A. Yee and Fr. Peter E. Wang. Dr. James Limburg and Dr. Terrence E. Fretheim of Luther Northwestern Theological Seminary were generous with their suggestions and the sharing of bibliographical lists from their own research. Dr. David M. Howard of

Bethel Theological Seminary and Dr. Chris A. Franke of the College of St. Catherine were also helpful as was Dr. Walter A. Brueggemann of Columbia Theological Seminary in Decatur, Georgia. He reviewed the original book prospectus and made helpful suggestions. Dr. Bruce V. Malchow of Sacred Heart School of Theology in Hales Corners, Wisconsin, provided resources and helpful criticism of the original outline for the book.

I wish to thank and acknowledge the assistance of the staff of the John Ireland Memorial Library, especially Ms. Mary Martin, Ms. Betty Bigelbach and Ms. Karen Batdorf for their invaluable assistance in helping me with my research. I would also like to acknowledge the support and encouragement of my former faculty colleagues at the School of Divinity, Fr. Charles L. Froehle, Rector/ Vice President, Dr. Gene A. Scapanski, Dr. Victor J. Klimoski, Sr. M. Christine Athans, B.V.M., and Sr. Carol Rennie, O.S.B. A sincere thanks goes to my student research assistants Kevin Boucher and David L. Gottwalt as well as Kevin Donohue, Daniel Van Treeck, and Jeff Zyla who spent countless hours in word processing. Two people deserve special mention, Gerald J. Milske who as Office Coordinator and secretary to the Graduate Faculty at the School of Divinity gave of himself in countless hours of proofreading and preparation of the final text; and to my wife Kathleen Flannery Zannoni who helped me keep a sense of balance throughout the project.

It is my hope that this bibliography will prove to be a contribution to, and a ready resource for, the continued study of the Old Testament.

Arthur E. Zannoni

I. TEXTS AND TOOLS

1. ATLASES

Aharoni, Y. *The Macmillan Bible Atlas*. New York: Macmillan, 1977.

_____. *The Land of the Bible: A Historical Geography*. Philadelphia: Westminster; London: Burns & Oates, 1979–80.

Baly, D. *Atlas of the Biblical World*. New York: Word, 1971.

Beitzel, B. *The Moody Atlas of Bible Lands*. Chicago: Moody, 1987.

Blaiklock, E. M., ed. *Zondervan Pictorial Bible Atlas*. Grand Rapids: Zondervan, 1969.

Bruce, F. T. *Bible History Atlas*. New York: Crossroad, 1982.

Eerdmans' Atlas of the Bible. Grand Rapids: Eerdmans, 1983.

Frank, H., ed. *Atlas of the Bible Lands*. Maplewood: Hammond, 1990.

Gaener, J. L., ed. *Reader's Digest Atlas of the Bible*. Pleasantville: Reader's Digest, 1971.

Grollenberg, L. H. *Atlas of the Bible*. London: Nelson, 1957.

_____. *Shorter Atlas of the Bible*. New York: Nelson, 1961.

_____. *The Penguin Shorter Atlas of the Bible*. Harmondsworth–Baltimore: Penguin, 1978.

Hammond Incorporated. *Hammond's Atlas of the Bible Lands*. H. T. Frank, ed. Maplewood: Hammond, 1977.

Laney, J. *Baker's Concise Bible Atlas: A Geographical Survey of Bible History*. Grand Rapids: Baker, 1988.

May, H. G., ed. *Oxford Bible Atlas*. London–New York: Oxford University Press, 1962, 1974, 1984.

Negenman, J. H. *New Atlas of the Bible*. Garden City: Doubleday, 1980.

1

Paterson, J. and D. Wiseman, eds. *New Bible*. Wheaton: Tyndale, 1985.

Pfeiffer, C. F. *Baker's Pocket Atlas of the Bible*. Grand Rapids: Baker, 1973.

Pritchard, J. B., ed. *The Harper Atlas of the Bible*. New York: Harper & Row, 1987.

Rasmussen, C. G. *The Zondervan NIV Atlas of the Bible*. Grand Rapids: Zondervan, 1989.

Rogerson, J. W. *Atlas of the Bible*. New York: Facts on File, 1985, 1988.

Rowley, H. H. *Modern Reader's Bible Atlas*. New York: Association, 1961.

_____. *Student's Bible Atlas*. Cleveland: World, 1965.

_____. *The Teach Yourself Bible Atlas*. London: English Universities Press, 1960.

Wright, G. E. and F. V. Filson. *The Westminster Historical Atlas to the Bible*. Rev. ed. Philadelphia: Westminster, 1956.

2. BIBLIOGRAPHIES

Ackroyd, P. R. *Bible Bibliography 1967–1973. Old Testament Book Lists of the Society for Old Testament Study*. Oxford: Blackwell, 1974.

Anderson, G. W., ed. *A Decade of Bible Bibliography. (The Book Lists of the Society for Old Testament Studies, 1957–1966)*. Oxford: Blackwell, 1967.

Auld, A. G., ed. *The Society For Old Testament Study: Book List 1989*. Leeds: W. S. Maney, 1989.

Brock, S. P., C. T. Fritsch and S. Jellicoe. "A Classified Bibliography of the Septuagint." *Arbeiten zur Literatur und Geschichte des Hellenistischen Judentums, VI*. Leiden: Brill, 1973.

_____. *A Classified Bibliography of the Septuagint*. Leiden: Brill, 1973.

Childs, B. S. *Old Testament Books for Pastor and Teacher* Philadelphia: Westminster, 1977.

Dawsey, J. *A Scholar's Guide to Academic Journals in Religion.* Metuchen: Scarecrow, 1988.

Fitzmyer, J. A. *An Introductory Bibliography for the Study of Scripture.* Rev. ed. Rome: Biblical Institute Press, 1981.

Gottcent, J. H. *The Bible as Literature: A Selective Bibliography.* Boston: Hall, 1979.

Gotwald, N. K. *Theological Bibliographies; Essential Books for a Minister's Library.* Newton Centre, Mass.: Andover Newton Theological School, 1963, 1964, 1966.

Hupper, W. G. *Index to English Periodical Literature on the Old Testament and Ancient Near Eastern Studies.* 3 vols. Metuchen: Scarecrow, 1987, 1988, 1990.

Montalvo, D. E. *Index of Subject Indices: Old Testament, 1975–1983.* Philadelphia: Aloya, 1984.

North, R., ed. *Elenchus Bibliographicus Biblicus.* Rome: Biblical Institute Press, 1968 to present.

Old Testament Abstracts. Washington D. C.: The Catholic Biblical Association of America, 1978–to present.

Petersen, P. D. *Evangelicalism and Fundamentalism: A Bibliography Selected From the ATLA Religion Data Base.* Chicago: American Theological Library Association, 1983.

Purvis, J. D. *Jerusalem, The Holy City: A Bibliography.* Metuchen: Scarecrow, 1988.

Rounds, D. *Articles on Antiquity in Festschriften. The Ancient Near East. The Old Testament, Greece/Rome/Byzantium.* Cambridge: Harvard University Press, 1962.

Rowley, H. H., ed. *Eleven years of Bible Bibliography: The Book Lists of the Society for Old Testament Study, 1946–56.* Indian Hills: Falcon's Wing, 1957.

Suder, R. W. *Hebrew Inscriptions. A Classified Bibliography.* London–Toronto: Associated University Presses, 1984.

Van Der Wal, A. *Micah: A Classified Bibliography.* Amsterdam: Free University Press, 1990.

3. HEBREW TEXTS AND ANCIENT VERSIONS

Barock, S. P. "The Phenomenon of the Septuagint." *Old Testament Studies* 17 (1972) 11–36.

Biblia Hebraica. 3rd ed. Stuttgart: Württembergische Bibelanstalt, 1937.

Biblia Hebraica. London: Duncan, 1825, 1837.

Biblia Hebraica. Wien: Holzhausen, 1887, 1896, 1898.

Biblia Sacra Vulgata Editionis. Rome: Editiones Paulinae, 1957.

Brenton, L. C. *The Septuagint with Apocrypha: Greek and English.* Peabody: Hendrickson, 1986.

Brockington, L. H., ed. *The Hebrew Text of the Old Testament: The Readings Adopted for the Translators of the New English Bible.* London–New York: Oxford University Press, 1973.

Brooke, A. E., N. McLean and H. Thackeray. *The Old Testament in Greek According to the Text of the Codex Vaticanus.* Cambridge: The University Press, 1966.

————. *The Old Testament in Greek.* Cambridge: Cambridge University Press, 1906–1940.

Brown, R. E., D. W. Johnson and K. G. O'Connell. "Text and Versions." *The New Jerome Biblical Commentary,* ed. by R. Brown et al. Englewood Cliffs: Prentice Hall, 1990. Pp. 1083–1112.

Bruce, F. F. *The Books and the Parchments.* Rev. ed. Old Tappan: Revell, 1984.

Bulletin of the International Organization for Septuagint and Cognate Studies. (A learned journal that reviews annually the latest developments in Septuagint Research.)

Colunga, A. and T. Laurentio, eds. *Biblia Vulgata.* Madrid: Biblioteca de Autores Cristianos, 1965.

Conybeare, F. C. *A Grammar of Septuagint Greek.* Grand Rapids: Zondervan, 1980.

Danker, F. W. *Multipurpose Tools for Bible Study.* 3rd ed. St. Louis: Concordia, 1970.

Elliger, K. and W. Rudolph, eds. *Biblia Hebraica Stuttgartensis.* Stuttgart: Deutsche Bibelstiftung, 1967–1977.

Fisher, L. R. *Ras Shamra Parallels: The Texts from Ugarit and the Hebrew Bible.* 3 vols. Rome: Biblical Institute Press, 1972–75.

_____. *The Claremont Ras Shamra Tablets.* Rome: Biblical Institute Press, 1971.

Gordis, R. *The Biblical Text in the Making.* New York: Ktav, 1971.

Green, J. P., gen. ed. *The Interlinear Bible: Hebrew/English.* Evansville: Associated, 1976; reprinted Baker, 1979.

_____., ed. *The Interlinear Hebrew/Greek English Bible.* 4 vols. Wilmington–Evansville: Associated, 1976–78.

Hoftijzer, J. and G. Van der Kooij. *Aramaic Texts from Deir 'Alla.* Leiden: Brill, 1976.

Holmes, R. *Vetus Testamentum Graecum cum Variis Lectionibus.* Oxford: Clarendon, 1798–1827.

Jeffrey, A. "Text and Ancient Versions of the Old Testament." *The Interpreter's Bible* Vol. I, New York: Abingdon–Cokesbury, 1951–57. Pp. 46–62.

Jellicoe, S., ed. *Studies in the Septuagint: Origins, Recension and Interpretations: Selected with a Prolegomenon.* New York: Ktav, 1974.

_____. *The Septuagint and Modern Study.* Oxford: Clarendon, 1968.

Kenyon, F. *Our Bible and the Ancient Manuscripts.* London: Eyre & Spottiswoock, 1962.

Kittel R., ed. *Biblia Hebraica.* Lipsiae: Hinrichs, 1909, 1962.

Klein, R. W. *Textual Criticism of the Old Testament: The Septuagint After Qumran.* Philadelphia: Fortress, 1974.

Kohlenberger, J. R., III. *The NIV Interlinear Hebrew-English Old Testament.* 4 vols. Grand Rapids: Zondervan, 1979.

Magil, J. *The Englishman's Linear Hebrew Old Testament.* Grand Rapids: Zondervan, 1974.

McCarter, P. K., Jr. *Textual Criticism: Recovering the Text of the Hebrew Bible.* Philadelphia: Fortress, 1986.

Nova Vulgata Bibliorum Sacrorum Editio. Vatican City: Libreria Editrice Vaticana, 1979, 1986.

Ottley, R. R. *A Handbook to the Septuagint.* London: Methuen, 1920.

Peshitta Institute of Leiden, eds. *The Old Testament in Syriac.* Leiden: Brill, 1972.

Roberts, B. J. "The Textual Transmission of the Old Testament." In *Tradition and Interpretation.* G. W. Anderson. London–New York: Oxford University Press, 1979. Pp. 1–30.

Septuaginta: Vetus Testamentum Graecum Auctoritate Societatis Litterarum Gottengensis Editum. Gottingen: Vandenhoeck & Ruprecht, 1931.

Sivete, H. B. *An Introduction to the Old Testament in Greek.* Cambridge: University Press, 1914.

Sollamo, R. *Renderings of Hebrew Semiprepositions in the Septuagint.* Helsinki: Suomalainen Tiedeakatemia, 1979.

Sperber, A., ed. *The Bible in Aramaic.* 4 vols. Leiden: Brill, 1959–1973.

Swete, H. B. *The Old Testament in Greek According to the Septuagint.* 2nd ed. Cambridge: Cambridge University Press, 1895–1899.

The Collective Catalogue of Hebrew Manuscripts. Paris–Cambridge–Alexandria: Chadwych Healey, 1989.

The Holy Scriptures According to the Masoretic Text. 2 vols. Philadelphia: Jewish Publication Society of America, 1955.

The Septuagint Version of the Old Testament with an English Translation. New York: Pott, 1896.

The Septuagint Versions of the Old Testament. Grand Rapids: Zondervan, 1970.

Thomas, D. R. *A Primer of Old Testament Text Criticism.* Oxford: Blackwell, 1965.

Tove, E. *The Text-Critical Use of the Septuagint in Biblical Research.* Jerusalem: Simor, 1981.

Vetus Testamentum Syriace et Neosyriace. London: Trinitarian Bible Society, 1954.

Waldman, N. M. *The Recent Study of Hebrew: A Survey of the Literature with Selected Bibliography.* Cincinnati: Hebrew Union College Press, 1989.

Weber, R. et al., eds. *Biblia Sacra Juxta Vulgatam Versionem.* 2 vols. Stuttgart: Würtenbergische Bibelanstalt, 1969.

Weingren, J. *Introduction to the Critical Study of the Text of the Hebrew Bible.* London–New York: Oxford University Press, 1982.

Wonneberger, R. *Understanding BHS. A Manual for the Users of Biblia Hebraica Stuttgartensia.* Rome: Biblical Institute Press, 1984.

Wurthwein, E. *The Text of the Old Testament.* Oxford: Blackwell, 1957; Rev. ed. Grand Rapids: Eerdmans, 1979.

4. HEBREW, GREEK AND LATIN CONCORDANCES

Baird, A. and D. N. Freedman, eds. *The Computer Bible: A Critical Concordance.* Wooster: Biblical Research Associates, 1970.

Davidson, B. *A Concordance of the Hebrew and Chaldee Scriptures.* London: Bagster, 1876.

Even-Shoshan, A. *A New Concordance of the Bible.* Jerusalem: Kiryat Sepher, 1980.

Fischer, B. *Novae Concordantiae Bibliorum Sacrorum Juxta Vulgatum Versionem Critice Editam.* 5 vols. Stuttgart–Bart Cannstatt: Friedrich Frommann Verlag Gunther Holzbooz, 1977.

Furst, J. *Librorum sacrorum Veteris Testamenti concordantiae Hebraicae atque Chaldaicae adito lexico linguae sacrae Hebraicae et Chaldaicae duplici uno Neohebraice altero latine scripto.* Lipsiae: Sumtibus et Typis Caroli Tauchnitii, 1840.

Hatch, E. and H. A. Redpath. *A Concordance to the Septuagint and Other Greek Versions of the Old Testament.* 3rd ed. 2 vols. Graz: Akademische Druck u. Verlagsanstalt, 1955.

Hatch, E. *A Concordance to the Septuagint and the other Greek versions of the Old Testament (including the apocryphal books).* Graz: Akademische Druck u. Verlagsanstalt, 1954–75.

Lisowsky, G. *Konkordanz zum hebräischen Alten Testament.* Stuttgart: Württembergische Bibelanstalt, 1958.

Loewenstamm, S. E., ed. *Thesaurus of the Language of the Bible: Complete Concordance Hebrew Bible Dictionary, Hebrew-English Bible Dictionary.* Jerusalem: Bible Concordance, 1957.

Mandelkern, S. *Veteris Testamenti: Concordantiae Hebraicae atque Chaldaicae.* 8th ed. Jerusalem: Schocken, 1969.

Mohrish, G. *A Concordance of the Septuagint.* London: Bagster; reprinted Grand Rapids: Zondervan, 1976.

Santos, E. C. *An Expanded Hebrew Index for the Hatch-Redpath Concordance for the Septuagint.* Jerusalem: Dugith, 1973.

Taylor, J. *The Hebrew Concordance, Adapted to the English Bible.* London: Waugh & Fenner, 1754–1757.

The Englishman's Hebrew and Chaldee Concordance of the Old Testament. London: Bagster, 1874.

Tov, E. *A Computerized Data Base for Septuagint Studies: The Parallel Aligned Text of the Greek and Hebrew Bible.* Stellenbosch: JNSL, 1986.

Wigram, G. V. *The Englishman's Hebrew and Chaldee Concordance of the Old Testament.* London: Bagster, 3rd ed., 1874; reprinted Grand Rapids: Zondervan, 1978; Baker, 1980.

_____, ed. *The Hebraist's Vademecum.* London: Groombridge, 1867.

_____. *The Englishman's Hebrew and Chaldee Concordance of the Old Testament Numerically Coded to Strong's Exhaustive Concordance.* Milford: Mott Media, 1980.

_____. *The Englishman's Hebrew and Chaldee Concordance of the Old Testament.* London: Bagster, 1952.

_____. *The New Englishman's Hebrew Concordance: Coded to Strong's Concordance Numbering System.* Peabody: Hendrickson, 1984.

Young, G. D. *Concordance of Ugaritic.* Rome: Pontifical Biblical Institute, 1956.

5. HEBREW LEXICA AND GRAMMARS

Anderson, F. I. and A. D. Forbes. *Spelling in the Hebrew Bible.* Rome: Biblical Institute Press, 1986.

Armstrong, T. A. *A Reader's Hebrew-English Lexicon of the Old Testament.* Grand Rapids: Zondervan, 1980–1982.

Armstrong, T. A., D. L. Busby and C. F. Carr. *Reader's Hebrew-English Lexicon of the Old Testament.* 4 vols. in 1. Grand Rapids: Zondervan, 1989.

Avishur, Y. *Stylistic Studies of Word-Pairs in Biblical and Ancient Semitic Literatures.* Neukirchen-Vlyn: Neukirchner-Kevelaer, Butzon & Bercker, 1984.

Brown, F., S. R. Driver, and C. A. Briggs. *Hebrew and English Lexicon of the Old Testament.* Oxford: Clarendon, 1966.

Carlson, E. L. *Elementary Hebrew.* Grand Rapids: Baker, 1956.

Claassen, W. T., ed. *Text and Context. Old Testament and Semitic Studies for F. C. Fensham.* Sheffield: JSOT, 1988.

Creager, H. L. *Beginner's Hebrew Grammar.* New York: Heath, 1927.

Dahood, M. *Ugaritic-Hebrew Philology.* Rome: Biblical Institute Press, 1965.

Davidson, A. B. *A Key to the Exercises in the Introductory Hebrew Grammar.* Edinburgh: T & T Clark, 1991.

_____. *An Introductory Hebrew Grammar.* Edinburgh: T & T Clark, 1991.

Davidson, B. *The Analytical Hebrew and Chaldee Lexicon.* London: Bagster, 1848, 2nd ed. 1850; reprinted Grand Rapids: Zondervan, 1970; Lynn: Hendrikson, 1981.

Einspahr, B. *Index to the Brown, Driver and Briggs Hebrew Lexicon.* Chicago: Moody, 1976.

Gesenius, F. H. *Gesenius' Hebrew Grammar.* London: Asher, 1885.

Gesenius' Hebrew and Chaldee Lexicon to the Old Testament Scriptures: Numerically Coded to Strong's Exhaustive Concordance. Grand Rapids: Baker, 1979.

_____ and E. Kautzsch. *Gesenius' Hebrew Grammar.* 2nd ed. London–New York: Oxford University Press, 1910, 15th printing [1980].

Goodrick, E. W. *Do it Yourself Hebrew and Greek: Everybody's Guide to the Language Tools.* Grand Rapids: Zondervan; Portland: Multnomah, 1980.

Gordon, C. H. *Ugaritic Textbook.* Rome: Biblical Institute Press, 1965.

Green, J. P. and M. A. Robinson. *A Concise Lexicon to the Biblical Languages.* Lynn: Hendrickson, 1987.

Greenberg, M. *Introduction to Hebrew.* Englewood Cliffs: Prentice Hall, 1965.

Harper, W. R. *Introductory Hebrew Method and Manual.* Chicago: University of Chicago Press, 1969.

Harris, R. L., G. L. Archer and B. J. Waltke, eds. *Theological Wordbook of the Old Testament.* Chicago: Moody, 1980.

Holladay, W. L. *A Concise Hebrew and Aramaic Lexicon of the Old Testament.* Grand Rapids: Eerdmans, 1971.

Hunter, A. V. *Biblical Hebrew Workbook. An Inductive Study for Beginners.* Lanham: University Press of America, 1988.

Johns, A. F. *A Short Grammar of Biblical Aramaic.* Berrien Springs: Andrews University Press, 1972.

Kittel, B. P., V. Hoffer, and R. A. Wright. *Biblical Hebrew: A Text and Workbook.* New Haven: Yale University Press, 1989.

Koehler, L. and W. Baumgartner. *Supplementum ad Lexicon in Veteris Testamenti Libros.* Leiden: Brill, 1958.

Koehler, L. H. *Lexicon in Veteris Testamenti Libros.* Leiden: Brill, 1948.

La Sor, W. S. *Handbook of Biblical Hebrew.* 2 vols. Grand Rapids: Eerdmans, 1978.

Lambdin, T. O. *Introduction to Biblical Hebrew.* New York: Scribner's, 1971.

Liddell, H. G. and R. Scott. *A Greek–English Lexicon.* Rev. ed. augmented by H. S. Jones. Oxford: Clarendon, 1940.

Mansoor, M. *Biblical Hebrew Step by Step. Vol. 1.* Grand Rapids: Baker, 1957, 1978.

_____. *Biblical Hebrew Step by Step. Vol. 2.* 3rd ed. Grand Rapids: Baker, 1984.

Martinez, E. R. *Hebrew-Ugaritic Index to the Writings of Mitchell J. Dahood.* Rome: Biblical Institute Press, 1967, 1981.

Mauchline, J. *An Introductory Hebrew Grammar with Progressive Exercises in Reading, Writing and Printing.* Edinburgh: Clark, 1962.

Moulton, H. K., ed. *The Analytical Greek Lexicon Revised.* Grand Rapids: Zondervan, 1978.

Muraoka, T. *Emphatic Words and Structures in Biblical Hebrew.* Jerusalem: Magnes, 1985.

_____. *Modern Hebrew for Biblical Scholars.* Sheffield: The University Press, 1982.

Osburn, W., Jr. *A Hebrew-English Lexicon to the Old Testament.* Grand Rapids: Zondervan, 1982.

Polzin, R. *Late Biblical Hebrew: Toward an Historical Typology of Biblical Hebrew Prose.* Missoula: Scholars, 1976.

Robinson, M. A. *Indexes to All Editions of Brown-Driver-Briggs Hebrew Lexicon and Thayer's Greek Lexicon.* Grand Rapids: Baker, 1981.

Rooker, M. *Biblical Hebrew in Transition: The Language of the Book of Ezekiel.* JSOT Supp. Sheffield: JSOT, 1990.

Rosenthal, F. *A Grammar of Biblical Aramaic.* Wiesbaden: Otto Harrassowitz, 1961.

Sawyer, J. F. *A Modern Introduction to Biblical Hebrew.* Boston: Oriel, 1976.

Schacther, H. *The New Universal Hebrew English Dictionary.* 2 vols. 2nd ed. Tel-Aviv, Israel: Yavneh, 1962.

Shisha-Halevy, A. *Coptic Grammatical Categories.* Rome: Biblical Institute Press, 1986.

Sperber, A. *A Historical Grammar of Biblical Hebrew.* Leiden: Brill, 1966.

Vasholz, R. I. *Hebrew Exercises. A Programmed Approach.* Grand Rapids: Baker, 1981.

Vogt, E. *Lexicon Linguae Aramaicae Veteris Testamenti Documentis Antiquis Illustratum.* Rome: Pontifical Biblical Institute, 1971.

Waltke, B. K. and M. O'Connor. *Introduction to Biblical Hebrew Syntax.* Winona Lake: Eisenbrauns, 1989.

Watts, J. D. *Lists of Words Occurring Frequently in the Hebrew Bible.* Grand Rapids: Eerdmans, 1959.

Weingren, J. *A Practical Grammar for Classical Hebrew.* Oxford: Clarendon, 1959.

Williams, R. J. *Hebrew Syntax: An Outline.* 2nd ed. Toronto–Buffalo–London: University of Toronto Press, 1976.

Yates, K. M. *The Essentials of Biblical Hebrew.* New York: Harpers, 1956.

6. MODERN ENGLISH TRANSLATIONS

Albright, W. F. and D. N. Freedman, eds. *The Anchor Bible.* Garden City: Doubleday, 1964. (A multi–volume ongoing series.)

Arbez, E. "Modern Translations of the Old Testament: V. English Language Translations." *Catholic Biblical Quarterly* 17 (1955) 456–485.

Bailey, L. R., ed. *The Word of God: A Guide to English Versions of the Bible.* Atlanta: Knox, 1982.

Beekman, J. and J. Callow. *Translating the Word of God.* Grand Rapids: Zondervan, 1974.

Bruce, F. F. *History of the Bible in English: From the Earliest Versions.* 3rd ed. New York–London: Oxford University Press, 1978.

Christian Community Bible. Philippines: Claretian; Bloomington: Meyer Stone, 1989.

Frank, H. T. and W. L. Reed, eds. *Translating and Understanding the Old Testament.* New York: Abingdon, 1970.

Good News Bible with Deuterocanonicals/Aprocrypha. The Bible in Today's English Version. New York: American Bible Society,1979.

Goodspeed, E. J. *The Complete Bible, an American Translation.* Chicago: University of Chicago Press, 1948.

Hann, R. R. *The Bible: An Owner's Manual. What You Need to Know Before You Buy and Read Your Own Bible.* New York: Paulist, 1983.

Harper Study Bible. (Revised Standard Version.) San Francisco: Harper & Row, 1964.

Holy Bible from the Ancient Eastern Text. New York: Harper, 1957.

Huberman, B. "Translating the Bible." *Atlantic Monthly* 253 (1985) 43–58.

Kohlenberger, J. R. *The NIV Triglot Old Testament.* Grand Rapids: Zondervan, 1981.

Kubo, S. and W. Specht. *So Many Versions?* Grand Rapids: Zondervan, 1975.

Lewlis, J. P. *The English Bible: From KJV to NIV.* Grand Rapids: Baker, 1981.

May, H. G., and B. M. Metzger. *The New Oxford Annotated Bible with the Apocrypha.* New York: Oxford University Press, 1973.

New American Standard Bible. Rev. ed. Philadelphia: Holman, 1976.

New American Standard Bible. New York: World, 1972.

New Revised Standard Version. New York: Collins, 1989.

New Revised Standard Version. The New Oxford Annotated Bible with the Apocrypha. New York: Oxford University Press, 1991.

Pope, H. *English Versions of the Bible.* St. Louis: Herder, 1952.

Roberts, B. J. *The Old Testament Text and Versions.* Cardiff: University of Wales Press, 1951.

Robinson, H. W. *The Bible in Its Ancient and English Versions.* London–New York: Oxford University Press, 1954.

Scofield, C. I., ed. *The New Scofield Reference Bible.* New York: Oxford University Press, 1967.

Senior, D., gen. ed. *The Catholic Study Bible.* New York: Oxford University Press, 1990.

The Holy Bible Containing the Old and New Testaments. Revised Standard Version. Division of Christian Education of the National Council of Churches of Christ in the United States of America, 1946, 1952, 1971.

The Holy Bible. New International Version. Containing the Old Testament and the New Testament. Grand Rapids: Zondervan, 1978.

The Holy Bible, Translated From the Original Languages with Critical Use of All the Ancient Sources by members of the Catholic Biblical Association of America sponsored by the Episcopal Committee of the Confraternity of Christian Doctrine. Paterson: St. Anthony Guild, 1952.

The Jerusalem Bible. Garden City: Doubleday, 1966.

The New American Bible. Translated From the Original Languages with Critical Use of all the Ancient Sources by members of the Catholic Biblical Association of America, sponsored by the Bishops' Committee of the Confraternity of Christian Doctrine. New York: Catholic Book, 1970.

The New English Bible with the Apocrypha. New York: Oxford University Press and Cambridge University Press, 1970.

The New English Bible. New York: Oxford University Press, 1961.

The New Jerusalem Bible. Garden City: Doubleday, 1985.

The NIV Study Bible. London: Hodder & Stoughton, 1987; Grand Rapids: Zondervan, 1989.

The Prophets – Nevi'im. A New Translation of the Holy Scriptures According to the Traditional Hebrew Text. 2nd ed. Philadelphia: Jewish Publication Society, 1978.

The Thompson Chain Reference Bible. 5th ed. New York: Kirkbridge, 1964.

Wikgran, A. "The English Versions of the Bible." *Peake's Commentary on Holy Scripture*. London–New York: Nelson, 1962. Pp. 24–28.

Wikgren, A. "The English Bible." *The Interpreter's Bible*. Vol. I. New York: Abingdon–Cokesbury, 1952. Pp. 84–105.

Zimmermann, F. *Biblical Books Translated from the Aramaic*. New York: Ktav, 1975.

7. ENGLISH LANGUAGE CONCORDANCES

Baily, L. R. "What a Concordance Can Do For You. The Bible Word by Word." *Biblical Archaeology Review* 10 (1984) 60–67.

Concordance to the Aprocrypha/Deuterocanonical Books of the Revised Standard Version. Grand Rapids: Eerdmans, 1982.

Cruden, A. *Complete Concordance to the Old and New Testaments*. Guildford: Lutterworth, 1930; Grand Rapids: Baker, 1953.

Davidson, B. *A Concordance to the Hebrew and Chaldee Scriptures*. London: Bagster, 1876.

Elder, E., ed. *Concordance to the New English Bible*. Grand Rapids: Zondervan, 1964.

Ellison, J. W. *Nelson's Complete Concordance of the Revised Standard Version Bible*. Nashville: Nelson, 1984.

Even-Soshan, A. *A New Concordance of the Old Testament: Using the Hebrew and Aramaic Text*. Jerusalem: Kiryat Sepher, 1982; Grand Rapids: Baker, 1984.

Goodrick, E. W. and J. R. Kohlenberger, eds. *The NIV Complete Concordance. The Complete English Concordance to the New International Version*. Grand Rapids: Zondervan, 1981.

Goodrick, E. W. *The NIV Concordance: The Complete English Concordance to the New International Version.* Grand Rapids: Zondervan, 1981.

Griffith, H. K. *The New World Idea Index to the Holy Bible.* New York: Word, 1972.

Hartdegen, S. J. *Nelson's Complete Concordance of The New American Bible.* Nashville–New York: Nelson; Collegeville: The Liturgical Press, 1977.

Metzger, B. M. *The Oxford Concise Concordance to the Revised Standard Version of the Holy Bible.* New York: Oxford University Press, 1962.

New American Standard Bible Concordance to the Old and New Testaments. La Habra: Foundation, 1972.

Robinson, D., ed. *Concordance to the Good News Bible.* Swindon: Bible Society, 1983.

Speer, J. A. *The Living Bible Concordance Complete.* Poolesville: Poolesville Presbyterian Church, 1973.

Strong, J. *The New Strong's Exhaustive Concordance of the Bible.* Nashville: Nelson, 1984.

Strong, J. *Strong's Exhaustive Concordance.* Grand Rapids: Baker, 1976.

Thomas, R. L., ed. *New American Standard Exhaustive Concordance of the Bible.* Nashville: Holman, 1981.

Whitaker, R. E. and J. E. Goehring, comp. *The Eerdmans Analytical Concordance to the Revised Standard Version of the Bible.* Grand Rapids: Eerdmans, 1988.

Young, R. *Young's Analytical Concordance to the Bible.* Grand Rapids: Eerdmans, 1971, 1977, 1982.

a. Topical Concordances

Most persons are familiar with word concordances. A word concordance can serve both to facilitate word studies and to guide the reader to biblical context data.

In addition to word concordances, however, there are topical concordances, which group together biblical passages related to one another by a common topic or theme. These can be immensely valuable in suggesting to the reader other passages related to the one on which you are working.

Useful topical concordances are listed below.

Hitchcock, R. D. *Baker's Topical Bible.* Grand Rapids: Baker, 1952.

Joy, C. R. *Harper's Topical Concordance.* Rev. ed. San Francisco: Harper & Row, 1976.

Nave, O. J. *Nave's Topical Bible.* Chicago: Moody, 1974.

The Holman Topical Concordance. Philadelphia: Holman, 1973.

Viening, E. *The Zondervan Topical Bible.* Grand Rapids: Zondervan, 1969.

Wigram, G. V. and R. D. Winter. *The Word Study Concordance.* Wheaton: Tyndale; Pasadena: William Carey Library, 1978.

8. BIBLICAL DICTIONARIES AND ENCYCLOPEDIAS

Achtemeier, P. J. *Harper's Bible Dictionary.* San Francisco: Harper & Row, 1985.

Ackroyd, P., C. Evans, G. Lampe and S. Greenslade, eds. *Cambridge History of the Bible.* 3 vols. Cambridge: University Press, 1963–1970.

Anderson, B. W. *The Books of the Bible.* New York: Scribners, 1989.

Bauer, J. B., ed. *Encyclopedia of Biblical Theology: The Complete Sacramentum Verbi.* New York: Crossroad, 1981.

Blair, E. P., ed. *Abingdon Bible Handbook.* Nashville: Abingdon, 1975.

Botterweck, G. J. and H. Ringgren, eds. *Theological Dictionary of the Old Testament.* Vols. I–VI complete. Work is still in progress. Grand Rapids: Eerdmans, 1974–1980.

Bromiley, G. W., ed. *The International Standard Bible Encyclopedia.* 4 vols. Grand Rapids: Eerdmans, 1979.

Buttrick, G. A. et al., eds. *The Interpreter's Dictionary of the Bible. An Illustrated Encylopedia.* 5 vols. New York–Nashville: Abingdon, 1962, 1976.

Cheyne, T. K. *Encyclopedia Dictionary of the Bible.* New York: Mc-Graw Hill, 1963.

Crim, K., ed. *The Interpreter's Dictionary of the Bible.* Supplementary volume. Nashville: Abingdon, 1976.

Douglas, J. D. *The New Bible Dictionary.* Grand Rapids: Eerdmans, 1962, 1965.

Douglas, J. D., rev. ed. and M. Tenney, gen. ed. *The NIV Compact Dictionary of the Bible.* Grand Rapids: Eerdmans, 1987.

Eerdman's Family Encyclopedia of the Bible. Grand Rapids: Eerdmans, 1978.

Elwell, W. A., ed. *Baker Encyclopedia of the Bible.* 2 vols. Grand Rapids: Baker, 1988.

Encyclopedia Judaica. 16 vols. Jerusalem: Keter; New York: Macmillan, 1971.

Gehman, H. S., ed. *The New Westminster Dictionary of the Bible.* Philadelphia: Westminster, 1970, 1982.

Grant, F. and H. H. Rowley. *Dictionary of the Bible.* Rev. ed. New York: Scribner's, 1963.

Gray, J. C. *The Biblical Encyclopedia.* Cleveland: Barton, 1903.

Harper's Bible Dictionary. San Francisco: Harper & Row, 1985.

Harris, R. L., ed., G. L. Archer, Jr., and B. K. Waltke, assoc. eds. *Theological Wordbook of the Old Testament.* Chicago: Moody, 1980.

Hartman, L. F., ed. *Encyclopedic Dictionary of the Bible.* New York–London: McGraw Hill, 1963.

Hastings, J. A., ed. *A Dictionary of the Bible.* 5 vols. Edinburgh: Clark, 1931.

Hillyer, N. et. al., eds. *The Illustrated Bible Dictionary.* 3 vols. Leicester: Inter-Varsity, 1980.

Jastrow, M., ed. *A Dictionary of the Targumim.* New York: Padres, 1950.

Kasher, M. M. *Encyclopedia of Biblical Interpretation, A Millennial Anthology.* Translated under the editorship of Harry Freedman. New York: American Biblical Encyclopedia Society, 1953.

Léon-Defour, X., ed. *Dictionary of Biblical Theology.* New York–Tournai: Desclée, 1967.

McKenzie, J. L. *Dictionary of the Bible.* Milwaukee: Bruce, 1965.

Miller, M. S. and J. L. Miller, eds. *Harper's Dictionary of the Bible.* Rev. ed. San Francisco: Harper & Row, 1978.

Mills, W., et al., eds. *Mercer Dictionary of the Bible.* Macon: Mercer University Press, 1990.

Myers, A. C. *The Eerdmans Bible Dictionary.* Grand Rapids: Eerdmans, 1987.

Pick, A. *Dictionary of Old Testament Words for English readers.* Grand Rapids: Kregel, 1845, 1977.

Richardson, A., ed. *A Theological Word Book of the Bible.* London: SCM, 1950; New York: Macmillan, 1951.

Rowley, H. H. *Dictionary of Bible Place Names.* Old Tappon: Revell, 1970.

_____. *Dictionary of Bible Themes.* London: Nelson, 1968.

_____ and F. C. Grant, eds. *A Dictionary of the Bible.* 1 vol. New York: Scribner's, 1963.

Smith, B. *The Westminster Concise Bible Dictionary.* Philadelphia: Westminster, 1965.

Steinmueller, J. E. and K. Sullivan. *Catholic Biblical Encyclopedia.* New York: Wagner, 1950–1956.

Tenney, M. C. *The Zondervan Pictorial Encyclopedia of the Bible.* 5 vols. Grand Rapids: Zondervan, 1975.

Thompson, D. W. *A Dictionary of Famous Bible Places.* Boston: Whittemore, 1965.

Vine, W. E. et al. *Vine's Expository Dictionary of Biblical Words.* Nashville: Nelson, 1985.

von Allmen, J. J., ed. *The Vocabulary of the Bible: A Companion to the Bible*. London: Lutterworth; New York: Oxford University Press, 1958.

Walker, W. O., Jr., ed. *Harper's Bible Pronunciation Guide*. Grand Rapids: Zondervan, 1989.

Wigoder, G., ed. *Illustrated Dictionary and Concordance of the Bible*. New York: Macmillan, 1986.

Wilson, W. *New Wilson's Old Testament Word Studies: Keyed to Strong's Numbering System and to Theological Wordbook of the Old Testament*. Grand Rapids: Kregel, 1987.

9. OLD TESTAMENT INTRODUCTIONS

Anderson, B. W. *The Books of the Bible*. Vol. 1: The OldTestament/ Hebrew Bible; Vol. 2: The Apocrypha and the New Testament. New York: Charles Scribner's Sons, 1989.

Anderson, B. W. *Understanding the Old Testament*. Englewood Cliffs: Prentice Hall, 1976, 1986.

_____. *The Unfolding Drama of the Bible*. Philadelphia: Fortress, 1988.

Anderson, G. W. *A Critical Introduction to the Old Testament*. London: Duckworth, 1959, 1962.

Archer, G. *A Survey of Old Testament Introduction*. Chicago: Moody, 1964.

Barclay, W. *Introducing the Bible*. Nashville: Abingdon, 1979.

Barr, J. *Old and New in Interpretation*. New York: Harper & Row; London: SCM, 1966.

Barr, R. R. *What Is The Bible?* Minneapolis: Winston, 1984.

Beebe, H. K. *The Old Testament: An Introduction to Its Literary, Historical and Religious Traditions*. Belmont: Dickenson, 1970.

Bennet, B. M. *Bennett's Guide to the Bible*. New York: Seabury, 1982.

Bentzen, A. *Introduction to the Old Testament*. 2 vols. Copenhagen: Gad, 1948, 1952, 1959.

Bergant, D. *Introduction to the Bible.* Collegeville: The Liturgical Press, 1985.

Bewer, J. A. *The Literature of the Old Testament.* New York: Columbia University Press, 1933, 1949, 1962.

Bigger, S. *Creating the Old Testament: The Emergence of the Hebrew Bible.* Cambridge: Blackwell, 1989.

Bimson, J. *The Compact Handbook of the Old Testament.* Minneapolis: Bethany, 1988.

Blanch, S. *For All Mankind. A New Approach to the Old Testament.* New York: Oxford University Press, 1978.

Boadt, L. *Reading the Old Testament: An Introduction.* New York: Paulist, 1984.

Brooks, R. and J. Collins, eds. *Hebrew Bible or Old Testament? Studying the Bible in Judaism and Christianity.* Notre Dame: University of Notre Dame Press, 1990.

Bruce, F. F. *Israel and the Nations.* Grand Rapids: Eerdmans, 1963.

Brueggemann, W. *The Bible Makes Sense.* Winona: St. Mary's College Press; Atlanta: John Knox, 1977.

Buck, H. M. *People of the Lord; The History, Scriptures and Faith of Ancient Israel.* New York: Macmillan, 1965, 1966.

Campbell, A. F. *A Study Companion to Old Testament Literature. An Approach to the Writing of Pre-Exilic and Exilic Israel.* Collegeville: The Liturgical Press/Michael Glazier, 1990.

Carmody, J., D. L. Carmody and R. J. Cohn. *Exploring the Hebrew Bible.* Englewood Cliffs: Prentice Hall, 1988.

Childs, B. S. *Introduction to the Old Testament as Scripture.* Philadelphia: Fortress, 1979.

Coggins, R. *Introducing the Old Testament.* Oxford: Oxford University Press, 1990.

Craigie, P. C. *The Old Testament. Its Background, Growth and Content.* Nashville: Abingdon, 1986.

Crenshaw, J. L. *Story and Faith. A Guide to the Old Testament.* New York: Macmillan, 1986.

Cuming, J. and P. Burns, eds. *The Bible Now. Its Meaning and Use for Christians Today.* New York: Seabury, 1981.

Davidson, R. *The Old Testament.* London: Hodder & Stoughton–Lippincott, 1964.

Drane, J. *Introducing the Old Testament.* San Francisco: Harper & Row, 1988.

Driver, S. R. *Introduction to the Literature of the Old Testament.* Rev. ed. New York: Scribner's, 1913; Meridian, 1956.

Dumbrell, W. J. *The Faith of Israel.* Grand Rapids: Baker, 1988.

Eissfeldt, O. *The Old Testament: An Introduction.* New York: Harper & Row, 1965.

Ellis, P. *The Men and Message of the Old Testament.* Collegeville: The Liturgical Press, 1963.

Feuillet, R. A. *Introduction to the Old Testament.* New York: Doubleday, 1970.

Flanders, H. J., R. W. Crapps and D. A. Smith. *People of the Covenant: An Introduction to the Old Testament.* 3rd ed. New York–Oxford: Oxford University Press, 1988.

Fohrer, G. *Introduction to the Old Testament.* Nashville: Abingdon, 1968.

Fosdick, H. E. *A Guide to Understanding the Bible.* New York: Harper, 1938.

_____. *The Modern Use of the Bible.* New York: Macmillan, 1924.

Freedman, D. N. *God Has Spoken: An Introduction to the Old Testament for Young People.* Philadelphia: Westminster, 1949.

Fretheim, T. *Our Old Testament Heritage.* 2 vols. Minneapolis: Augsburg, 1970–72.

Gabel, J. B. and C. B. Wheeler. *The Bible as Literature: An Introduction.* New York: Oxford University Press, 1986.

Gilles, A. *The People of the Book.* Cincinnati: St. Anthony Messenger, 1983.

Goldingay, J. *Old Testament Commentary Survey.* London: Theological Students Fellowship, 1975.

Goldman, S. *The Book of Human Destiny.* New York: Harper, 1948.

Gordon, D. R. *The Old Testament: A Beginning Survey.* Englewood Cliffs: Prentice Hall, 1985.

Gottwald, N. K. *A Light to the Nations: An Introduction to the Old Testament.* San Francisco: Harper, 1959.

_____. *The Hebrew Bible: A Socio-Literary Introduction.* Philadelphia: Fortress, 1985.

Gray, G. B. *A Critical Introduction to the Old Testament.* New York: Scribner, 1924.

Gross, H. *A Biblical Introduction to the Old Testament.* Notre Dame: University of Notre Dame Press, 1968.

Gunneweg, A. H. *Understanding the Old Testament.* Philadelphia: Westminster, 1978.

Guthrie, D. et al., eds. *The New Bible Commentary.* 3rd rev. ed. Grand Rapids: Eerdmans, 1970.

Hann, R. R. *The Bible: An Owner's Manual.* New York: Paulist, 1983.

Hanson, P. D. *The People Called: The Growth of Community In The Bible.* San Francisco: Harper & Row, 1987.

Harrelson, W. J. *Interpreting the Old Testament.* NewYork: Holt, Rinehart & Winston, 1964.

Harrington, D. *Interpreting the Old Testament—a Practical Guide.* Wilmington: Michael Glazier, 1991.

Harrington, W. J. *Key to the Bible. (The Old Testament Record of Promise).* 3 vols. Garden City: Doubleday, 1976.

_____. *The New Guide to Reading and Studying the Bible.* London: Sheed & Ward, 1978, 1982; Dublin: Veritas, 1982; Wilmington: Michael Glazier, 1978, 1984.

Harrison, R. K. *Introduction to the Old Testament: with a comprehensive review of Old Testament studies and a special supplement on the Apocrypha.* Grand Rapids: Eerdmans, 1969.

Hayes, J. H. *An Introduction to Old Testament Study*. Nashville: Abingdon, 1979.

_____. *Introduction to the Bible*. Philadelphia: Westminster, 1971.

Hiers, R. H. *Reading the Bible Book by Book*. Philadelphia: Fortress, 1988.

Hinson, D. F. *The Books of the Old Testament*. London: S.P.C.K., 1974.

Humphreys, W. L. *Crisis and Story: Introduction to the Old Testament*. Palo Alto: Mayfield, 1979.

Japhet, S., ed. *Studies in the Bible*. Jerusalem: Magnes, 1986.

Jensen, J. *God's Word to Israel*. Collegeville: Michael Glazier, 1991.

Kaiser, O. *Introduction to the Old Testament*. Minneapolis: Augsburg, 1975.

_____. *Introduction to the Old Testament. A Presentation of its Results and Problems*. Trans. by J. Sturdy. Oxford: Blackwell,1975.

Keil, K. F. *Introduction to the Old Testament*. 2 vols. Lynn: Hendrickson, 1988.

Koch, K. *The Book of Books: The Growth of the Bible*. Philadelphia: Westminster, 1969.

Kuhatschek, J. *How to Study the Bible*. Downers Grove: Inter–Varsity, 1985.

_____. *Taking the Guesswork Out of Applying the Bible*. Downers Grove: Inter–Varsity, 1990.

Kuhl, C. *The Old Testament: Its Origins and Composition*. Trans. by C. Herriott. Richmond: John Knox, 1961.

Kuntz, J. K. *The People of Ancient Israel*. New York: Harper & Row, 1974.

La Sor, W. S., D. A. Hubbard and F. W. Bush. *Old Testament Survey, The Message, Form, and Background of the Old Testament*. Grand Rapids: Eerdmans, 1982.

Lace, J. O. *Understanding the Old Testament*. Cambridge: University Press, 1972.

Laffey, A. L. *An Introduction to the Old Testament. A Feminist Perspective.* Philadelphia: Fortress, 1988.

Larue, G. A. *Old Testament Life and Literature.* Boston: Allyn & Bacon, 1968.

Levenson, J. D. *Sinai and Zion. An Entry into the Jewish Bible.* San Francisco: Harper & Row, 1987.

Marshall, C. B. *A Guide Through the Old Testament.* Louisville: Westminster–Knox, 1989.

McCall, T. S. *The Bible Jesus Read is Exciting!: A Popular Introduction to the Old Testament.* Garden City: Doubleday, 1978.

McKenting, H. *Studying the Old Testament.* Minneapolis: Augsburg, 1982.

McKenzie, J. L. *The Old Testament Without Illusion.* Chicago: More, 1979.

_____. *The Two-edged Sword: An Introduction of the Old Testament.* Milwaukee: Bruce, 1956.

Moriarity, F. L. *Introducing the Old Testament.* Milwaukee: Bruce, 1960.

Napier, B. D. *Song of the Vineyard: A Theological Introduction to the Old Testament.* New York: Harper, 1962.

Neusner, J. *The Oral Torah. The Sacred Books of Judaism: An Introduction.* New York: Harper, 1985.

Ohlsen, W. *Perspectives on Old Testament Literature.* New York: Harcourt, Brace, Jovanovich, 1978.

Olher, A. *Studying The Old Testament From Tradition to Canon.* Edinburgh: T & T Clark, 1991.

Pfeiffer, R. H. *Introduction to the Old Testament.* New York: Harper & Row, 1941, 1948.

Propp, W., B. Halpern, and D. Freedman. *The Hebrew Bible and Its Interpreters.* Winona Lake: Eisenbrauns, 1990.

Rendtorff, R. *The Old Testament: An Introduction.* Philadelphia: Fortress, 1986.

Robert, A. *Introduction to the Old Testament.* New York: Desclée, 1968.

Robinson, H. W. *The Old Testament: Its Making and Meaning.* Nashville: Cokesbury, 1937.

Rogerson, J., ed. *Beginning Old Testament Study.* Philadelphia: Westmister, 1982.

_____ and P. Davies. The Old Testament World. Englewood Cliffs: Prentice Hall, 1989.

Rohr, R. and J. Martos. *The Great Themes of Scripture. Old Testament.* Cincinnati: St. Anthony Messenger, 1991.

Rowley, H. H. *The Growth of the Old Testament.* New York: Harper & Row, 1963.

Sandmel, S. *The Enjoyment of Scripture.* New York: Oxford University Press, 1972.

_____. *The Hebrew Scriptures. An Introduction to their Literature and Religious Ideas.* New York: Knopf, 1963; Oxford University Press, 1978.

Schmidt, W. H. *Old Testament Introduction.* New York: Crossroad, 1984.

_____. *The Faith of the Old Testament: A History.* Philadelphia: Westminster, 1983.

Schultz, S. J. *Message of the Old Testament.* (Abridgement of *The Old Testament Speaks.*) San Francisco: Harper & Row, 1986.

_____. *The Old Testament Speaks.* San Francisco: Harper & Row, 1990.

Selby, D. J. *Introduction to the Bible.* New York: Macmillan, 1971.

Sellin, E. *Introduction to the Old Testament.* London: Hodder & Stoughton, 1923; Nashville: Abingdon, 1968.

Soggin, J. A. *Introduction to the Old Testament.* Philadelphia: Westminster; Knox, 1974, 1976, 1980, 1982, 1989.

Stuhlmueller, C. *New Paths Through the Old Testament.* Mahwah: Paulist, 1989.

Tucker, G. M. and D. A. Knight, eds. *The Hebrew Bible and Its Modern Interpreters*. Philadelphia: Fortress, 1985.

Turner, N. *Handbook for Biblical Studies*. Philadelphia: Westminster, 1982.

von Allmen, J. J. *A Companion to the Bible*. Cambridge: Oxford University Press, 1958.

Walton, R. C. *A Basic Introduction to the Old Testament*. London: SCM, 1970, 1980.

Weiser, A. *The Old Testament: Its Formation and Development*. New York: Association, 1961.

West, J. K. *Introduction to the Old Testament*. New York: Macmillan, 1971, 1981.

Westermann, C. *Handbook to the Old Testament*. Minneapolis: Augsburg, 1976.

_____. *A Thousand Years and a Day*. Philadelphia: Muhlenberg, 1962.

Wolff, H. W. *The Old Testament. A Guide to its Writings*. Philadelphia: Westminster, 1973.

Yoder, P. *From Word to Life: A Guide to the Art of Bible Study*. Scottsdale: Herald, 1982.

Young, E. J. *An Introduction to the Old Testament*. Grand Rapids: Eerdmans, 1958; London: Tyndale, 1960, 1965.

10. ONE-VOLUME COMMENTARIES

Bigger, S. *Creating the Old Testament: The Emergence of the Hebrew Bible*. Oxford: Blackwell, 1989.

Black, M. and H. H. Rowley, eds. *Peake's Commentary on the Bible*. New York–London: Nelson, 1962.

Brown, R. E., J. A. Fitzmyer and R. E. Murphy, eds. *The Jerome Biblical Commentary*. Englewood Cliffs: Prentice Hall, 1969.

_____, eds. *The New Jerome Biblical Commentary*. Englewood Cliffs: Prentice Hall, 1989.

Brown, R. M. *The Bible Speaks to You.* Philadelphia: Westminster, 1985.

Buttrick, G. A. *The Interpreter's Bible.* New York: Abingdon, 1952–57.

Davidson, F. *The New Bible Commentary.* Grand Rapids: Eerdmans, 1960.

Driver, S. R., A. Plummer and C. A. Briggs, eds. *The International Commentary on the Holy Scriptures of the Old and New Testaments.* Edinburgh: Clark, 1956.

Finegan, J. *Handbook of Biblical Chronology.* Princeton: Princeton University Press, 1964.

Fuller, R. C., L. Johnston and C. Kearns, eds. *A New Catholic Commentary on Holy Scripture.* Camden–London: Nelson, 1969.

Goldingay, J. *Old Testament Commentary Survey.* M. Branson and R. Hubbard, eds. 2nd ed. Madison: Theological Fellowship, Inter–Varsity, 1981.

Hauer, C. E. and W. A. Young. *An Introduction to the Bible. A Journey into Three Worlds.* Englewood Cliffs: Prentice Hall, 1986.

Layman, C. M., ed. *The Interpreter's One Volume Commentary on the Bible.* Nashville: Abingdon, 1971.

Mays, J. L., gen. ed. *Harper's Bible Commentary.* San Francisco: Harper & Row, 1988.

Miller, J. M. *The Old Testament and the Historian.* Philadelphia: Fortress, 1976.

Rhymer, J. and A. Bullen. *Companion to the Good News Old Testament.* Cleveland: Collins–World, 1976.

Richards, L. O. *The Teacher's Commentary.* Wheaton: Victor, 1989.

Riley, W. *The Tale of Two Testaments.* Mystic: Twenty-Third, 1985.

Rowley, H. H. *From Moses to Qumran: Studies in the Old Testament.* London: Lutterworth, 1963.

_____. *The Rediscovery of the Old Testament.* Philadelphia: Westminster, 1964.

Stuart, D. *Favorite Old Testament Passages. A Popular Commentary for Today.* Philadelphia: Westminster, 1985.

Ward, M., ed. *A Companion to the Bible.* New York: Alba, 1985.

11. MULTI-VOLUME COMMENTARIES

Ackroyd, P. R., A. R. Leaney and J. W. Packer, gen. eds. *The Cambridge Bible. Commentary on the New English Bible.* Cambridge: University Press, 1972.

Ackroyd, P. R. and C. F. Evans. *The Cambridge History of the Bible.* Vol. 1, "From Beginnings to Jerome." Cambridge: University Press, 1970.

Ackroyd, P., B. W. Anderson and J. L. Mays. *The Old Testament Library.* Philadelphia: Westminster. (Still in process of compilation.)

Albright, W. F. and D. N. Freedman, eds. *The Anchor Bible.* Garden City: Doubleday, 1964. (Still in process of compilation.)

Allen, C. J. et al., eds. *The Broadman Bible Commentary.* 12 vols. Nashville: Broadman, 1969.

Anderson, B. W. "The Problem and Promise of Commentary." *Interpretation* 36 (1982) 341–55.

Barclay, W. and F. F. Bruce, eds. *Bible Guides.* 22 vols. New York: Abingdon, 1969–1965.

Buttrick, G. A. et al., eds. *The Interpreter's Bible.* 12 vols. New York: Abingdon–Cokesbury, 1951–1957.

Clements, R. E. and M. Black, eds. *The New Century Bible Commentary.* Grand Rapids: Eerdmans, 1967–

Cohen, A., ed. *Soncino Book of the Bible.* 14 vols. London: Soncino, 1945–1952.

Cross, F. M. et al., eds. *Hermeneia.* Multi-Volume Series. Philadelphia: Fortress, 1971. (A multi-volume critical commentary still in the process of compilation.)

Fretheim, T. E. "Old Testament Commentaries, Their Selection and Use." *Interpretation* 36 (1982) 356–71.

Gabelstein, F. E., gen. ed. *Expositor's Bible Commentary.* Grand Rapids: Zondervan, 1979, 1989.

Greenslade, S. L. *The Cambridge History of the Bible.* Vol. 3. "The West From the Reformation to the Present Day." Cambridge: University Press, 1963.

Harrison, R. K., gen. ed. *The New International Commentary on the Old Testament.* Grand Rapids: Eerdmans, 1986. (Still in process.)

International Critical Commentary on the Holy Scriptures. New York: Scribner's, 1896–1951.

Keil, C. F. and F. Delitzsch. *A Commentary on the Old Testament.* 10 vols. Grand Rapids: Eerdmans, 1975.

Lampe, G. W. *The Cambridge History of the Bible.* Vol. 2. Cambridge: University Press, 1969.

Layman's Bible Commentary. 25 vols. Richmond: John Knox, 1959–1964.

Marsh, J. and C. A. Richardson, eds. *Torch Bible Commentaries.* London: SCM, 1952.

Mayes, J. L., P. D. Miller and P. J. Achtemeier. *Interpretation: A Bible Commentary for Teaching and Preaching.* Atlanta: John Knox, 1980–

Ogilvie, L. J., gen. ed. *The Communicator's Commentary.* Dallas: Word, 1982.

Plummer, A. et al., eds. *The International Critical Commentary.* New York: Scribner's, 1910.

Proclamation Commentaries. Old Testament Witness for Preaching Series. Philadelphia: Fortress, 1977–

Steinmuller, J. E. and K. Sullivan. *The Catholic Biblical Encyclopedia.* 2 vols. New York: Wagner, 1950.

Stuhlmueller, C. and M. McNamara, eds. *Old Testament Message: A Biblical–Theological Commentary.* Wilmington: Michael Glazier, 1981.

The Daily Study Bible Series. Philadelphia: Westminster, 1982.

The Interpreter's Bible. New York: Abingdon–Cokesbury, 1951–1957.

The Cambridge History of the Bible. Cambridge: Cambridge University Press, 1963–70.

The Westminster Commentary. London: Methuen, 1904.

van der Woude, A. S., gen. ed. *Text and Interpretation. A Practical Commentary.* Grand Rapids: Eerdmans. (still in process.)

Watts, J. D., ed. *Word Biblical Commentary.* Waco: Word, 1982.

Wright, G. E. et al., eds. *The Old Testament Library.* Philadelphia: Westminster, 1973.

II. INTERPRETATION OF THE OLD TESTAMENT

12. EXEGETICAL METHODOLOGY

Achtemeier, E. *The Old Testament and the Proclamation of the Gospel.* Philadelphia: Westminster, 1973.

Alonso-Schökel, L. *Understanding the Biblical Research.* New York: Herder, 1963.

Alter, R. *The Art of Biblical Narrative.* New York: Basic, 1981.

Anderson, G. W., ed. *Tradition and Interpretation.* Oxford: Clarendon, 1979.

Armerding, C. E. *The Old Testament and Criticism.* Grand Rapids: Eerdmans, 1983.

Barr, J. *Comparative Philology and the Text of the Old Testament.* Winona Lake: Eisenbrauns, 1987.

_____. *The Bible and the Modern World.* New York: Harper & Row, 1973.

Barton, J. *Reading the Old Testament. Method in Biblical Study.* Philadelphia: Westminster, 1984.

Brown, R. E. *Biblical Exegesis and Church Doctrine.* New York: Paulist, 1985.

Brueggemann, W. *Revelation and Violence: A Study in Contextualization.* Milwaukee: Marquette University Press, 1986.

Bultmann, R. K. "Is Exegesis Without Presuppositions Possible?" *Existence and Faith.* S. Ogden., ed. New York: Meridian, 1960. Pp. 189–96.

Buss, M. J. *Encounter with the Text: Form and History in the Hebrew Bible.* Missoula: Scholars, 1979.

Campbell, D. B. *The Old Testament for Modern Readers.* Atlanta: John Knox, 1972.

Carson, D. A. *Exegetical Fallacies.* Grand Rapids: Baker, 1984.

Clemens, T. and M. Wyschogrod, eds. *Understanding Scripture: Explorations of Jewish and Christian Traditions of Interpretation.* New York: Paulist, 1987.

Clements, R. E. *One Hundred Years of Old Testament Interpretation.* Philadelphia: Westminster, 1976.

Collins, J. T. and J. D. Crossman, eds. *The Biblical Heritage in Modern Catholic Scholarship.* Wilmington: Michael Glazier, 1986.

Coppens, J. *The Old Testament and the Critics.* Paterson: St. Anthony Guild, 1942.

Danker, F. W. *Multipurpose Tools for Bible Study.* St Louis: Concordia, 1970.

Emerton, J. A. and S. C. Reif. *Interpreting the Hebrew Bible.* Essays in Honor of E. I. Rosenthal. Cambridge: University Press, 1982.

Engnell, I. *A Rigid Scrutiny: Critical Essays on the Old Testament.* Nashville: Vanderbilt University Press, 1969.

Evans, C. D., W. W. Hallo and J. B. White, eds. *Scripture in Context: Essays on the Comparative Method.* Pittsburgh: Pickwick, 1980.

Evans, G. R. *The Language and Logic of the Bible: Earlier Middle Ages.* Cambridge–NewYork: Cambridge University Press, 1985.

Fishbane, M. *Biblical Interpretation In Ancient Israel.* Oxford–New York: Oxford University Press, 1986.

_____. "Jewish Biblical Exegesis: Presuppositions and Principles." *Scripture in the Jewish and Christian Traditions: Authority, Interpretation, Relevance.* Ed. by F. E. Greenspahn. Nashville: Abingdon, 1982. Pp. 91–110.

Froehlich, K. *Biblical Interpretation in the Early Church.* Philadelphia: Fortress, 1984.

Grant, R. M. and D. Tracy. *A Short History of the Interpretation of the Bible.* Philadelphia: Fortress, 1984.

Grant, R. M., J. T. McNeill and S. Terrian. "History of the Interpretation of the Bible." *The Interpreter's Bible.* Vol. I. Pp. 106–141.

Greenspahn, F., ed. *Scripture in the Jewish and Christian Traditions: Authority, Interpretation, Relevance.* Nashville: Abingdon, 1982.

Hahn, H. F. *The Old Testament in Modern Research.* Philadelphia: Fortress; London: SCM, 1966.

Hallo, W. W. et al., eds. *Scripture in Context II. More Essays on the Comparative Methodology.* Winona Lake: Eisenbrauns, 1983.

Hanson, P. D. *The Diversity of Scripture: A Theological Interpretation.* Philadelphia: Fortress, 1982.

Harrelson, W. J. *Interpreting the Old Testament.* New York: Holt, Rinehart & Winston, 1964.

Hayes, J. H. and Carl R. Holladay. *Biblical Exegesis a Beginner's Handbook.* Atlanta: John Knox, 1982.

Hyatt, J. P. *The Bible in Modern Scholarship.* Papers read at the 100th meeting of the Society of Biblical Literature, December 20–30, 1984. Nashville: Abingdon, 1984.

"Interpretation, History of." (Various contributors.) *The Interpreter's Dictionary of the Bible.* New York: Abingdon, 1962. Pp. 436–456.

Kraeling, E. G. *The Old Testament Since the Reformation.* New York: Harper & Row, 1955; Schocken, 1969.

Kaiser, O. and W. G. Kümmel. *Exegetical Method: A Student's Handbook.* New York: Seabury, 1981.

Kaiser, W. C., Jr. *Toward an Exegetical Theology.* Grand Rapids: Baker, 1981.

Keck, L. E. and G. M. Tucker. "Exegesis." *The Interpreter's Dictionary of the Bible.* New York: Abingdon, 1962. Pp. 196–303.

Klein, R. W. *Textual Criticism of the Old Testament.* Philadelphia: Fortress, 1974.

Knierim, R. and G. Tucker, eds. *The Forms of the Old Testament Literature.* 24 volumes. Grand Rapids: Eerdmans, 1983. (Work on the series is still in process.)

Knight, D. A. and G. M. Tucker, eds. *The Hebrew Bible and Its Modern Interpreters.* Philadelphia: Fortress, 1985; Atlanta: Scholars, 1989.

Krentz, Edgar. *The Historical Critical Method.* Philadelphia: Fortress, 1977.

Küng, H. and J. Moltmann. *Conflicting Ways of Interpreting the Bible.* New York: Seabury, 1980.

Malherbe, A. J. "An Introduction: The Task and Method of Exegesis." *Restoration Quarterly* 5 (1961) 169–178.

Marrow, S. B. *Basic Tools of Biblical Exegesis: A Student's Manual.* Rome: Biblical Institute Press, 1976.

Mayes, J. L. *Exegesis as a Theological Discipline.* Richmond: Union Theological Seminary, 1960.

McCarthy, D. and W. Callen. *Modern Biblical Studies.* Milwaukee: Bruce, 1967.

Mickelson, A. B. *Interpreting the Bible.* Grand Rapids: Eerdmans, 1963.

Miller, J. *The Old Testament and the Historian.* Philadelphia: Fortress, 1976.

Murphy, R. E. "Reflections on the History of the Exposition of Scripture." *Studies in Catholic History.* N. Minnich, R. Eno, R. Trisco, eds., 1985.

_____, ed. "Theology, Exegesis, and Proclamation." *Concilium* 70. New York: Herder, 1971.

Neusner, J., B. Levine and E. Frerichs, eds. *Judaic Perspectives on Ancient Israel.* Philadelphia: Fortress, 1987.

Nielsen, E. *Oral Tradition.* London: SCM, 1954.

Polzin, R. M. and E. Rothmann, eds. *The Biblical Mosaic: Changing Perspectives.* Philadelphia: Fortress; Chico: Scholars, 1982.

Reman, J. "Methods In Studying the Biblical Text Today." *Concordia Theological Monthly* 40 (1969) 655–681.

Ricoeur, P. *Essays on Biblical Interpretation.* Philadelphia: Fortress, 1980.

Rogerson, J., ed. *Beginning Old Testament Study.* Philadelphia: Westminster, 1983.

_____, *Old Testament Criticism in the Nineteenth Century: England and Germany.* London: S.P.C.K, 1984; Philadelphia: Fortress, 1985.

Rohrbaugh, R. L. *The Biblical Interpreter.* Philadelphia: Fortress, 1978.

Rowley, H. H., ed. *The Old Testament and Modern Study.* Oxford: Clarendon, 1951; London: Oxford University Press, 1961.

Soulen, R. N. *Handbook of Biblical Criticism.* 2 ed., revised and augmented. Atlanta: John Knox, 1981.

Stock, A. "The Limits of Historical Critical Exegesis." *Biblical Theology Bulletin 13* (1983) 28–31.

Stuart, D. K. *Old Testament Exegesis: A Primer for Students and Pastors.* Philadelphia: Westminster, 1984.

Stuhlmacher, P. *Historical Criticism and Theological Interpretation of Scripture.* Philadelphia: Fortress, 1977.

Suelzer A. and J. S. Kselman. "Modern Old Testament Criticism." *The New Jerome Biblical Commentary,* ed. by R. Brown et al. Englewood Cliffs: Prentice Hall, 1990. Pp. 1113–29.

Trigg, J. W. *Biblical Interpretation.* Wilmington: Michael Glazier, 1988.

Vawter, B. *The Path of Wisdom: Biblical Investigations.* Wilmington: Michael Glazier, 1986.

Weingreen, J. *Introduction to the Critical Study of the Text of the Hebrew Bible.* New York: Oxford University Press, 1982.

Yoder, P. *From Word to Life: A Guide to the Art of Bible Study.* Scottsdale: Herald, 1982.

13. LITERARY APPROACHES

a. General

Aichele, G., Jr. *The Limits of Story.* Chico: Scholars; Philadelphia: Fortress, 1985.

Alonso-Schökel, L. *A Manual of Hebrew Poetics.* Rome: Biblical Institute Press, 1988.

Alter, R. *The Art of Biblical Narrative.* New York: Basic, 1981.

Alter, R. and F. Kermode. *The Literary Guide to the Bible.* Cambridge Belknap, 1987.

Amihai, M., G. W. Coats and A. M. Solomon, eds. *Narrative Research on the Hebrew Bible. Semeia* 46. Atlanta: Scholars, 1989.

Benoit, P. *Exegèse et Théologie.* 3 vols. Paris: Cerf, 1961–1968.

Berlin, A. *Poetics and Interpretation of Biblical Narrative.* Sheffield: Almond Press, 1983.

Brams, S. J. *Biblical Games: A Strategic Analysis of Stories in the Old Testament.* Cambridge: MIT, 1980.

Busas, M. J. *Encounter with the Text: Form and History in the Hebrew Bible.* Philadelphia: Fortress, 1979.

Caird, G. B. *The Language and Imagery of the Bible.* Philadelphia: Westminster, 1980.

Campbell, A. F. *The Study Companion to Old Testament Literature.* Wilmington: Michael Glazier, 1988.

Carmi, T., ed. *The Penguin Book of Hebrew Verse.* London: Lane & Penguin, 1981.

Coats, G. W., ed. *Saga, Legend, Tale, Novella, Fable. Narrative Forms in Old Testament Literature.* Sheffield: JSOT Press, 1985.

Culley, R. C. *Studies in the Structure of Hebrew Narrative.* Philadelphia: Fortress, 1976.

Davidson, R. and A. R. Leaney. *Biblical Criticism.* Harmondsworth: Penguin, 1970.

Exum, J. C., ed. *Signs and Wonders. Biblical Texts in Literary Focus.* Atlanta: Scholars, 1989.

Fisch, H. *Poetry with a Purpose: Biblical Poetics and Interpretation.* Bloomington–Indianapolis: Indiana University, 1982.

Fontaine, C. R. *Traditional Sayings in the Old Testament.* Sheffield: Almond Press, 1982.

Frei, H. *The Eclipse of Biblical Narrative.* New Haven: Yale University Press, 1974.

Gabel, J. B. and C. B. Wheeler. *The Bible as Literature: An Introduction.* New York: Oxford University Press, 1986.

Geller, S. A., E. L. Greenstein and A. Berlin. *A Sense of Text: The Art of Language in the Study of Biblical Literature.* Winona Lake: Eisenbrauns, 1983.

Gerhart, M. and J. G. Williams, eds. *Genre, Narrativity, and Theology. Semeia 43.* Atlanta: Scholars, 1989.

Good, E. M. *Irony in the Old Testament.* Sheffield: Almond, 1981.

Kirkpatrick, P. G. *The Old Testament and Folklore Study.* Sheffield: JSOT Press, 1988.

Klein, R. W. *Textual Criticism of the Old Testament.* Philadelphia: Fortress, 1974.

Knight, D. *Rediscovering the Traditions of Israel.* Missoula: Scholars, 1973.

Koch, K. *The Growth of the Biblical Tradition. (The Form Critical Method).* New York: Scribners, 1969.

Krentz, E. *The Historical-Critical Method.* Philadelphia: Fortress, 1975.

Kugel, J. L. *Idea of Biblical Poetry: Parallelism and its History.* New Haven: Yale University Press, 1981.

Licht, J. *Storytelling in the Bible.* Jerusalem: Magnes, 1978.

Lohfink, G. *The Bible: Now I Get It.* Garden City: Doubleday, 1979.

Lord, A. *The Singer of Tales.* Cambridge: Harvard University Press, 1964; Atheneum, 1973.

Lowenstamm, S. E. *Comparative Studies in Biblical and Ancient Oriental Literatures.* Neukirchen/Vluyn: Neukirchener, 1980.

Maier, G. *The End of Historical Critical Method.* St. Louis: Concordia, 1977.

Maier, J. and V. Tollers, eds. *The Bible in its Literary Milieu. Contemporary Essays.* Grand Rapids: Eerdmans, 1979.

Miller, J. M. *The Old Testament and the Historian.* Philadelphia Fortress, 1976.

Milne, P. J. *Vladimir Propp and the Study of Structure in Hebrew Biblical Narrative.* Sheffield: Sheffield, 1988.

Miscall, P. D. *The Working of Old Testament Narrative.* Philadelphia: Fortress; Chico: Scholars, 1983.

Nickelsburg, G. W. *Jewish Literature Between the Bible and the Mishnah: A Historical and Literary Introduction.* Philadelphia: Fortress, 1981.

Niditch, S. *Underdogs and Tricksters: A Prelude to Biblical Folklore.* San Francisco: Harper & Row, 1987.

Robertson, D. A. *Linguistic Evidence in Dating Early Hebrew Poetry.* Missoula: Scholars, 1973.

Robertson, E. *The Text of the Old Testament and Methods of Textual Criticism.* London: Shapiro–Valentine, 1939.

Rogerson, J. W. *Myth in Old Testament Interpretation.* Berlin–New York: Gruyter, 1974.

Savran, G. W. *Telling and Retelling: Quotation in Biblical Narrative.* Bloomington–Indianapolis: Indiana University, 1988.

Soulen, R. N. *Handbook of Biblical Criticism.* Atlanta: John Knox, 1976.

Stuhlmacher, P. *Historical Criticism and Theological Interpretation of Scripture.* Philadelphia: Fortress, 1977.

Warshaw, T. S. *Handbook for Teaching the Bible in Literature Class.* Nashville: Abingdon, 1978.

Watson, W. G. *Classical Hebrew Poetry. A Guide to Its Techniques.* Sheffield: JSOT Press, 1985.

Wurthwein, E. *The Text of the Old Testament.* Grand Rapids: Eerdmans, 1980.

b. Literary Criticism

Alter, R. *The Art of Biblical Narrative.* New York: Basic Books; London: Allen & Univen, 1981, 1985.

Barr, J. "Reading the Bible as Literature." *Bulletin of the John Rylands University Library* 56 (1973) 10–33.

Fishbane, M. *Text and Texture: Close Readings of Selected Biblical Texts.* New York: Schocken, 1979.

Frye, N. *The Great Code: The Bible and Literature.* New York–London: Harcourt, Brace, Jovanovich, 1982.

Funk, R. W., ed. *Literary Critical Studies of Biblical Texts. Semeia* 8. Missoula: Scholars, 1977.

GrosLouis, K. R. and J. S. Ackerman, eds. *Literary Interpretations of Biblical Narratives.* Volume II. Nashville: Abingdon, 1974, 1984.

Habel, N. C. *Literary Criticism of the Old Testament.* Philadelphia: Fortress, 1971.

Long, B. O., ed. *Images of Man and God: Old Testament Short Stories in Literary Focus.* Sheffield: JSOT Press, 1981.

Louis, K. R., J. S. Ackerman and T. S. Warshaw. *Literary Interpretations of Biblical Narratives.* 2 vols. Nashville: Abingdon, 1974, 1982.

McKnight, E. V. *The Bible and the Reader: An Introduction to Literary Criticism.* Philadelphia: Fortress, 1985.

Miscall, P. D. *The Workings of Old Testament Narrative.* Chico: Scholars; Philadelphia: Fortress, 1983.

Preminger, A. and E. L. Greenstein. *The Hebrew Bible in Literary Criticism.* New York: Ungar, 1986.

Robertson, D. *The Old Testament and the Literary Critic.* Philadelphia: Fortress, 1977.

Sternberg, M. *The Poetics of Biblical Narrative.* Bloomington: Indiana University Press, 1985.

c. Form Criticism

Coats, G. W., ed. *Saga, Legend, Tale, Novella, Fable: Narrative Forms in Old Testament Literature.* Sheffield: JSOT Press, 1985.

Doty, W. G. "The Concept of Genre in Literary Analysis." *Society of Biblical Literature Proceedings*. Society of Biblical Literature, 1972. Pp. 413–418.

Gunkel, H. "Fundamental Problems of Hebrew Literary History." *What Remains of the Old Testament and Other Essays*. New York: Basic Books; London: Allen & Univen, 1928. Pp. 57–68.

Hayes, J. H., ed. *Old Testament Form Criticism*. San Antonio: Trinity University Press, 1974.

Knierlim, R. "Old Testament Form Criticism Reconsidered." *Interpretation* 27 (1973) 435–468.

Knierim, R. and G. M. Tucker, ed. *The Forms of the Old Testament Literature*. 24 vols. Grand Rapids: Eerdmans, 1981.

Koch, K. *The Growth of the Biblical Tradition*. New York: Black; London: Schribner's, 1969.

Lohfink, G. *The Bible:* Now *I Get It! A Form Criticism Handbook*. Garden City: Doubleday, 1979.

McKnight, E. *What is Form Criticism?* Philadelphia: Fortress, 1971.

Muilenburg, J. "Form Criticism and Beyond." *Journal of Biblical Literature* 88 (1969) 1–18.

Tucker, G. M. *Form Criticism of the Old Testament*. Philadelphia: Fortress, 1971.

_____. "Form Criticism, OT." *The Interpreter's Dictionary of the Bible. Supplementary Volume*, 342–345.

Von Rad, G. "The Form–critical Problem of the Hexateuch." In *The Problem of the Hexateuch and Other Essays*. New York: McGraw Hill, 1966. Pp. 1–78.

d. Tradition Criticism

Brueggemann, W. and H. W. Wolff. *The Vitality of Old Testament Traditions*. Atlanta: John Knox, 1975.

Coats, G. W. "Tradition Criticism, O.T." *The Interpreter's Dictionary of the Bible. Supplementary Volume*, 912–914.

Clements, R. E. "Pentateuchal Problems." *Tradition and Interpretation* G. Anderson, ed. Oxford: Claredon, 1979. Pp. 96–124.

Culley, R. C., ed. *Oral Tradition and the Old Testament Studies. Semeia* 5. Missoula: Scholars, 1976.

Gunkel, H. *The Legends of Genesis: The Biblical Saga and History.* New York: Schocken, 1964.

Halpern, B. and J. D. Levenson, eds. *Traditions in Transformation: Turning Points in Biblical Faith.* Winona Lake: Eisenbrauns, 1984.

Jeppesen, K. and B. Otzen, eds. *The Productions of Time: Tradition in Old Testament Scholarship.* Sheffield: Almond Press, 1984.

Knight, D. A. *Rediscovering the Traditions of Israel.* 2nd edition. Missoula: Scholars, 1975.

_____, ed. *Tradition and Theology in the Old Testament.* Philadelphia: Fortress, 1977.

Mendenhall, G. E. *The Tenth Generation: The Origins of the Biblical Tradition.* Baltimore: Johns Hopkins University Press, 1973.

Mowinckel, S. "Tradition, Oral." *The Interpreter's Dictionary of the Bible* 4. Nashville: Abingdon, 1962. Pp. 683–685.

_____. *Prophecy and Tradition: The Prophetic Books in the Light of the Study of the Growth and History of the Tradition.* Oslo: Dybwad, 1946.

Nielson, E. *Oral Tradition: A Modern Problem in Old Testament Interpretation.* London: SCM, 1954.

Noth, M. "Analysis of the Elements of the Traditions." *A History of Pentateuchal Traditions.* Chico: Scholars, 1981. Pp. 52 ff.

Ohler, A. *Studying the Old Testament: From Tradition to Canon.* Edinburgh: Clark, 1985.

Rast, W. *Tradition, History and the Old Testament.* Philadelphia: Fortress, 1972.

Wolff, H. W. and W. Brueggemann. *The Vitality of Old Testament Traditions.* 2nd ed. Atlanta: John Knox, 1982.

e. Redaction Criticism

March, W. E. "Redaction Criticism and the Formation of the Prophetic Books." *Society of Biblical Literature Seminar Papers* (1977) 87–101.

Mayes, A. D. *The Story of Israel Between Settlement and Exile: A Redactional Study of the Deuteronomistic History.* London: SCM, 1983.

Nelson, R. D. *The Double Redaction of the Deuteronomistic History.* Sheffield: JSOT Press, 1981.

Noth, M. *The Deuteronomistic History.* Sheffield: JSOT Press, 1981.

Perrin, N. *What is Redaction Criticism?* Philadelphia: Fortress, 1969.

Rendsburg, G. A. *The Redaction of Genesis.* Winona Lake: Eisenbraums, 1985.

Wharton, J. A. "Redaction Criticism, O.T." *The Interpreter's Dictionary of the Bible. Supplementary Volume.* Nashville: Abingdon, 1976. Pp. 729–732.

f. Structuralist Criticism

Alonso-Schökel, L. "The Poetic Structure of Psalms 42–44." *Journal For The Study of The Old Testament* 1 (1976) 4–11; 3 (1977) 61–65.

Bar-Efrat, S. "Some Observations on the Analysis of Structure in Biblical Narrative." *Vetus Testamentum* 30 (1980), 154–73.

Bartels, R., et al. *Structural Analysis and Biblical Exegesis: Interpretational Essays.* Pittsburgh: Pickwick; Edinburgh: Clark, 1974.

Barthes, R. and F. Boyon, et al. *Structural Analysis and Biblical Exegesis.* Interpretational Essays. Pittsburgh: Pickwick, 1974.

Barthes, R. *Writing Degree Zero and Elements of Semiology.* London: Jonathan Cape, 1967; Boston: Beacon, 1970.

Buss, M., ed. *Encounter With the Text: Form and History In The Hebrew Bible.* Missoula: Scholars Press; Philadelphia: Fortress, 1979.

Calloud, J. *Structural Analysis of Narrative.* Philadelphia: Fortress, 1976.

Clines, D. J., D. M. Gunn and A. J. Hauser, eds. *Art and Meaning: Rhetoric in Biblical Literature.* Sheffield: JSOT Press, 1982.

Culler, J. D. *Structural Poetics: Structuralism, Linguistics and the Story of Literature.* Ithaca: Cornell University Press; London: Routledge & Kegan Paul, 1975.

Culley, R. C. "Structural Analysis: Is it Done with Mirrors?" *Interpretation* 28 (1974) 165–181.

Detweiler, R. *Story, Sign, and Self: Phenomenology and Structuralism as Literary Critical Methods.* Philadelphia: Fortress; Missoula: Scholars, 1978.

Fokkelman, J. P. *Narrative Art and Poetry in the Books of Samuel: A Full Interpretation Based on Stylistic and Structural Analyses.* 4 vols. Assen: Van Gorcum, 1975, 1980.

Gottwald, N. "Sociological Method in the Study of Ancient Israel." In *Encounter with the Text: Form and History in the Hebrew Bible.* M. Buss, ed. Philadelphia: Fortress, 1979. Pp. 69–82.

Greenwood, D. *Structuralism and the Biblical Text.* New York: Mouton, 1985.

Hadidian, D. Y., gen. ed. *Structural Analysis and Biblical Exegesis.* Pittsburgh: Pickwick, 1974.

Jacobson, R. "The Structuralists and the Bible." *Interpretation* 28 (1974) 146–64.

Jobling, D. *The Sense of Biblical Narrative: Three Structural Analyses in the Old Testament.* Sheffield: JSOT Press, 1978.

_____. *The Sense of Biblical Narrative: Structural Analyses in the Hebrew Bible II.* Sheffield: JSOT Press, 1986.

Johnson, A. M. *A Bibliography of Semiological and Structural Studies of Religion.* Pittsburgh: The Clifford E. Barbour Library of Pittsburgh Theological Seminary, 1979.

_____. *Structuralism and Biblical Hermeneutics.* Pittsburgh: Pickwick, 1979.

Lane, M., ed. *Introduction To Structuralism: A Reader.* New York Basic Books; London, Jonathan Cape, 1970.

Leach, E. R. and D. A. Aycock, *Structuralist Interpretations of Biblical Myth*. Cambridge–New York: Cambridge University Press, 1983.

Leach, E. R. *Genesis As Myth and Other Essays*. London: Jonathan Cape, 1969.

Mc Knight, E. V. *Meaning In Texts*. Philadelphia: Fortress, 1978.

Ohler, A. *Studying the Old Testament from Tradition to Canon*. Edinburgh: T & T Clark, 1985.

Patte, D. *What Is Structural Exegesis?* Philadelphia: Fortress, 1976.

_____, ed. *Genesis 2 and 3, Kaleidoscopic Structural Readings. Semeia* 18. Chico: Scholars, 1980.

_____ and A. Patte. *Structural Exegesis: From Theory to Practice*. Philadelphia: Fortress, 1978.

Polzin, R. M. *Biblical Structuralism: Method and Subjectivity in the Study of Ancient Texts*. Philadelphia: Fortress, 1977.

Robey, D., ed. *Structuralism: An Introduction*. London–New York: Oxford University Press, 1973.

Rogerson, J. W. "Recent Literary Structuralist Approaches to Biblical Interpretation." *The Churchman* 90 (1976) 165–77.

Roth, W. "Structural Interpretation of Jacob at the Jabbok' (Genesis 32: 22–32)." *Biblical Research* 22 (1977) 51–62.

Scholes, R. *Structuralism in Literature: An Introduction*. New Haven–London: Yale University Press, 1974.

Seung, T. K. *Structuralism and Hermeneutics*. New York: Columbia University Press, 1982.

Spivey, R. A. "Structuralism and Biblical Studies' Uninvited Guest." *Interpretation* 28 (1974) 133–145.

Tollers, V. L. and J. R. Maier. *The Bible In Its Literary Milieu*. Grand Rapids: Eerdmans, 1979.

van der Meer, W. and J. C. de Moor, eds. *The Structural Analysis of Biblical and Canaanite Poetry*. Sheffield: JSOT Press, 1989.

g. Canonical Criticism

Ackroyd, P. A. "Original Text and Canonical Text." *Union Seminary Quarterly* 32 (1977) 166–73.

Brueggemann, W. *The Bible Makes Sense.* Atlanta: John Knox, 1977.

_____. *The Creative Word: Canon as a Model for Biblical Education.* Philadelphia: Fortress, 1982.

Childs, B. S. "The Exegetical Significance of the Canon for the Study of the Old Testament." *Supplement to Vetus Testamentum.* Vol. 29. Leiden: Brill, 1978. Pp. 66–80.

_____. "The Old Testament As Scripture of The Church." *Concordia Theological Monthly* 43 (1972) 709–22.

_____. *Old Testament Theology in a Canonical Context.* Philadelphia: Fortress, 1986.

Coats, G. W. and B. O. Long, eds. *Canon and Authority: Essays in Old Testament Religion and Theology.* Philadelphia: Fortress, 1977.

Sanders, J. A. *Canon and Community: A Guide to Canonical Criticism.* Philadelphia: Fortress, 1984.

_____. "The Nature and Function of Canon," *Magnalia Dei* 157, 531–560.

Spina, F. A. " Canonical Criticism: Childs Versus Sanders." *Interpreting God's Word For Today: An Inquiry Into Hermeneutics From a Biblical Theological Perspective.* Anderson: Warner, 1982, 165–94.

Tucker, G. M., ed. *Canon, Theology, and Old Testament Interpretation: Essays In Honor of Brevard S. Childs.* Philadelphia: Fortress, 1988.

Vasholz, R. *The Old Testament Canon in the Old Testament Church: The Internal Rationale for Old Testament Canonicity.* Lewiston: Edwin Mellen, 1990.

h. Rhetorical Criticism

Allen, L. C. "The Value of Rhetorical Criticism in Psalm 69." *Journal of Biblical Literature* 105 (1986) 577–598.

Black, E. *Rhetorical Criticism: A Study in Method.* Madison: University of Wisconsin Press, 1978.

_____. *Rhetorical Criticism: A Study in Method.* New York: Macmillan, 1965.

Cheresko, A. R. "A Rhetorical Analysis of David's 'Boast' (I Samuel 17: 34-37). Some Reflections on Method." *Catholic Biblical Quarterly* 47 (1985) 49–74.

Clines, D. J., D. M. Gunn and A. J. Hauser, eds. *Art and Meaning: Rhetoric in Biblical Literature.* Sheffield: JSOT Press, 1982.

Jackson, J. J. and M. Kessler, eds. *Rhetorical Criticism, Essays in Honor of James Muilenberg.* Pittsburgh: Pickwick, 1974.

Kselman, J. S. "Psalm 146 in its Context." *Catholic Biblical Quarterly* 50 (1988) 587–599.

Lewin, E. D. "Arguing for Authority a Rhetorical Study of Jeremiah 1:4-19 and 20:7-18." *Journal for the Study of the Old Testament* 32 (1985) 105–119.

Nilsen, T. R., ed. *Essays on Rhetorical Criticism.* New York: Random, 1968.

Ogden, G. S. "Psalm 60: Its Rhetoric Form and Function." *Journal for the Study of the Old Testament* 31 (1985) 82–94.

Scott, R. L. *Methods of Rhetorical Criticism: A Twentieth Century Perspective.* New York: Harper & Row, 1972.

Viviano P. A. "II Kings 17: A Rhetorical and Form–Critical Analysis." *Catholic Biblical Quarterly* 49 (1987) 548–559.

Wuellner, W. " Where is Rhetorical Criticism Taking Us?" *Catholic Biblical Quarterly* 49 (1987) 448–463.

i. Sociological Criticism (Social Science Approaches)

Brueggemann, W. "Social Criticism and Social Vision in the Deuteronomic Formula of the Judges (Judg. 3: 12, 4:1-2, 6:1; Deut. 32)." *Die Botschaft und die Boten.* Ed. by J. Jeremias and L. Perlit. 1981.

_____. "Trajectories in Old Testament Literature and the Sociology of Ancient Israel." *Journal of Biblical Literature* 98 (1979) 161–185.

Clements, R., ed. *The World of Ancient Israel: Sociological, Anthropological and Political Perspectives.* Cambridge: Cambridge University Press, 1989.

Frick, Frank S. "Social Science Methods and Theories of Significance For The Study of The Israelite Monarchy: A Critical Review Essay." *Semeia* 37 (1986) 9–52.

Gottwald, N. K. "Religious Conversion and the Societal Origins of Ancient Israel." *Perspectives in Religious Studies* 15 (1988) 49–65.

_____. "Sociological Criticism of the Old Testament." *Christian Century* 99 (1982) 474–477.

_____. "Sociological Method in Biblical Research and Contemporary Peace Studies." *American Baptist Quarterly* 2 (1983) 142–156.

_____. "Sociological Method in the Study of Ancient Israel." *Encounter With The Text.* Ed. by M. J. Buss. Philadelphia: Fortress, 1979. Pp. 69–81.

_____. *The Hebrew Bible: A Socio Literary Introduction.* Philadelphia: Fortress, 1985.

Kimbrough, S. T. *Israelite Religion in Sociological Perspective: The Work of Antonin Causse.* Wiesbaden: Otto Hahrassowitz, 1978.

Lang, B. *Monotheism and the Prophetic Minority. An Essay in Biblical History and Sociology.* Sheffield: Almond Press, 1983.

North, Robert. *Sociology of the Biblical Jubilee.* Rome: Pontifical Biblical Institute, 1954.

Wallis, Louis. *God and the Social Process: A Study In Hebrew History.* Chicago: University of Chicago Press, 1935.

_____. *Sociological Study of the Bible.* Chicago: University of Chicago Press, 1912.

_____. *The Bible Is Human.* New York: AMS Press, 1972.

Wilson, R. R. *Sociological Approaches to the Old Testament.* Philadelphia: Fortress, 1984.

14. HERMENEUTICS

Achtemeier, E. *The Old Testament and the Proclamation of the Gospel.* Philadelphia: Westminster, 1973.

Achtemeier, P. *An Introduction to the New Hermeneutic.* Philadelphia: Westminster, 1969.

_____. *The Old Testament Roots of Our Faith.* New York: Abingdon, 1962; London: S.P.C.K., 1964; Philadelphia: Fortress, 1962, 1979.

Barr, J. *Holy Scripture Canon Authority Criticism.* Philadelphia: Westminster, 1983.

_____. *Old and New in Interpretation.* New York: Harper & Row, 1966.

_____. *The Bible in the Modern World.* New York: Harper Row, 1973.

Barton, J. *Reading the Old Testament: Method in Biblical Study.* Philadelphia: Westminster, 1984.

Braaten, C. *History and Hermeneutics.* Philadelphia: Westminster, 1966.

Bright, J. *The Authority of the Old Testament.* Grand Rapids: Baker 1975.

Brown, R. E. and S. M. Schneiders. "Hermeneutics." *The New Jerome Biblical Commentary.* Ed. by R. Brown et al. Englewood Cliffs: Prentice Hall, 1990. Pp. 1146–1165.

_____. "Hermeneutics." *The Jerome Biblical Commentary.* Ed. by R. Brown et al. Englewood Cliffs: Prentice Hall, 1968. Pp. 605–623.

_____. *Biblical Exegesis and Church Doctrine.* New York: Paulist, 1985.

Caird, G. B. *The Language and Imagery of the Bible.* Philadelphia: Westminster, 1980.

Campbell, D. B. *The Old Testament for Modern Readers.* Atlanta: John Knox, 1972.

Carson, D. A. and J. D. Woodbridge, eds. *Hermeneutics, Authority, and Canon*. Grand Rapids: Academie, 1986.

Childs, B. *Biblical Theology in Crisis*. Philadelphia: Westminster, 1970.

Clements, R. E. *One Hundred Years of Old Testament Interpretation*. Philadelphia: Westminster, 1976.

Croatto, J. S. *Biblical Hermeneutics*. Maryknoll: Orbis, 1987.

Crossan, J. D., ed. *Paul Ricoeur on Biblical Hermeneutics*. Missoula: Scholars, 1975.

Dyer, G. J. *The Pastoral Guide to the Bible*. Mundelein, IL: Civitas Dei, 1978.

Fiorenza, E. S. "Contemporary Biblical Scholarship: Its Roots, Present Understandings and Future Directions." *Modern Biblical Scholarship*. Villanova, PA: Villanova University Press, 1984.

_____. "For the Sake of Our Salvation: Biblical Interpretation as Theological Task." *Sin, Salvation and the Spirit*. D. Durken, ed. Collegeville: The Liturgical Press, 1979. Pp. 21–40.

Fishbane, M. *Text and Texture. Close Readings of Selected Biblical Texts*. New York: Schocken, 1979.

Friedman, R. E., ed. *The Creation of Sacred Literature: Composition and Redaction of the Biblical text*. Berkeley–Los Angeles–London: University of California Press, 1981.

Funk, R. W. *Language, Hermeneutic, and Word of God*. New York: Harper & Row, 1966.

Funk, R. and G. Ebeling. *History and Hermeneutic*. New York: Harper & Row, 1967.

Furguson, D. S. *Biblical Hermeneutics: An Introduction*. Atlanta: John Knox, 1986.

Gasque, W. W. and W. S. La Sor, eds. *Scripture, Tradition, and Interpretation. Essays Presented to Everett F. Harrison by His Students and Colleagues in Honor of His Seventy-Fifth Birthday*. Grand Rapids: Eerdmans, 1978.

Gowan, D. E. *Reclaiming the Old Testament for the Christian Pulpit*. Atlanta: John Knox, 1980.

Grant, R. M. and D. Tracy. *A Short History of the Interpretation of the Bible.* 2nd ed. Philadelphia: Fortress, 1984.

Harrington, D. J. *Interpreting the Old Testament.* (*Old Testament Message: A Biblical Theological Commentary.*) Wilmington: Michael Glazier, 1981.

Hassel, G. *Old Testament Theology: Basic Issues in the Current Debate.* Grand Rapids: Eerdmans, 1972.

Hayes, J. H. and W. Holladay, eds. *Biblical Exegesis: A Beginner's Handbook.* Atlanta: John Knox, 1982.

Johnson, E. E. *Expository Hermeneutics. An Introduction.* Grand Rapids: Zondervan, 1989.

Keck. L. E. *The Bible and the Pulpit: The Renewal of Biblical Preaching.* Nashville: Abingdon, 1978.

Keegan, T. J. *Interpreting the Bible: A Popular Introduction to Biblical Hermeneutics.* Mahwah: Paulist, 1985.

Kimbrough, S. T., Jr. *Israelite Religion in Sociological Perspective.* Wiesbaden: Harrassowitz, 1978.

Kuyper, L. J. *The Scripture Unbroken.* Grand Rapids: Eerdmans, 1978.

Lehmann, K. "Hermeneutics." *Sacramentum Mundi.* New York: Herder, 1968. Pp. 23–26.

Lys, D. *The Meaning of the Old Testament, an Essay on Hermeneutics.* Nashville: Abingdon, 1967.

Marle, R. *Introduction to Hermeneutics.* New York: Herder, 1967.

Mc Kim, D. K. *A Guide To Contemporary Hermeneutics: Major Trends In Biblical Interpretation.* Grand Rapids: Eerdmans, 1986.

_____. *What Christians Believe About The Bible.* Nashville: Nelson, 1985.

McKnight, E. V. *Meaning in Texts: The Historical Shaping of a Narrative Hermeneutics.* Philadelphia: Fortress, 1978.

Murphy, R. E., ed. *Theology, Exegesis and Proclamation.* New York: Herder, 1971.

Ricoeur, P. *Essays on Biblical Interpretation.* Philadelphia: Fortress, 1980.

_____. *The Conflict of Interpretations: Essays in Hermeneutics.* Evanston: Northwestern University Press, 1974.

_____. *Interpretation Theory: Discourse and the Surplus of Meaning.* Fort Worth: Texas Christian University, 1976.

Sanders, J. A. "Hermeneutics." *The Interpreter's Dictionary of the Bible. Supplementary Volume.* Nashville: Abingdon, 1976. Pp. 402–407.

Smart, J. D. *The Strange Silence of the Bible in the Church.* Philadelphia: Westminster, 1980.

Smart, J. *The Interpretation of Scripture.* Philadelphia: Westminster, 1961.

Stuart, D. K. *Old Testament Exegesis: A Primer for Students and Pastors.* Philadelphia: Westminster, 1980.

Stuhlmacher, P. *Historical Criticism and Theological Interpretation of Scripture.* Philadelphia: Fortress, 1977.

Tracy, D. *Plurality and Ambiguity: Hermeneutics, Religion, Hope.* San Francisco: Harper & Row, 1987.

Uffenheimer, B. and H. G. Reventlow, eds. *Creative Biblical Exegesis: Christian and Jewish Hermeneutics Through the Centuries.* Sheffield: JSOT Press, 1988.

von Rad, G. *Biblical Interpretations in Preaching.* Nashville: Abingdon, 1977.

Westermann, C., ed. *Essays on Old Testament Hermeneutics.* Richmond: John Knox, 1973.

15. BIBLICAL AUTHORITY AND INSPIRATION

Abraham, W. *The Divine Inspiration of Holy Scripture.* Oxford: University Press, 1981.

Achtemeier, P. J. *The Inspiration of Scripture: Problems and Proposals.* Philadelphia: Westminster, 1980.

Alley, R. *Revolt Against the Faithful: A Biblical Case for Inspiration as Encounter.* New York: Lippincott, 1970.

Alonso-Schökel, L. *The Inspired Word: Scripture in the Light of Language and Literature.* Trans. by F. Martin. New York: Herder, 1972.

Anderson, B. W., ed. *The Old Testament and Christian Faith.* New York: Herder, 1969.

Barr, J. *Old and New Interpretation.* New York: Harper & Row, 1982.

_____. *The Scope and Authority of the Bible.* Philadelphia: Westminster, 1980.

Bartlett, D. L. *The Shape of Scriptural Authority.* Philadelphia: Fortress, 1983.

Barton, J. *People of the Book. The Authority of the Bible in Christianity.* Louisville: Westminster–John Knox, 1988.

Bea, A. *The Word of God and Mankind.* Chicago: Franciscan, 1967.

Beegle, D. *The Inspiration of Scripture.* Philadelphia: Westminster, 1963.

Benoit, P. *Aspects of Biblical Inspiration.* Chicago: Priory, 1965.

_____. "Inspiration and Revelation." *The Human Reality of Sacred Scripture. Concilium.* Vol. 10. New York: Paulist, 1965. Pp. 6–24.

_____. *Inspiration and the Bible.* New York: Sheed and Ward, 1965.

Boer, H. R. *The Bible and Higher Criticism.* Grand Rapids: Eerdmans, 1981.

Bright, J. *The Authority of the Old Testament.* Nashville: Abingdon, 1967.

Bryant, R. *The Bible's Authority Today.* Minneapolis: Augsburg, 1968.

Burtchaell, J. T. *Catholic Theories of Biblical Inspiration since 1810: A Review and Critique.* Cambridge: University Press, 1969.

Carson, D. A. and J. Woodbridge, eds. *Scripture and Truth.* Grand Rapids: Zondervan, 1983.

Collins, R. F. "Inspiration." *The New Jerome Biblical Commentary.* Ed. by R. Brown et al. Englewood Cliffs: Prentice Hall, 1990. Pp. 1023–33.

Countryman, W. *Biblical Authority or Biblical Tyranny?* Philadelphia: Fortress, 1981.

Cunliffe-Jones, H. *The Authority of the Biblical Revelation.* Boston: Pilgrim, 1948.

Farmer, H. H. "The Bible and its Significance and Authority." *The Interpreter's Bible.* Vol. 1. New York: Abingdon, 1952. Pp. 3–31.

Friedman, R. E. *Who Wrote the Bible?* Englewood Cliffs: Prentice Hall, 1987.

Gaussen, L. *The Inspiration of the Holy Scriptures.* London: Farncombe & Son, 1912.

Geisler, N., ed. *Inerrancy.* Grand Rapids: Zondervan, 1979.

Gnuse, R. *The Authority of the Bible: Inspiration, Revelation, and the Canon of Scripture.* New York: Paulist, 1985.

Goldingay, J. *Theological Diversity and the Authority of the Old Testament.* Grand Rapids: Eerdmans, 1987.

Greenspahn, F. E., ed. *Scripture in the Jewish and Christian Traditions: Authority, Interpretation, Relevance.* Nashville: Abingdon, 1962.

Hagen, K., ed. *The Bible in the Churches: How Different Christians Interpret the Scriptures.* New York: Paulist, 1985.

Harris, R. L. *Inspiration and the Canonicity of the Bible: an Historical and Exegetical Study.* Grand Rapids: Zondervan, 1976.

Henry, C. *God, Revelation and Authority.* Vol. 2. *God Who Speaks and Shows.* Waco: Word, 1976.

Herbert, A. G. *The Authority of the Old Testament.* London: Faber, 1947.

Hoffman, T. "Inspiration, Normativeness, Canonicity, and the Unique Sacred Character of the Bible." *Catholic Biblical Quarterly* 44 (1982) 447–469.

Inch, M. and R. Youngblood, *The Living and Active Word of God* (Studies in Honor of S. J. Schultz). Winona Lake: Eisenbrauns, 1983.

Jensen, R. "On the Problem(s) of Scriptural Authority." *Interpretation* 31 (1977) 237–250.

Loretz, O. *The Truth of the Bible.* New York: Herder, 1968.

Mayo, S. M. *The Relevance of the Old Testament for the Christian Faith.* Washington, D.C.: University Press of America, 1982.

McKenzie, J. "Inspiration." *Dictionary of the Bible.* New York: MacMillan, 1965. Pp. 389–93.

McKim, D., ed. *The Authoritative Word: Essays on the Nature of Scripture.* Grand Rapids: Eerdmans, 1983.

Miller, D. G. *The Authority of the Bible.* Grand Rapids: Eerdmans, 1972.

Montgomery, J. W. *God's Inerrant Word: An International Symposium on the Trustworthiness of Scriptures.* Minneapolis: Bethany, 1974.

Newman, J. H. *On the Inspiration of Scripture.* Washington: Corpus, 1966.

Orr, J. *Revelation and Inspiration.* Grand Rapids: Eerdmans, 1952.

Pache, R. *The Inspiration and Authority of Scripture.* Chicago: Moody, 1969.

Pinnock, C. A. *The Scripture Principle.* San Francisco: Harper & Row, 1984.

Pirot, J. "Inspiration." *Guide to the Bible: An Introduction to the Study of Holy Scripture.* 2 vols. Rome: Desclée, 1951. Pp. 9–65.

Rahner, K. *Inspiration in the Bible.* 2nd rev. ed. New York: Herder & Herder, 1964.

Ramsey, A. M. "The Authority of the Bible." *Peake's Commentary on Holy Scripture.* London-New York: Nelson, 1962. Pp. 1–7.

Reventlow, H. G. *The Authority of the Bible and the Rise of the Modern World.* Philadelphia: Fortress, 1984, 1985.

Ridderbos, H. *Studies in Scripture and its Authority.* Grand Rapids: Eerdmans, 1978.

Robinson, H. W. *Inspiration and Revelation in the Old Testament.* London: Oxford University Press, 1946; Oxford: Clarendon, 1950.

Rogers, J. B. and D. K. McKim. *The Authority and Interpretation of the Bible: An Historical Approach.* San Francisco: Harper & Row, 1979.

Rogers, J., ed. *Biblical Authority.* Waco: Word, 1977.

Rome and the Study of Scripture. St. Meinrad: Abbey, 1964.

Saarnivaara, U. *Can the Bible Be Trusted?* Minneapolis: Osterhuis, 1983.

Smart, J. D. *The Past Present and Future of Biblical Theology.* Philadelphia: Westminster, 1979; Edinburgh: Clark, 1980.

Snaith, N. H. *The Inspiration and Authority of the Bible.* London: Epsworth, 1956.

Syme, G. S. and C. U. Syme. *The Scripture of Truth.* Milford: Mott Media, 1983.

Terrien, S. *The Elusive Presence: Towards a New Biblical Theology.* New York: Harper & Row, 1978.

Vatican II: Dogmatic Constitution on Divine Revelation. (Dei Verbum.) Vatican Council II, the Conciliar and Post-Conciliar Documents. A. Flannery. Northport: Costello, 1984. Pp. 750–765.

von Campenhausen, H. *The Formation of the Christian Bible.* Philadelphia: Fortress, 1972.

Warfield, B. B. *The Inspiration and Authority of the Bible.* Philadelphia: Presbyterian and Reformed, 1970.

Winegreen, J., et al. "Interpretation, History of." *Interpreter's Dictionary of the Bible.* Supplementary Volume. Nashville: Abingdon, 1976. Pp. 436–56.

Wood, J. D. *The Interpretation of the Bible.* London: Duckworth, 1958.

16. ARCHAEOLOGY, HISTORY AND GEOGRAPHY

Aharmi, J. *The Land of the Bible: A Historical Geography.* London: Burnes & Oates, 1966; Philadelphia: Westminster, 1980.

Aharoni, Y. and Avi–Yonah, M. *The Macmillan Bible Atlas.* London: Collier-Macmillan; New York: Macmillan, 1968.

_____. *The Land of the Bible: A Historical Geography*. 2nd. ed. enlarged and rev. London: Burns & Oates, Ltd.; Philadelphia: Westminster, 1979.

_____. *The Archaeology of the Land of Israel*. Philadelphia: Westminster, 1982.

Albright, W. F. *Archaeology and the Religion of Israel*. Baltimore: Johns Hopkins, 1968; Garden City: Doubleday, 1969.

_____. *From the Stone Age to Christianity*. Baltimore: The Johns Hopkins Press, 1940, 1946, 1957; Garden City: Doubleday, 1957.

_____. *The Archaeology of Palestine*. Harmondsworth: Penguin, 1949, 1961.

_____. *The Archaeology of Palestine and the Bible*. Rev. ed. Cambridge: American Schools of Oriental Research, 1974.

_____. *The Biblical Period*. Pittsburgh: Biblical Colloquium, 1950.

Alt, A. *Essays on Old Testament History and Religion*. Garden City: Doubleday, 1968.

Avi-Yonah, M. *The Holy Land From the Persian to the Arab Conquests (536 BC to AD 640): A Historical Geography*. Grand Rapids: Baker, 1977.

_____, ed. *Encyclopedia of Archaeological Excavations in the Holy Land*. 4 vols. Englewood Cliffs: Prentice Hall, 1975; London: Oxford University Press, 1975–1978.

Axelsson, L. E. *The Lord Rose up from Seir. Studies in History and Traditions of the Negev and Southern Judah*. Stockholm: Almqvist & Wiksell, 1987.

Baez-Camargo, G. *Archaeological Commentary on the Bible*. New York: Doubleday, 1984.

Baly, D. *Geographical Companion to the Bible*. New York: McGraw-Hill; London: Lutterworth, 1963, 1979.

_____. *The Geography of the Bible*. London: Lutterworth, 1962; New York: Harper & Row, 1957, 1974.

Bartlett, J. R. *Jericho*. Grand Rapids: Eerdmans, 1983.

Beld, S. G., W. W. Hallo and P. Michalowski. *The Tablets of Ebla. Concordance and Bibliography.* Winona Lake: Eisenbrauns, 1984.

Bilde, P. *Flavius Josephus Between Jerusalem and Rome.* Sheffield: JSOT Press, 1988.

Blaiklock, E. M. and R. K. Harrison, eds. *The New International Dictionary of Biblical Archaeology.* Grand Rapids: Zondervan, 1984.

Boling, R. G. *The Early Biblical Community in Transjordan.* Sheffield: Almond Press, 1988.

Borowski, O. *Agriculture in Iron Age Israel.* Winona Lake: Eisenbrauns, 1987.

Brauner, R. A., ed. *Jewish Civilization: Essays and Studies.* Vol. 2. Philadelphia: Reconstructionist Rabbinical College, 1981.

Brown, R. E. and R. North. "Biblical Geography." *The New Jerome Biblical Commentary.* Ed. by R. Brown, et al. Englewood Cliffs: Prentice Hall, 1990. Pp. 1175–95.

Brown, R. *Recent Discoveries and the Biblical World.* Wilmington: Michael Glazier, 1983.

Bultmann, R. *Primitive Christianity in its Contemporary Setting.* Philadelphia: Fortress, 1980.

Campbell, E. F., D. N. Freedman and G. E. Wright., eds. *The Biblical Archaeologist Reader.* 3 vols. Garden City: Doubleday, 1961–1970.

Cate, R. L. *A History of the Bible Lands In the Interbiblical Period.* Nashville: Broadman, 1989.

Cervicek, P. *Rock Pictures of Upper Egypt and Nubia.* Rome: Herder, 1986.

Collins, J. J. "The Historical Character of the Old Testament in Recent Biblical Theology." *Catholic Biblical Quarterly* 41 (1979) 185–204.

Coote, R. *Early Israel: A New Horizon.* Philadelphia: Fortress, 1990.

Coote, R. and D. Ord. *The Bible's First History.* Philadelphia: Fortress, 1989.

_____. *The Bible's First History.* Philadelphia: Fortress, 1989.

Cornfeld, G. and D. N. Freedman. *Archaeology of the Bible: Book by Book.* San Francisco: Harper & Row, 1976, 2nd ed. 1982.

Coulson, W. D. and A. Leonard, Jr. *Cities of the Delta, I. Naukratis.* Malibu: Undena, 1981.

Craigie, P. C. *Ugarit and the Old Testament.* Grand Rapids: Eerdmans, 1983.

Cross, F. M. *The Ancient Library at Qumran and Modern Biblical Studies.* Garden City: Doubleday, 1961.

Curtis, A. H. *Ugarit (Ras Shamra).* Grand Rapids: Eerdmans, 1985.

Darrell, L. H. *The Old Testament and the Archaeologist.* Philadelphia: Fortress, 1981.

Davies, G. I. *The Way of the Wilderness. A Geographical Study of the Wilderness Itineraries in the Old Testament.* London: Cambridge University Press, 1979.

_____. *Megiddo.* Cambridge: Lutterworth; Grand Rapids: Eerdmans, 1986.

Davies, P. R. *Qumran.* Grand Rapids: Eerdmans, 1983.

de Vaux, R. "On Right and Wrong Use of Archaeology." *Near Eastern Archaeology in the Twentieth Century.* J. A. Sanders, ed. Garden City: Doubleday, 1970. Pp. 64–80.

Dever, W. G. *Archaeology and Biblical Studies: Retrospects and Prospects.* Evanston: Seabury, 1974.

_____. "Archaeology." *The Interpreter's Dictionary of the Bible.* Supplementary Volume. Nashville: Abingdon, 1976. Pp. 44–52.

_____. "Biblical Theology and Biblical Archaeology." *Harvard Theological Review* 73 (1980) 1–15.

_____ and H. D. Lance, eds. *A Manual of Field Excavation.* New York: Hebrew Union College, 1978.

DeVries, S. J. *Yesterday, Today and Tomorrow: Time and History in the Old Testament.* Grand Rapids: Eerdmans, 1975.

Dowley, T., ed. *Discovering the Bible. Archaeologists Look at Scripture.* Grand Rapids: Eerdmans, 1986.

Edersheim, A. *Old Testament Bible History.* Grand Rapids: Eerdmans, 1972.

Eliade, M. *Cosmos and History: the Myth of the Eternal Return.* New York: Harper, 1954, 1959.

Feinberg, C. L. "The Value of Archaeological Studies for Biblical Research." *Tradition and Testament.* Ed. by C. L. Feinberg and P. Feinberg. Chicago: Moody, 1981. Pp. 265–292.

Finegan, J. *Archaeological History of the Ancient Middle East.* Boulder: Westview; Folkestone: Dawson, 1979.

Finkelstein, I. *The Archaeology of the Israelite Settlement.* Jerusalem: Israel Exploration Society, 1988.

Fishbane, M. *Biblical Interpretation in Ancient Israel.* Oxford: Clarendon, 1985.

Frank, H. T. *An Archaeological Companion to the Bible.* Nashville: Abingdon, 1971.

Freedman, D. N. and J. C. Greenfield, eds. *New Directions in Biblical Archaeology.* Garden City: Doubleday, 1969.

_____ and E. F. Campbell, Jr., eds. *The Biblical Archaeologist Reader,* vol 1, Garden City: Doubleday, 1961; vol. 2, Garden City: Doubleday, 1964; vol 3, Garden City: Doubleday, 1970; vol. 4, Sheffield: Almond Press, 1983.

_____. *Pottery, Poetry, and Prophecy.* Winona Lake: Eisenbrauns, 1980.

Friedman, E. *El-Muhraga (The Sacrifice–Keren Ha-Karmel); Here Elijah Raised His Altar.* Rome: Edizioni del Teresianum, 1985.

Garbini, G. *History and Ideology in Ancient Israel.* New York: Crossroad, 1988.

Garstang, J. *The Story of Jericho.* London: Hodder & Stoughton, 1940.

Gernty, L.T. and L. G. Herr, eds. *The Archaeology of Jordan and Other Studies Presented to Siegfried H. Horn.* Berrian Springs: Andrews University, 1986.

Gibson, J. C. *Canaanite Myths and Legends.* Edinburgh: Clark, 1978.

Glueck, N. *The Other Side of the Jordan.* New Haven: American Schools of Oriental Research, 1940; rev. ed., 1970.

_____. *Exploration in Eastern Palestine, IV.* New Haven: American Schools of Oriental Research under the Jane Dows Nies Publication Fund, 1951.

Gray, J. *Archaeology and the Old Testament World.* London–New York: Nelson, 1962.

_____. "Recent Archaeological Discoveries and Their Bearing on the Old Testament." *Tradition and Interpretation.* G. W. Anderson, ed. Oxford: Clarendon, 1979. Pp. 65–95.

Halpern B. *The First Historians: The Hebrew Bible and History.* San Francisco: Harper & Row, 1988.

Haran, M., ed. *Eretz-Israel.* Vol XLII. Jerusalem: Israel Exploration Society, 1978.

Hayes, J. H. and J. M. Miller, eds. *Israelite and Judaean History.* Philadelphia: Westminster, 1977.

Herzog, Z., et. al. *Excavations at Tel Michal, 1977.* Tel Aviv: University Institute of Archaeology, 1979.

Hopkins, D. C. *The Highlands of Canaan: Agricultural Life in the Early Iron Age.* Sheffield: Almond Press, 1985.

Hoppe, L. J. *What Are They Saying About Biblical Archaeology?* New York–Ramsey: Paulist, 1984.

Jeppesen, K. and B. Otzen, eds. *The Production of Time. Tradition History in the Old Testament Scholarship.* Sheffield: Almond Press, 1984.

Kallai, Z. *Historical Geography of the Bible: The Tribal Territories of Israel.* Leiden: Brill, 1986.

Kenyon, F. G. *Our Bible and the Ancient Manuscripts.* London: Eyre & Spottiswoode; New York: Harper, 1958.

Kenyon, K. M. *Archaeology in the Holy Land.* London: Benn, 1960,

_____. *Beginning in Archaeology.* New York: Praeger, 1953.

_____. *Digging Up Jericho.* New York: Praeger, 1957.

_____. *Digging Up Jerusalem*. London: Benn, 1974.

_____. *The Bible and Recent Archaeology*. Atlanta: John Knox, 1978.

Kitchen, K. A. *The Bible in its World. The Bible & Archaeology Today*. Downers Grove: Inter–Varsity, 1977; Exeter: Paternoster, 1977.

Knibb, M. A. *The Qumran Community*. Cambridge: University Press, 1987.

Kochavi, M., et al. *Aphek-Antipartis 1974–1977. The Inscriptions*. Tel Aviv: University Institute of Archaeology, 1978.

Lance, H. D. *The Old Testament and the Archaeologist*. Philadelphia: Fortress, 1981.

Lapp, N. L., ed. *The Tale of the Tell. Archaeological Studies by Paul W. Lapp*. Pittsburgh: Pickwick, 1975.

Lapp, P. W. *Archaeology and History*. New York: World, 1969.

_____. *Biblical Archaeology and History*. New York: World, 1969.

Malamat, A., ed. *The Age of the Monarchies: Culture and Society*. Jerusalem: Massada, 1979.

Mazar, A. *Archaeology of the Land of the Bible: 10,000–586 B.C.E.* The Anchor Bible Reference Library. New York: Doubleday, 1990.

_____ and Y. Yadin, eds. *Nahman Avigad Volume*. Jerusalem: The Hebrew University, 1985.

Milik, J. T. *Ten Years of Discovery in the Wilderness of Judaea*. Naperville: Allenson, 1959.

Miller, J. M. *The Old Testament and the Historian*. Philadelphia: Fortress Press, 1976.

Moorey, R. and P. Parr, eds. *Archaeology in the Levant. Essays for Kathleen Kenyon*. Warminster: Aris & Phillips, 1978.

Moorey, R. *Excavations in Palestine*. Grand Rapids: Eerdmans, 1983.

Negev, A., ed. *Archaeological Encyclopedia of the Holy Land*. Jerusalem: The Jerusalem Publishing House; New York: Putnam, 1972.

Nielsen, E. *Law, History and Tradition. Selected Essays*. Copenhagen: GAD, 1983.

North, R. and P. J. King. "Biblical Archaeology." *The New Jerome Biblical Commentary*. Ed. by R. Brown et al. Englewood Cliffs: Prentice Hall, 1990. Pp. 1196–1218.

Osman, A. *Stranger in the Valley of the Kings*. San Francisco: Harper & Row, 1987.

Payne, D. F. *Kingdoms of the Lord*. Grand Rapids: Eerdmans, 1981.

Perdue, L. G., L. E. Toombs and G. L. Johnson, eds. *Archaeology and Biblical Interpretation: Essays in Memory of D. Glenn Rose*. Atlanta: John Knox, 1987.

Porter, J. R. "Old Testament Historiography." *Tradition and Interpretation*. Oxford: Clarendon, 1979. Pp. 125–162.

Pritchard, J. B. *Archaeology and the Old Testament*. Princeton: Princeton University Press, 1958.

Rainey, A. F. *Egypt, Israel, Sinai: Archaeological and Historical Relationships in the Biblical Period*. Jerusalem: Tel Aviv University, 1987.

_____. *El Amarma Tablets 359–379*. Kevalaer: Butzon & Bercker; Neukirchen-Vluyn: Neukirchener, 1978.

Ramsey, G. W. *The Quest for the Historical Israel*. Atlanta: John Knox, 1981.

Rast, W. E. *Preliminary Reports of ASOR-Sponsored Excavations 1980–1984*. Winona Lake: Eisenbrauns, 1986.

_____. *Preliminary Reports of ASOR-Sponsored Excavations 1982–1985*. Baltimore: Johns Hopkins, 1988.

Robinson, J. M., gen. ed. *The Nag Hammadi Library in English*. San Francisco: Harper & Row, 1988.

Rothenberg, B. *Timna: Valley of the Biblical Copper Mines*. London: Thomas & Hudson, 1972.

Russell, D. S. *The Jews from Alexander to Herod*. London: Oxford University Press, 1967.

Sanders, J. A., ed. *Near Eastern Archaeology in the Twentieth Century: Essays in Honor of Nelson Glueck.* Garden City: Doubleday, 1970.

Sawyer, J. F. and D. J. Clines, eds. *Midian, Moab and Edom: The History and Archaeology of Late Bronze and Iron Age Jordan and Northwest Arabia.* Sheffield: JSOT Press, 1983.

Schley, D. G. *Shiloh, A Biblical City in Tradition and History.* Sheffield: JSOT, 1989.

Schoville, K. N. *Biblical Archaeology in Focus.* Grand Rapids: Baker, 1978.

Shanks, H. *The City of David: A Guide to Biblical Jerusalem.* Washington, D. C.: The Biblical Archaeology Society, 1975.

Simons, J. *The Geographical and Topographical Texts of the Old Testament.* Leiden: Brill, 1959.

Slingerland, H. D. *The Testaments of the Twelve Patriarchs: A Critical History of Research.* Missoula: Scholars, 1977.

Smith, G. A. *Historical Geography of the Holy Land.* 4th ed. London: Hoder & Stoughton, 1896.

Stiebing, W. *Out of the Desert? Archaeology and the Exodus/Conquest Narratives.* Buffalo: Prometheus, 1989.

Teeple, H. M. *The Historical Approach to the Bible.* Evanston: Religion and Ethics Institute, 1982.

The Cambridge History of the Bible. 3 vols. Cambridge: Cambridge University Press, 1963–70.

Thomas, D. W., ed. *Archaeology and Old Testament Study.* Oxford: Clarendon, 1967.

Thompson, H. *Biblical Archaeology: The World, the Mediterranean, the Bible.* New York: Paragon, 1987.

Thompson, J. *The Bible and Archaeology.* 3rd rev ed. Grand Rapids: Eerdmans, 1982.

Tomabechi, Y. *Catalogue of Artifacts in the Babylonion Collection of the Lowie Museum of Anthropology.* Malibu: Undena, 1984.

Towner, W. S. *Archaeology and Old Testament Study.* Oxford: Clarendon, 1967.

Van Seters, J. *In Search of History: Historiography in the Ancient World and the Origins of Biblical History.* London–New Haven: Yale University Press, 1983.

Wacholder, B. Z. *The Dawn of Qumran; The Sectarian Torah and the Teacher of Righteousness.* Cincinnati: Hebrew Union College, 1983.

Williams, W. G. *Archaeology in Biblical Research.* New York: Abingdon, 1965.

Winton, T. D., ed. *Archaeology and Old Testament Study.* Oxford: Clarendon, 1967.

Wright, G. E. *Biblical Archaeology.* Rev. and expanded ed. London: Duckworth; Philadelphia: Westminster, 1962. (The best survey of the subject.)

_____. "What Archaeology Can and Cannot Do." *Biblical Archaeologist* 34 (1971) 70–76.

_____ and D. N. Freedman, eds. *The Biblical Archaeologist Reader.* Vol. 1. Garden City: Doubleday, 1964.

_____. *Biblical Archaeology.* London: Duckworth, 1957; Philadelphia: Westminster, 1957, 1962, 1963.

Yadin, Y. *Hazor: The Rediscovery of a Great Citadel of the Bible.* London: Weidenfeld & Nicolson, 1975.

_____. *Jerusalem Revisited.* Jerusalem: Israel Exploration Society, 1975.

17. CANON

Alexander, A. *Evidences of the Authenticity, Inspiration, and Canonical Authority of the Holy Scriptures.* Philadelphia: Presbyterian Board of Publication, 1836.

Barr, J. *Holy Scripture: Canon, Authority, Criticism.* Philadelphia: Westminster, 1983.

_____. *The Bible in the Modern World.* New York: Harper & Row, 1973.

Beckwith, R. T. *The Old Testament Canon of the New Testament Church.* Grand Rapids: Eerdmans, 1985, 1986.

Blenkinsopp, J. *Prophecy and Canon: A Contribution to the Study of Jewish Origins.* Notre Dame: University Press, 1977.

Brown, R. E. and R. F. Collins. "Canonicity." *The New Jerome Biblical Commentary.* Ed. by R. Brown, et al. Englewood Cliffs: Prentice Hall, 1990. Pp. 1034–54.

Bruce, F. F. *The Canon of Scripture.* Downers Grove: Inter-Varsity, 1988.

Brueggemann, W. *The Creative Word: Canon as a Model for Biblical Education.* Philadelphia: Fortress, 1982.

Coats, G. W. and B. O. Long, eds. *Canon and Authority.* Philadelphia: Fortress, 1977.

Filson, F. V. *Which Books Belong in the Bible? A Study of the Canon.* Philadelphia: Westminster, 1957.

Flack, E. E. and B. M. Metzger, et al. *The Text Canon and Principal Versions of the Bible.* Grand Rapids: Baker, 1956.

Freedman, D. N. "Canon of the Old Testament." *Interpreter's Dictionary of the Bible.* Supplementary Volume. Nashville: Abingdon, 1976. Pp. 130–136.

Green, W. H. *General Introduction to the Old Testament; the Canon.* New York: Scribner, 1916.

Haran, M., ed. *Eretz-Israel.* Vol XLII. Jerusalem: Israel Exploration Society, 1978.

Heidt, W. *Inspiration, Canonicity, Texts, Versions, Hermeneutics: A General Introduction to Sacred Scripture.* Collegeville: The Liturgical Press, 1970.

Jeffery, A. "The Canon of the Old Testament" and "Texts and Ancient Versions of the Old Testament." *The Interpreter's Bible.* Vol. 1. New York: Abingdon, 1952. Pp. 32–62.

Leiman, S. Z. *The Canonization of Hebrew Scripture: The Talmudic and Midrashic Evidence.* Hamden: Archon, 1976.

_____. *The Canon and Masorah of the Hebrew Bible: An Introductory Reader.* New York: Ktav, 1974.

Meade, D. G. *Pseudonymity and Canon.* Grand Rapids: Eerdmans, 1987.

Neusner, J. *From Politics to Piety: The Emergence of Pharisaic Judaism.* Englewood Cliffs: Prentice Hall, 1973.

Ostborn, G. *Cult and Canon: A Study in the Canonization of the Old Testament.* Uppsala: Lundequistska, 1951.

Roberts, B. J. "The Canon and Text of the Old Testament." *Peake's Commentary on Holy Scripture.* London–New York: Nelson, 1962. Pp. 73–75 (section 58d).

Rowley, H. H. *The Growth of the Old Testament.* New York: Harper & Row; London: Hutchinson's University Library, 1950, 1964, 1967.

Sanders, E. P. *Canon and Community.* Philadelphia: Fortress, 1979.

Sanders, J. N. "The Literature and Canon of the New Testament." *Peake's Commentary on Holy Scripture.* London–New York: Nelson, 1962. Pp. 676–682.

Sanders, J. *Torah and Canon.* Philadelphia: Fortress, 1972.

_____. "Adaptable for Life: The Nature and Function of Canon." *Magnalia Dei: The Mighty Acts of God.* Garden City: Doubleday, 1976.

Sundberg, A. Z., Jr. *The Old Testament of the Early Church.* Cambridge–London: Harvard University Press, 1964.

_____. "The Old Testament: A Christian Canon." *Catholic Biblical Quarterly* 30 (1968) 143–55.

_____. "The Bible Canon and the Christian Doctrine of Inspiration." *Interpretation* 29 (1975) 358–371.

_____. "The Protestant Old Testament Canon: Should It Be Reexamined?" *Catholic Biblical Quarterly* 28 (1966) 194–203.

Tucker, G. M., D. L. Peterson and R. R. Woods, eds. *Canon, Theology, and Old Testament Interpretation.* Essays in Honor of Brevard S. Childs. Philadelphia: Fortress, 1988.

Weingren, J. *From Bible to Mishnah: The Continuity of Tradition.* Manchester: Manchester University Press, 1976.

Wright, G. E. "The Canon as Theological Problem." *The Old Testament and Theology.* New York: Harper & Row, 1969.

III. PENTATEUCH

18. GENERAL

Aalders, G. C. *A Short Introduction to the Pentateuch.* London: Tyndale, 1949.

Albright, W. F. *The Biblical Period From Abraham to Ezra.* New York: Harper & Row, 1963.

Alt, A. "The God of the Father." *Essays on Old Testament History and Religion.* Garden City: Doubleday, 1967. Pp. 1–100.

_____. *Noah: The Person and the Story in History and Tradition.* Columbia: University of South Carolina Press, 1989.

Beck, M. H. and L. Williamson, Jr. *Mastering Old Testament Facts. Book 1: Introduction, Genesis–Deuteronomy.* Atlanta: John Knox, 1978.

Blenkinsopp, J. *From Adam to Abraham.* New York: Paulist, 1965.

Brueggemann, W. and H. W. Wolff. *The Vitality of the Old Testament.* Atlanta: John Knox, 1975.

Carpenter, E. E. "Recent Pentateuchal Studies." *Ashbury Theological Journal* 41 (1986) 19–35.

Cassuto, U. *The Documentary Hypothesis and the Composition of the Pentateuch.* Jerusalem: Magnes, 1961, 1972.

Clines, D. *The Theme of the Pentateuch.* JSOT Supplement 10. Sheffield: University of Sheffield, Department of Biblical Studies, 1978, 1984.

Coote, R. B. and D. R. Ord. *The Bible's First History.* Philadelphia: Fortress, 1989.

Cross, F. M. *Canaanite Myth and Hebrew Epic: Essays in the History of the Religion of Israel.* Cambridge: Harvard University Press, 1973.

_____, "The Cultus of the Israelite League." *Canaanite Myth and Hebrew Epic.* Cambridge: Harvard University Press, 1973. Chs. 4–6.

Ellis, P. *The Yahwist.* Notre Dame: Fides, 1968.

Emerton, J., ed. *Studies in the Pentateuch.* Leiden: Brill, 1990.

Gaebelein, F. E., gen. ed. *The Exposition's Bible Commentary.* Vol. 2. Grand Rapids: Zondervan, 1990.

Guinan, M. D. *Pentateuch.* Collegeville: The Liturgical Press/Michael Glazier, 1990.

Habel, N. *Literary Criticism of the Old Testament.* Philadelphia: Fortress, 1971.

Hamilton, P. V. *Handbook on the Pentateuch: Genesis, Exodus, Leviticus, Numbers, Deuteronomy.* Grand Rapids: Baker, 1982.

Hasel G. F. "The Sabbath in the Pentateuch." *The Sabbath in Scripture and History.* K. Strand, ed. Washington, D. C.: Review and Herald Publication Association, 1982. Pp. 21–43.

Herrmann, S. *Israel In Egypt.* Naperville: Allenson, 1973.

Hirsch, S. R. *The Pentateuch.* London: Levy, 1963.

Holborn, A. *The Pentateuch in the Light of Today.* Edinburgh: Clark, 1902.

Jackson, B. S. "The Ceremonial and the Judicial: Biblical Law as Sign and Symbol." *Journal for the Study of the Old Testament* 30 (1984) 25–50.

Jacobson, B. S. *Meditation on the Torah.* Tel Aviv: Sinai, 1956.

Jenks, A. W. *The Elohist and North Israelite Traditions.* Missoula: Scholars, 1977.

Johnson, M. D. *The Purpose of the Biblical Genealogies.* Cambridge: Cambridge University Press, 1969.

Johnston, L. *The God of Our Fathers.* New York: Paulist, 1975.

Johnstone, W. *Exodus.* Sheffield: JSOT, 1990.

Klein, M. *The Fragment-Targums of the Pentateuch According to their Extant Sources.* 2 vols. Rome: Biblical Institute Press, 1980.

La Verdiere, E. *Introduction to the Pentateuch.* Collegeville: The Liturgical Press, 1971.

Lazar, M. *The Ladino Pentateuch.* Culver City: Labyrinthos, 1988.

Levenson, J. D. *Sinai and Zion: An Entry into the Jewish Bible.* Minneapolis: Winston, 1985.

Livingston, G. H. *The Pentateuch In Its Cultural Environment.* Grand Rapids: Baker, 1974.

Mackintosh, C. H. *Genesis to Deuteronomy: Notes on the Pentateuch.* Neptune: Loigeaux, 1972.

Mann, T. W. *The Book of the Torah: The Narrative Integrity of the Pentateuch.* Atlanta: John Knox, 1988.

Marks, J. H. *The Pentateuch: A Commentary on Genesis, Exodus, Leviticus, Numbers, Deuteronomy.* Charles Laymon, ed. Nashville: Abingdon, 1983.

McEvenue, S. *Interpreting the Pentateuch.* Collegeville: The Liturgical Press/Michael Glazier, 1990.

_____. *The Narrative Style of the Priestly Writer.* Rome: Biblical Institute Press, 1971.

McKane, W. *Studies in the Patriarchal Narratives.* Edinburgh: Handsel, 1979.

Mendanhall, G. E. *Law and Covenant in Israel and the Ancient Near East.* Pittsburgh: Biblical Colloquium, 1955.

Millard, A. R. and D. J. Wiseman, eds. *Essays on the Patriarchal Narratives.* Winona Lake: Eisenbrauns, 1980.

Miller, P. *Deuteronomy.* Louisville: John Knox, 1990.

Murphy, R. E. "Introduction to the Pentateuch." *The New Jerome Biblical Commentary.* Ed. by R. Brown, et al. Englewood Cliffs: Prentice Hall, 1990. Pp. 3–7.

Nelson, R. D. *The Double Redaction of the Deuteronomistic History.* Sheffield: JSOT Press, 1981.

North, C. R. "Pentateuchal Criticism." *Old Testament and Modern Study.* H. H. Rowley, ed. Oxford: Clarendon Press, 1951. Pp. 48–83.

Noth, M. *A History of Pentateuchal Traditions.* Trans. by B. W. Anderson. Chico: Scholars, 1981.

_____. *The Laws in the Pentateuch and Other Essays.* Edinburgh: Oliver & Boyd, 1966; Philadelphia: Fortress, 1967.

Owens, J. *Analytical Key to the Old Testament.* Vol. 1. Genesis-Joshua. Grand Rapids: Baker, 1990.

Patrick, D. *Old Testament Law.* Atlanta: John Knox, 1985.

Plaut, H. G., ed. *The Torah: A Modern Commentary.* Commentaries by W. G. Plaut; Leviticus by B.J. Bamberger; Essays on ancient Near Eastern literature by W. W. Hallo. New York: Union of American Hebrew Congregations, 1974–1981.

Sanders, J. A. *Torah and Canon.* Philadelphia: Fortress, 1972.

Sarna, N. M., gen. ed. *The JPS Torah Commentary.* 5 volumes (still in process). Philadelphia: Jewish Publication Society, 1989– .

Segal, M. H. *The Pentateuch. Its Composition and its Authorship and other Biblical Studies.* Jerusalem: Magnes; London: Oxford University Press, 1967.

Seters, J. V. *Abraham in History and Tradition.* New Haven: Yale University Press, 1975.

Suelzer, A. *The Pentateuch: A Study In Salvation History.* New York: Herder, 1964.

Tigay, J. H. "The Evolution of the Pentateuchal Narratives in Light of the Evolution of the Gilgamesh Epic." *Empirical Models For Biblical Criticism.* Ed. by J. Tigay. Philadelphia: University of Pennsylvania Press, 1985. Pp. 21–52.

von Rad, G. *The Problem of the Hexateuch and Other Essays.* New York: McGraw Hill, 1966.

Whybray, R. N. *The Making of the Pentateuch: A Methodological Study.* Sheffield: JSOT Press, 1987.

Wiener, H. M. *Essays In Pentateuchal Criticism.* Oberlin, OH: Bibliotheca Sacra , 1910, 1912.

Wilson, R. A. *Genealogy and History in the Biblical World.* New Haven: Yale University Press, 1977.

Winnet, F. V. *The Mosaic Tradition.* Toronto: University of Toronto Press, 1949.

Yahuda, A. S. *The Accuracy of the Bible: The Stories of Joseph, the Exodus and Genesis Confirmed and Illustrated by Egyptian Monuments and Language.* London: Heinemann, 1934.

19. SPECIFIC WORKS ON SPECIFIC BOOKS OF THE PENTATEUCH

a. Genesis

Abela, A. *The Themes of the Abraham Narrative.* Malta: Studia Editions, 1989.

Allis, O. T. "The Blessing of Abraham." *Princeton Theological Review* 25 (1927) 26–98.

Alt, A. "The God of the Fathers." *Essays on Old Testament History and Religion* Garden City: Doubleday, 1967. Pp. 1–100.

Anderson, B. W. "A Stylistic Study of the Priestly Creation Story." *Canon and Authority.* Ed. by G. Coats and B. O. Long. Philadelphia: Fortress, 1977.

_____. *Creation Versus Chaos. The Reinterpretation of Mythical Symbolism in the Bible.* New York: Association, 1967.

_____. "Creation and the Noachic Covenant." *Cry of the Environment: Rebuilding the Christian Creation Tradition.* Ed. by P. N. Joranson and K. Butigan. Santa Fe: Bear, 1984. Pp. 45–61.

_____. *Creation Versus Chaos, the Reinterpretation of Mythical Symbolism in the Bible.* Philadelphia: Fortress, 1989.

_____. "From Analysis to Synthesis: the Interpretation of Genesis 1–11." *Journal of Biblical Literature* 97 (1978) 230–39.

_____, ed. *Creation in the Old Testament.* Philadelphia: Fortress, 1984.

Arieti, S. *Abraham and the Contemporary Mind.* New York: Basic, 1981.

Aviezar, N. *In the Beginning: Biblical Creation and Science.* New York: Ktav, 1990.

Bailey, L. R. *Where Is Noah's Ark?* Nashville: Abingdon, 1978.

_____. *Noah: The Person and The Story In History and Tradition.* Columbia: University of South Carolina Press, 1989.

Baldwin, J. G. *The Message of Genesis 12–50: from Abraham to Joseph.* Leicester–Downers Grove: Inter-Varsity, 1986.

Bird, P. "Male and Female, He Created Them: Genesis 1:27b in the Context of the Priestly Account of Creation." *Harvard Theological Review* 74, 2 (1981) 129–59.

Boice, J. M. *Genesis: An Expositional Commentary. Vol. I Genesis 1:1–11:32.* Grand Rapids: Zondervan, 1982.

Brandon, S. G. *Creation Legends of The Ancient Near East.* London: Hodder & Stoughton, 1963.

Brueggemann, W. *Genesis: A Bible Commentary for Preaching and Teaching.* Atlanta: John Knox, 1982.

_____. "Genesis 3: A Foray into Psychology and Biblical Theology." *Colloquium* 19 (1987), 48–56.

_____. "The Keygma of the Priestly Writers." *The Vitality of Israel's Traditions.* 2nd ed. W. Brueggemann and H. W. Wolff. Atlanta: John Knox, 1982. Ch. 6.

Calvin, J. *Commentaries on the First Book of Moses Called Genesis.* Trans. by J. King. Grand Rapids: Eerdmans, 1948; Grand Rapids: Baker, 1984.

Cassuto, U. *Commentary on the Book of Genesis.* 2 vols. Jerusalem: Magnes, 1961.

Clark, M. "A Legal Background of the Yahwist's Use of 'God and Evil' in Genesis 2–3." *Journal of Biblical Literature* 88 (1969) 266–78.

Clark, M. "The Flood and the Structure of the Pre-Patriarchal History." *Zeitschrift für die Alttestamentliche Wissenschaft* 83 (1971) 204–210.

Clements, R. E. *Abraham and David.* Naperville: Allenson, 1967.

Clifford, R. J. and R. E. Murphy. "Genesis." *The New Jerome Biblical Commentary.* Ed. by R. Brown, et al. Englewood Cliffs: Prentice Hall, 1990. Pp. 8–43.

Clines, D. *What Does Eve Do To Help: And Other Readerly Questions to the Old Testament.* Sheffield: JSOT, 1990.

Coats, G. W. *Genesis with an Introduction to Narrative Literature.* Grand Rapids: Eerdmans, 1983.

Coats, W. *From Canaan to Egypt. Structural and Theological Context for the Joseph Story. The Catholic Biblical Quarterly* Monograph Series #4. Washington, D.C.: The Catholic Biblical Association, 1967.

Cochrane, C. C. *The Gospel According to Genesis.* Grand Rapids: Eerdmans, 1984.

Cohen, H. H. *The Drunkenness of Noah.* University: University of Alabama Press, 1974.

Cross, F. M. "The Religion of Canaan and the God of Israel." *Canaanite Myth and Hebrew Epic: Essays in the History of the Religion of Israel.* Cambridge: Harvard University Press, 1973. Pp. 1–76.

_____. "Yahweh and the God of the Patriarchs." *Harvard Theological Review* 55 (1962) 225–259.

Dahlberg, B. T. "On Recognizing the Unity of Genesis." *Theology Digest* 24 (1976) 360–67.

Davidson, R. *Genesis 1–11 The Cambridge Bible Commentary, NEB.* Cambridge: Cambridge University Press, 1973.

_____. *Genesis 12–50 The Cambridge Bible Commentary, NEB.* Cambridge: Cambridge University Press, 1979.

Day, J. *God's Conflict with the Dragon and the Sea. Echoes of a Canaanite Myth in the Old Testament.* New York: Cambridge University Press, 1985.

Delitzch, F. *A New Commentary on Genesis.* Grand Rapids: Eerdmans, 1978.

DeVaux, R. "The Hebrew Patriarchs and History." *The Bible and the Ancient Near East.* Garden City: Doubleday, 1960. Pp. 111–121.

Driver, S. R.*The Book of Genesis.*. London: Methuen, 1904.

Ellison, H. L. *Fathers of the Covenant, Studies in Genesis and Exodus.* Exeter: Paternoster, 1978.

Fitzmyer, J. A. *The Genesis Apocryphon of Qumran Cave: A Commentary.* Rome: Biblical Institute Press, 1971.

Franxman, T. W. *Genesis and the "Jewish Antiquities" of Flavius Josephus.* Rome: Biblical Institute Press, 1979.

Frye, R. M., ed. *Is God a Creationist?* New York: Scribner's, 1983.

Gage, W. A. *The Gospel of Genesis. Studies in Protology and Eschatology.* Winona Lake: Carpenter, 1984.

Gibson, J. C. *Genesis.* Volume 1. Edinburgh: St. Andrew; Philadelphia: Westminster, 1981.

_____. *Genesis.* Volume 2. Edinburgh: St. Andrew; Philadelphia: Westminster, 1982.

Goldman, S. *In the Beginning.* Philadelphia: Jewish Publication Society, 1949.

Gowan, D. E. *From Eden to Babel: A Commentary on the Book of Genesis 1–11.* Grand Rapids: Eerdmans, 1988.

Greenburg, M. *The Hab/piru.* New Haven: American Oriental Society, 1955.

Gunkel, H. *The Legends of Genesis: The Biblical Saga and History.* New York: Schoken, 1964.

_____. "The Influence of Babylonian Mythology Upon the Biblical Creation Story." *Creation in the Old Testament.* Ed. by B. W. Anderson. Philadelphia: Fortress, 1984.

Habel, N. C. "Yahweh, Maker of Heaven and Earth." *Journal of Biblical Literature* 91 (1972) 321–37.

Hamilton, V. P. *The Book of Genesis, Chapters 1–17.* Grand Rapids: Eerdmans, 1989.

Heidel, A. *The Babylonian Genesis.* 2nd ed. Chicago: University of Chicago Press, 1951; Phoenix Books, 1963.

_____. *The Gilgamesh Epic and Old Testament Parallels.* 2nd ed. Chicago: University of Chicago Press, 1946; Phoenix Books,1963.

Hendel, R. S. *The Epic of the Patriarch. The Jacob Cycle and the Traditions of Canaan and Israel.* Atlanta: Scholars, 1987.

Herbert, A. S. *Genesis 12–50. Abraham and His Heirs.* London: SCM, 1962.

Hildebrand, D. R. "A Summary of Recent Findings in Support of and Early Date for the So-Called Priestly Material of the Pentateuch." *Journal of Evangelical Theology* 29 (1986) 129–138.

Holt, J. *The Patriarchs of Israel.* Nashville: Vanderbilt University Press, 1964.

Hooke, S. H. *In the Beginning.* Oxford: Clarendon, 1948, 1955.

Horton, F. *The Melchizedek Tradition. A Critical Examination of the Sources to the Fifth Century A.D. and in the Epistle to the Hebrews.* Cambridge: Cambridge University Press, 1976.

Humphreys, W. L. *Joseph and His Family: A Literary Study.* Columbia: University of South Carolina Press, 1988.

Hunt, I. *The World of the Patriarchs.* Englewood Cliffs: Prentice Hall, 1964.

Hyers, C. "The Fall and Rise of Creationism." *Christian Century* 102 (1985) 411–415.

_____. *The Meaning of Creation: Genesis and Modern Science.* Atlanta: John Knox, 1984.

Jacob, B. *The First Book of the Bible: Genesis.* New York: Ktav, 1974.

Jeansonne, S. *The Women of Genesis from Sarah to Potiphar's Wife.* Philadelphia: Fortress, 1990.

Johnson, E. A. "The Incomprehensibility of God and the Image of God, Male and Female." *Theological Studies* 45 (1984) 441–65.

Johnston, L. *The God of Our Fathers.* New York: Paulist, 1975.

Jónsson, G. A. *The Image of God. Genesis 1:26-28 in a Century of Old Testament Research.* Stockholm: Almqvist & Wiksell, 1988.

Kidner, D. *Genesis.* London: Tyndale, 1967.

Kikawada, I. M. and A. Quinn. *Before Abraham Was: The Unity of Genesis 1–11.* Nashville: Abingdon, 1985.

Kobelski, P. J. *Melchizedek and Melchiresa. The Catholic Biblical Quarterly Monograph Series,* 10. Washington: The Catholic Biblical Association of America, 1981.

Kugel, J. *In Potiphar's House.* San Francisco: Harper & Row, 1990.

L'Heureux, C. E. *In and Out of Paradise.* New York–Ramsey: Paulist, 1983.

Lambert, W. G. and A. R. Millard. *Atra-Hasis: The Babylonian Story of the Flood.* Oxford: Clarendon, 1969.

Leach, E. R. *Genesis as Myth and Other Essays.* London: Cape, 1969.

Levenson, J. D. *Creation and the Persistence of Evil.* New York: Harper & Row, 1988.

Limburg, J. *A Good Land.* Minneapolis: Augsburg, 1981.

_____. *Old Stories for a New Time.* Atlanta: John Knox, 1983.

_____. "What Does it Mean to Have Dominion Over the Earth?" *Dialog* 10 (1971) 221–223.

Long, C. H. *Alpha: The Myths of Creation.* New York: Braziller, 1963.

Luke, J. T. "Abraham and the Iron Age: Reflections on the New Patriarchal Studies." *Journal for the Study of the Old Testament* 4 (1977) 35–47.

Luther, M. *Lectures on Genesis.* Ed. by Jaroslav Pelikan. 8 vols. St. Louis: Concordia, 1958–1965.

Maher, M. *Genesis.* Collegeville: Michael Glazier, 1991.

_____. *When God Made a Promise. A Christian Appreciation of Genesis.* Manchester: Koinonia, 1976.

_____. *Genesis.* Dublin: Gill & Macmillan, 1981; Wilmington: Michael Glazier, 1982.

Marks, J. H. *Genesis: A Commentary.* Philadelphia: Westminster, 1961.

Mazar, B. "The Historical Background of the Book of Genesis." *Journal of Near Eastern Studies* 28 (1969) 78–83.

McCurley, F. R. *Genesis, Exodus, Leviticus, Numbers.* Philadelphia: Fortress, 1979.

McEvenue, S. E. *The Narrative Style of the Priestly Writer. Analecta Biblica* 50. Rome: Biblical Institute Press, 1971.

McKane, W. *Studies in the Patriarchal Narratives.* Edinburgh: Handsel, 1979.

McKenting, H. *Why Bother with Adam and Eve?* Guildford: Lutterworth, 1982.

Meek, T. J. *Hebrew Origins* . Rev. ed. New York: Harper &Row, 1950.

Mellinkoff, R. *The Mark of Cain.* Berkeley: University of California Press, 1981.

Mendenhall, G. "The Shady Side of Wisdom: The Date and Purpose of Genesis 3." *A Light Unto My Path.* H. N. Bream, R. D. Heim, C. A. Moore. Philadelphia: Temple University Press, 1974. Pp. 319–334.

Millard, A. R. and D. J. Wiseman, eds. *Essays on the Patriarchal Narratives.* Winona Lake: Eisenbrauns, 1980, 1983.

Miller, P. D. *Genesis 1–11: Studies in Structure & Theme.* Sheffield: The University Press, 1978.

Molinie, M. D. *The Struggle of Jacob.* New York: Paulist, 1977.

Niditch, S. *Chaos to Cosmos: Studies in the Biblical Patterns of Creation.* Chico: Scholars, 1985.

Parrot, A. *Abraham and His Times.* Philadelphia: Fortress, 1968.

Quinn, A. and K. Isaac. *Before Abraham Was: The Unity of Genesis 1–11.* Nashville: Abingdon, 1985.

Radday, Y. and H. Shore. *Genesis: An Authorship Study in Computer-Assisted Statistical Linguistics.* Rome: Pontifical Biblical Institute, 1985.

Redford, D. B. *A Study of the Biblical Story of Joseph (Gen. 37–50).* Leiden: Brill, 1970.

Renckens, H. *Israel's Concept of the Beginning.* New York: Herder, 1964.

Rendsburg, G. A. *The Redaction of Genesis.* Winona Lake: Eisenbrauns, 1986.

Richardson, A. *Genesis 1–11. The Creation Stories and The Modern World View.* NewYork–London: Torch–SCM, 1953.

Robbins, G. *Genesis 1–3 in the History of Exegesis: Intrigue in the Garden.* Lewiston: Edwin Mellen, 1988.

Rowley, H. H. *From Joseph to Joshua.* London: Oxford University Press, 1950

Rudin-O'Brasky, T. *The Patriarchs in Hebron and Sodom (Gen. 18–19), A Study of the Structure and Composition of the Biblical Story.* Jerusalem–Tel-Aviv: Simor, 1982.

Sacks, R. *A Commentary on the Book of Genesis.* Lewiston: Edwin Mellen, 1900.

Sarna, N. M. *Genesis. The Jewish Publication Society Torah Commentary.* Vol 1. Philadelphia: Jewish Publication Society, 1989.

_____. *Understanding Genesis.* New York: Schocken, 1972.

_____. *Understanding Genesis: The Heritage of Biblical Israel.* New York: McGraw-Hill, 1966.

Schultz, S. J. "Sacrifice in the God–Man Relationship in the Pentateuch." *Interpretation and History.* R. Harris, S. H. Quek and R. Vannoy, eds. Singapore: Christian Life, 1986. Pp. 198–121.

Sheresk, I. *Dinah's Rebellion.* New York: Crossroad, 1990.

Skinner, J. *A Critical and Exegetical Commentary on the Book of Genesis. International Critical Commentary.* 1st ed. Edinburgh: Clark, 1st ed. 1910, rev. ed. 1930.

Speiser, E. A. *Genesis. The Anchor Bible.* Garden City: Doubleday, 1964.

Sproul, B. C. *Primal Myths: Creating the Word.* New York: Harper & Row, 1979.

Teubal, S. *Hagar the Egyptian: The Lost Tradition of Matriarchs.* San Francisco: Harper & Row, 1990.

Thielicke, H. *How the World Began.* Philadelphia: Fortress, 1970.

Thompson, T. L. *The Historicity of the Patriarchal Narratives. The Quest for the Historical Abraham.* Berlin–New York: de Gruyter, 1974.

_____. *The Origin Tradition of Ancient Israel. The Literary Formation of Genesis and Exodus 1–23.* Sheffield: JSOT Press, 1987.

Tsumura, D. T. *The Earth and the Waters in Genesis 1 & 2: A Linguistic Investigation.* Sheffield: JSOT Press, 1989.

Van Seters, J. *Abraham in History and Tradition.* New Haven: Yale University Press, 1975.

Vawter, B. *A Path Through Genesis.* New York: Sheed & Ward, 1956.

_____. *On Genesis: A New Reading.* Garden City: Doubleday, 1977.

_____. "Understanding Genesis." *Studies in Salvation History.* C. L. Salm, ed. Englewood-Cliffs: Prentice Hall, 1964. Pp. 57–67.

von Rad, G. *Genesis, A Commentary, Old Testament Library.* Trans. by J. H. Marks. Philadelphia: Westminster, 1972.

_____. *Genesis.* Philadelphia: Westminster, 1961.

_____. "The Primeval History." *Old Testament Theology.* Vol. 1. New York: Harper & Row, 1962, 1965. Pp. 136–164.

von Seters, J. *Abraham in History and Tradition.* New Haven: Yale University Press, 1975.

Wallace, H. *The Eden Narrative.* Atlanta: Scholars, 1985.

Walsh, J. T. "Genesis 2:46–3:24: A Synchronic Approach." *Journal of Biblical Literature* 96 (1977) 1611–77.

Walters, A. M. *Creation Regained.* Grand Rapids: Eerdmans, 1985.

Wcela, E. *Basic Beliefs in Genesis and Exodus.* New York: Pueblo, 1976.

Wenham, G. J. *Genesis 1–15.* Waco: Word, 1987.

Westermann, C. *Beginning and End in the Bible.* Trans. by K. Crim. Philadelphia: Fortress, 1972.

_____. *Creation.* Trans. by J. J. Scullion. Philadelphia: Fortress, 1974.

_____. *Genesis 1–11.* Minneapolis: Augsburg, 1984.

_____.*Genesis: A Practical Commentary.* Grand Rapids: Eerdmans, 1987.

_____. *Our Controversial Bible.* Minneapolis: Augsburg, 1969.

_____. *The Genesis Accounts of Creation.* Trans. by N. E. Wagner. Philadelphia: Fortress, 1964.

_____. *The Promises to the Fathers: Studies on the Patriarchal Narratives.* Trans. by D. E. Green. Philadelphia: Fortress, 1980.

Willis, J. T. *Genesis.* Austin: Sweet, 1979.

Wilson, R. R. *Genealogy and History in the Biblical World.* New Haven: Yale University Press, 1977.

Wiseman, P. J. *Ancient Records and the Structure of Genesis: A Case for Literary Unity.* Nashville: Nelson, 1985.

Wolff, H. W. "The Kerygma of the Yahwist." *Interpretation* 20 (1966) 131–158.

Wright, G. E. "History and the Patriarchs." *Expository Times* 71 (1960) 292–96.

Yohannan, J. D. *Joseph and Potiphar's Wife.* New York: New Directions, 1968.

Young, N. *Creator, Creation, and Faith.* Philadelphia: Westminster, 1976.

b. Exodus

Ackerman, J. "The Literary content of the Moses Birth Story." *Literary Interpretations of Biblical Narratives.* Ed. by K. R. Gros Louis, J. Ackerman, and T. S. Warshaw. Nashville: Abingdon, 1974. Pp. 74–119.

Alt, A. "The Origins of Israelite Law." *Essays in Old Testament History and Religion.* Garden City: Doubleday, 1967. Pp. 101–171.

Asimov, I. *Words from the Exodus.* Boston: Houghton Mifflin, 1963.

Auerbach, E. *Moses.* Translated and edited by R. A. Barclay and I. O. Lehman with annotations by I. O. Lehman. Detroit: Wayne State University Press, 1975.

Baltzer, K. *The Covenant Formulary in Old Testament, Jewish and Early Christian Writings.* Trans. by D. E. Green. Philadelphia: Fortress, 1971.

Beegle, D. M. *Moses, Servant of Yahweh.* Grand Rapids: Eerdmans, 1972.

Bently, J. *Secrets of Mt. Sinai.* Garden City: Doubleday, 1986.

Beyerlin, W. *Origins and History of the Oldest Sinaiatic Traditions.* Trans. by S. Rudman. Oxford: Blackwell, 1965.

Bimson, J. J. *Redating the Exodus and Conquest.* Sheffield: University of Sheffield, 1978; Sheffield: Almond Press, 1981.

Buber, M. *Moses.* London: East & West Library, 1946; New York: Harper, 1958.

Burden, J. J., ed. *Exodus 1–15: Text and Context.* Pretoria: Old Testament Society of South Africa, 1987.

Burns, R. *Exodus, Leviticus, Numbers with Excursus on Feasts/Rituals and Typology.* Collegeville: Michael Glazier, 1991.

Campbell, A. *The Ark Narrative.* Scholars, 1975.

Campbell, E. F. "Moses and the Foundations of Israel." *Interpretation* 29 (1975) 141–154.

Cassuto, U. *A Commentary on the Book of Exodus.* Trans. by I. Abrahams. Jerusalem: Magnes, 1967.

Childs, B. S. *The Book of Exodus. The Old Testament Library.* Philadelphia: Westminster, 1974.

Clements, R. E. *Exodus.* Cambridge: Cambridge University Press, 1972.

Clifford, R. J. "Exodus." *The New Jerome Biblical Commentary.* Ed. by R. Brown et al. Englewood Cliffs: Prentice Hall, 1990. Pp. 44–60.

Coats, G. "History and Theology in the Sea Tradition." *Studia Theologica* 29 (1975) 53–62.

_____. "The King's Loyal Opposition: Obedience and Authority in Exodus 32–34." *Canon and Authority.* G. Coats and B. O. Long, eds. Philadelphia: Fortress, 1977. Pp. 91–109.

_____. *Moses. Heroic Man, Man of God.* Sheffield: JSOT Press–Sheffield Academic Press, 1988.

_____. *Rebellion in the Wilderness.* New York: Abingdon, 1968.

Cole, A. *Exodus.* Downers Grove: Inter–Varsity, 1973.

Croatto, J. S. *Exodus, A Hermeneutics of Freedom.* Maryknoll: Orbis, 1981.

Daube, D. *The Exodus Pattern In the Bible.* London: Faber and Faber, 1963.

Dozeman, T. B. *God On The Mountain, A Study of Redaction, Theology and Canon in Exodus.* Atlanta: Scholars, 1989.

Driver, S. R. *The Book of Exodus.* Cambridge: University Press, 1911.

Durham, J. I. *Exodus.* Waco: Word, 1987.

Ellison, H. L. *Exodus.* Edinburgh: St. Andrew; Philadelphia: Westminster, 1982.

Exum, J. C. "You Shall Let Every Daughter Live: A Study of Ex. 1:8–2:10." *Semeia* 28 (1983) 63–82.

Fackenheim, E. L. *God's Presence in History: Jewish Affirmations and Philosophical Reflections.* New York: Harper & Row, 1970.

Fox, E. *Now These are the Names: A New English Rendition of the Book of Exodus.* New York: Schoken, 1986.

Freedman, D. N. "Divine Commitment and Human Obligation." *Interpretation* 18 (1964) 419–431.

Fretheim, T. "The Priestly Document: Anti–Temple?" *Vetus Testamentum* 18 (1968) 318–329.

Gerstenberger, E. "Covenant and Commandment." *Journal of Biblical Literature* 84 (1965) 38–51.

Gispen, W. H. *Exodus.* Grand Rapids: Zondervan; St. Catherines, Ontario: Paideia, 1982.

Goldman, S. *From Slavery to Freedom.* London–New York: Abelard & Schuman, 1958.

Greeley, A. M. *The Sinai Myth.* New York: Doubleday, 1975.

Greenberg, M. *Understanding Exodus.* New York: Behrman, 1969.

Gunn, D. "The Hardening of Pharaoh's Heart: Plot, Character and Theology in Exodus 1–14." *Art and Meaning: Rhetoric in Biblical Literature.* Ed. by D. Clines, D. Gunn, and A. Hauser. Sheffield: JSOT Press, 1982. Pp. 72–96.

Gutierrez, G. *The Power of the Poor in History.* Maryknoll: Orbis, 1983.

_____. *A Theology of Liberation.* Maryknoll: Orbis, 1973.

Halevi, Z. B. *Kabbalah and Exodus.* London: Rider, 1980.

Hanson, P. D. "The Theological Significance of Contradiction within the Book of the Covenant." *Canon and Authority.* Ed. by G. W. Coats and B. O. Long. Philadelphia: Fortress, 1977. Pp. 110–131.

Harrelson, W. *The Ten Commandments and Human Rights.* Philadelphia: Fortress, 1980.

Hillers, D. R. *Covenant: The History of a Biblical Idea.* Baltimore: Johns Hopkins, 1969.

Houtman, C. *Exodus I (1:1–7:13).* Kampen, Australia: Kok, 1987.

Huffmon, H. B. "The Exodus, Sinai and the Credo." *Catholic Biblical Quarterly* 27 (1965) Pp. 101–130.

Hyatt, J. P. *Exodus.* Grand Rapids: Eerdmans, 1980, 1981.

Isbell, C. "Exodus 1–2 in the context of Exodus 1–14: Story Lines and Key Words." *Art and Meaning: Rhetoric in Biblical Literature.* Ed. by D. Clines, D. Gunn and A. Hauser. Sheffield: JSOT Press, 1982. Pp. 37–61.

Janzen, J. G. "What's in a Name? 'Yahweh' in Exodus 3 and the Wider Biblical Context." *Interpretation* 33 (1979) 227–239.

Johnstone, W. *Exodus.* Sheffield: JSOT, 1990.

Kaplan, L. "And the Lord Sought to Kill Him (Ex. 4: 24): Yet Once Again." *Hebrew College Annual Review* 5 (1981) 65–74.

Kasher, M. M. *Encyclopedia of Biblical Interpretation. Exodus: Volume IX.* New York: Ktav, 1979.

Kearney, P. J. "Creation and Liturgy; The P Redaction of Ex. 25–40." *Zeitschrift für die Alttestamentliche Wissenschaft* 89 (1977) 375–387.

Knight, G. A. *Theology as Narration: A Commentary on the Book of Exodus.* Grand Rapids: Eerdmans, 1976.

McCarthy, D. J. "Exodus 3:14: History, Philology and Theology." *Catholic Biblical Quarterly* 40 (1978) 311–22.

_____. *Treaty and Covenant, A Study in Form in the Ancient Oriental Documents and in the Old Testament. Analecta Biblica* 21. Rome: Pontifical Biblical Institute, 1963.

McNeile, A. H. *The Book of Exodus with Introduction and Notes.* London: Methuen, 1908.

Mendenhall, G. *Law and Covenant in Israel and the Ancient Near East.* Pittsburgh: Biblical Colloquium, 1955.

Meyer, L. *The Message of Exodus.* Minneapolis: Augsburg, 1983.

Meyers, C. *The Tabernacle Menorah.* Missoula: Scholars, 1976.

Miller, P. D. *The Divine Warrior in Early Israel.* Cambridge: Harvard University Press, 1973.

Moberly, R. W. *At the Mountain of God. Story and Theology in Exodus 32–34.* Sheffield: JSOT Press, 1983.

Moore, M. *The Balaam Traditions: Their Character and Development.* Atlanta: Scholars, 1990.

Muilenburg, J. "The Form and Structure of the Covenantal Formulation." *Vetus Testamentum* 9 (1959) 347–65.

Newman, M. L., Jr. *The People of the Covenant: A Study of Israel from Moses to the Monarchy.* New York: Abingdon, 1962.

Nicholson, E. W. *Exodus and Sinai in History and Tradition.* Richmond: John Knox, 1973.

_____. "The Decalogue as the Direct Address of God." *Vetus Testamentum* 27 (1977) 422–33.

Nielson, E. *The Ten Commandments in New Perspective,* Trans. by D. J. Bourke. *Studies in Biblical Theology.* 2nd series, no. 17. Naperville: Allenson, 1968.

Noth, M. *Exodus.* Trans. by J. S. Bowden. *The Old Testament Library.* Philadelphia: Westminster, 1962.

Owens, J. J. *Analytical Key to the Old Testament: Exodus.* San Francisco: Harper & Row, 1977.

Patrick, D. "The Covenant Code Source." *Vetus Testamentum* 27 (1977) 145–57.

Plastaras, J. *The God of Exodus: The Theology of the Exodus Narratives.* Milwaukee: Bruce, 1966.

Plaut, W. G. *The Torah: A Modern Commentary.* New York: Union of American Hebrew Congregations, 1981.

Propp, W. *Water in the Wilderness.* Cambridge: Harvard University Press, 1988.

Rowley, H. H. *Moses and the Decalogue.* Manchester: The John Rylands Library, 1951.

_____. *From Moses to Qumran.* London: Lutterworth, 1963.

Rylaarsdam, J. C. "Introduction and Exegesis to the Book of Exodus." *Interpreter's Bible I.* New York: Abingdon, 1952. Pp. 833–1099.

Sarna, N. M. *Exodus. The JPS Torah Commentary.* Vol. 2. Philadelphia: Jewish Publication Society, 1990.

_____. *Exploring Exodus: The Heritage of Biblical Israel.* New York: Schocken, 1986.

Silver, A. H. *Moses and the Original Torah.* New York: Macmillan, 1961.

Silver, D. J. *Images of Moses.* New York: Basic, 1982.

Stamm, J. J. and M. E. Andrew. *The Ten Commandments in Recent Research. Studies in Biblical Theology.* 2nd series, no. 2. Naperville: Allenson, 1967.

Stiebing, W., Jr. *Out of the Desert? Archaeology and the Exodus/ Conquest Narratives.* Buffalo: Promethus, 1989.

Taylor-Parke, G. H. *Yahweh, The Divine Name in the Bible.* Waterloo, Ontario: Wilfrid Laurier University Press, 1975.

Thompson, R. J. *Moses and the Law in a Century of Criticism Since Graf.* Leiden: Brill, 1970.

Thompson, T. L. *The Origin Tradition of Ancient Israel. I. The Literary Formation of Genesis and Exodus 1–23.* Sheffield: JSOT Press, 1987.

Uris, L. *Exodus.* Garden City: Doubleday, 1958.

Van Iersel, B. and A. Weiler. *Exodus: A Lasting Paradigm.* Edinburgh: Clark, 1987.

Van Seters, J. "The Plagues of Egypt: Ancient Traditions or Literary Convention?" *Zeitschrift für die Alttestamentliche Wissenschaft* 98 (1986) 31–39.

Voegelin, E. *Israel and Revelation.* Louisiana State University Press, 1956. 3rd printing, 1969.

von Rad, G. *Moses.* London: Lutterworth; New York: Association, 1960.

Walzer, M. *Exodus and Revolution.* New York: Basic, 1985.

Wcela, E. *Basic Beliefs in Genesis and Exodus.* New York: Pueblo, 1976.

Wildavsky, A. *The Nursing Father: Moses as a Political Leader.* University, AL: University of Alabama Press, 1984.

Wildengren, G. "What Do We Know About Moses?" *Proclamation and Presence.* Richmond: John Knox, 1970. Pp. 21–47.

Wilson, R. "The Hardening of Pharoah's Heart." *Catholic Biblical Quarterly* 41 (1979) 19–36.

Wright, G. E. "Exodus." *Interpreter's Dictionary of the Bible,* 2. New York: Abingdon-Cokesbury, 1962. Pp. 189–199.

Zevit, Z. "The Priestly Redaction and Interpretation of the Plague Narrative in Exodus." *Jewish Quarterly Review* 66 (1975-76) 193–211.

c. Leviticus

Bailey, L. R. *Leviticus.* Atlanta: John Knox, 1987.

Bamburger, B. J. *Leviticus, The Torah: A Modern Commentary.* New York: Union of American Hebrew Congregations, 1981.

Bigger, S. F. "The Family Laws of Leviticus 18 in their Setting." *Journal of Biblical Literature* 98 (1979) 187–203.

Burns, R. *Exodus, Leviticus, Numbers.* Wilmington: Michael Glazier, 1983.

Chapman, A. T. and A. W. Streane. *The Book of Leviticus. Cambridge Bible.* Cambridge: Cambridge University Press, 1914.

Coats, G. W. *Moses. Heroic Man, Man of God.* Sheffield: Sheffield Academic Press, 1988.

Davies, D. "An Interpretation of Sacrifice in Leviticus." *Zeitschrift für die Alttestamentliche Wissenschaft* 89 (1977) 387–99.

de Vaux, R. *Ancient Israel: Its Life and Institutions.* New York: Longman & Todd–McGraw-Hill, 1961.

Ellinger, K. *Leviticus.* Tübingen: Mohr, 1966.

Faley, R. J. "Leviticus." *The New Jerome Biblical Commentary.* Ed. by R. Brown et al. Englewood Cliffs: Prentice Hall, 1990. Pp. 61–79.

Harrison, R. K. *Leviticus: An Introduction and Commentary.* Downers Grove: Inter-Varsity, 1980.

Kiuchi, N. *The Purification Offering in the Priestly Literature. Its Meaning and Interpretation.* Sheffield: JSOT Press, 1987.

Knight, G. A. *Leviticus.* Edinburgh: St. Andrew; Philadelphia: Westminster, 1981.

Levine, B. *In the Presence of the Lord: A Study of Cult and Some Cultic Terms in Ancient Israel.* Leiden: Brill, 1974.

_____. *Leviticus. The Jewish Publication Society Torah Commentary.* Vol. 3. Philadelphia: Jewish Publication Society, 1989.

Mays, J. L. "The Book of Leviticus/The Book of Numbers." *The Layman's Bible Commentary.* Vol. 4. Richmond: John Knox, 1963.

Michlem, N. "Introduction and Exegesis of the Book of Leviticus." *The Interpreter's Bible 2.* New York: Abingdon, 1952.

Milgrom, J. *Studies in Cultic Theology and Terminology.* Leiden: Brill, 1976.

_____. *Studies in Levitical Terminology.* Berkeley: University of California, 1970.

Noordtzij, A. *Leviticus.* Grand Rapids: Zondervan, 1982.

Noth, M. *Leviticus.* Trans. by J. E. Anderson. *Old Testament Library.* Philadelphia: Fortress, 1977.

Porter, J. R. *Leviticus.* Cambridge: Cambridge University Press, 1976.

Rendtorff, R. *Leviticus.* Neukirchen-Vluyn: Neukirchner, 1985.

Snaith, N. H. *Leviticus and Numbers.* London: Nelson, 1967.

Stuhlmueller, C. "Leviticus: The Teeth of Divine Will Into the Smallest Expectations of Human Courtesy." *The Bible Today* 80 (1977) 1082–88.

Wenham, G. J. *The Book of Leviticus.* Grand Rapids: Eerdmans, 1979.

Wilkinson, J. "Leprosy and Leviticus: A Problem of Semantics and Translation." *Scottish Journal of Theology* 31 (1978) 153–66.

d. Numbers

Albright, W. F. "The Oracles of Balaam." *Journal of Biblical Literature* 63 (1944) 207–33.

Asimov, I. *Words from the Exodus.* Boston: Houghton Mifflin, 1963.

Budd, P. J. *Numbers.* Waco: Word, 1984.

Burns, R. *Exodus, Leviticus, Numbers.* Wilmington: Michael Glazier, 1983.

Coats, G. W. "Balaam Sinner or Saint?" *Biblical Research* 18 (1973) 21–29.

Davies, G. I. *The Way of the Wilderness.* Cambridge: Cambridge University Press, 1979.

Elliot-Binns, L. E. *The Book of Numbers.* London: Methuen, 1927.

Flack, E. E. "Flashes of New Knowledge: Recent Study and the Book of Numbers." *Interpretation* 13 (1959) 3–23.

Gray, G. B. *A Critical and Exegetical Commentary on Numbers.* New York: Scribner's, 1906, 1909.

Grindel, J. A. "The Book of Numbers." *The Bible Today* 89 (1977) 1142–50.

Harrelson, W. "The Theology of Numbers." *Interpretation* 13 (1959) 24–36.

Hoftijzer, J. "The Prophet Balaam in a 6th Century Aramaic Inscription." *Biblical Archaeologist* 39 (1976) 11–17.

Jensen, I. L. *Numbers: Journey to God's Rest-land.* Chicago: Moody, 1964.

King, P. *The Book of Numbers.* Collegeville: The Liturgical Press, 1967.

L' Heureux, C. "Numbers." *The New Jerome Biblical Commentary.* Ed. by R. Brown et al. Englewood Cliffs: Prentice Hall, 1990. Pp. 80–93.

Maarsingh, B. *Numbers.* Grand Rapids: Eerdmans, 1987.

Marsh, J. "The Book of Numbers." *Interpreter's Bible* 2. New York: 1953. Pp. 135–308.

Milgrom, J. *Numbers. The Jewish Publication Society Torah Commentary.* Vol. 4. Philadelphia: Jewish Publication Society, 1989.

Moore, M. S. *The Balaam Traditions: Their Character and Development.* Altlanta: Scholars, 1988.

Moriarty, F. L. "Numbers." *The Jerome Biblical Commentary.* Englewood Cliffs: Prentice Hall, 1968. Pp. 86–100.

_____. *The Book of Numbers.* New York: Paulist, 1960.

Noordtzij, A. *Numbers.* Grand Rapids: Zondervan, 1984.

Noth, M. *Numbers: A Commentary.* Philadelphia: Westminster, 1968.

Olson, D. T. *The Death of the Old and the Birth of the New: The Framework of the Book of Numbers and the Pentateuch.* Chico: Scholars, 1985.

Plaut, W. G. *The Torah: A Modern Commentary.* New York: Union of American Hebrew Congregations, 1981.

Riggans, W. *Numbers.* Philadelphia: Westminster, 1983.

Rofé, A. *"The Book of Balaam" (Numbers 22:2–24:25).* Jerusalem: Simor, 1979.

Snaith, N. H. *Leviticus and Numbers.* London: Nelson, 1967.

Sturdy, J. *Numbers. The Cambridge Bible Commentary. The New English Bible.* New York–London: Cambridge University Press, 1976.

Tosato, A. "The Literary Structure of the First Two Poems of Balaam." *Vetus Testamentum* 29 (1979) 98–106.

Wenham, G. J. *Numbers: An Introduction and Commentary.* Downers Grove: Inter–Varsity, 1981.

Wharton, J. A. "The Command to Bless: An Exposition of Numbers 22:41–23:25." *Interpretation* 12 (1959) 37–48.

Zannoni, A. E. "Balaam: International Seer/Wizard Prophet." *St. Luke's Journal of Theology* 22 (1978) 5–19.

e. Deuteronomy

Abba, R. "Priests and Levites in Deuteronomy." *Vetus Testamentum* 27 (1977) 257–67.

Achtemeier, E. *Deuteronomy and Jeremiah.* Philadelphia: Fortress, 1978.

_____. "Plumbing the Richer Deuteronomy for the Preacher." *Interpretation* 441 (1987) 269–281.

Bee, R. E. "A Study of Deuteronomy Based on Statistical Properties of the Text." *Vetus Testamentum* 29 (1979) 1–22.

Blenkinsopp, J. "Deuteronomy." *The Jerome Biblical Commentary.* Ed. by R. Brown et al. Englewood Cliffs: Prentice Hall, 1968. Pp. 101–122.

_____. "Deuteronomy." *The New Jerome Biblical Commentary.* Ed. by R. Brown et al. Englewood Cliffs: Prentice Hall, 1990. Pp. 83–109.

Carmichael, C. M. "A Common Element in Five Supposedly Disparate Laws." *Vetus Testamentum* 29 (1979) 129–42.

Childs, B. *Introduction to the Old Testament as Scripture.* Philadelphia: Fortress, 1979. Pp. 205–255.

Clements, R. E. *Deuteronomy: God's Chosen People: A Theological Interpretation of the Book of Deuteronomy.* Sheffield: Sheffield Academic Press, 1989.

Clifford, R. *Deuteronomy, with an Excursus on Covenant and Law.* Wilmington: Michael Glazier; Dublin: Gill & Macmillan, 1982.

Craigie, P. C. *The Book of Deuteronomy.* Grand Rapids: Eerdmans, 1976.

Cunliffe-Jones, H. *Deuteronomy. Torch Bible Commentaries.* London: SCM, 1951.

Fretheim, T. E. *Deuteronomic History.* Nashville: Abingdon, 1983.

Halpern, B. "The Centralization Formula in Deuteronomy." *Vetus Testamentum* 31 (1981) 20–38.

Hidal, S. "Some Reflections on Deuteronomy 32." *Annual of the Swedish Theological Institute* 11 (1977–78) 15–21.

Hippe L. "The Meaning of Deuteronomy." *Biblical Theology Bulletin* 10 (1980) 111–17.

Kuyper, L. J. "The Book of Deuteronomy." *Interpretation* 6 (1952) 321–340.

MacKenzie, R. A. "The Messianism of Deuteronomy." *Catholic Biblical Quarterly* 19 (1957) 299–305.

Mayes, A. D. "Deuteronomy 4 and the Literary Criticism of Deuteronomy." New York: Seabury, 1978.

_____. *Deuteronomy.* London: Oliphants, 1979; Grand Rapids: Eerdmans, 1981.

Mc Bride, S. D. "Polity of the Covenant People: The Book of Deuteronomy." *Interpretation* 41 (1987) 220–244.

McConville, J. G. *Law and Theology in Deuteronomy.* Sheffield: JSOT Press, 1984.

McNeile, A. H. *Deuteronomy, Its Place in Revelation.* London: Longmans; New York: Green, 1912.

Miller, P. D. " 'Moses My Servant' The Deuteronomic Portrait of Moses." *Interpretation* 41 (1987) 245–255.

Miller, P. *Deuteronomy.* Louisville: John Knox, 1990.

Moran, W. "Deuteronomy." *A New Catholic Commentary on Holy Scripture.* R. C. Fuller, ed. London: Nelson, 1969.

Myers, J. M. "The Requisites for Response on the Theology of Deuteronomy." *Interpretation* 15 (1961) 14–31.

Nelson, R. D. *The Double Redaction of the Deuteronomistic History.* Sheffield: JSOT Press, 1981.

Nicholson, E. W. *Deuteronomy and Tradition.* Philadelphia: Fortress, 1967.

Noth, M. *The Deuteronomistic History.* Sheffield: JSOT Press, 1981.

Payne, D. F. *Deuteronomy.* Philadelphia: Westminster, 1985.

Peckham, B. *The Composition of the Deuteronomistic History.* Atlanta: Scholars, 1985.

Peifer, C. J. "The Book of Deuteronomy." *The Bible Today* 90 (1977) 1213–19.

Phillips, A. *Deuteronomy.* Cambridge: Cambridge University Press, 1973.

Polzin, R. *Moses and the Deuteronomist. A Literary Study of the Deuteronomic History Part One; Deuteronomy, Joshua, Judges.* New York: Seabury; San Francisco: Harper & Row, 1980.

Ridderbos, J. *Deuteronomy.* Grand Rapids: Zondervan, 1984.

Robinson, H. W. *Deuteronomy and Joshua.* Edinburgh: Jack, 1907; London: Oxford University Press, 1908.

Tigay, J. *Deuteronomy. The Jewish Publication Society Torah Commentary.* Vol. 5. Philadelphia: Jewish Publication Society, (to be published in 1991).

Thompson, J. A. *Deuteronomy.* London: Inter–Varsity, 1974.

von Rad, G. *Deuteronomy: A Commentary.* Philadelphia: Westminster, 1966.

_____. *Studies in Deuteronomy. Studies in Biblical Theology* No. 9. London: SCM, 1947, 1953; Chicago: Regnery, 1953.

Weinfield, M. *Deuteronomy and the Deuteronomic School.* Oxford: Clarendon, 1972.

Welch, A. C. *The Code of Deuteronomy.* London: Clarke, 1924.

_____. *Deuteronomy: The Framework to the Code.* London: Oxford University Press, 1932.

Westermann, C. *A Thousand Years and a Day.* Philadelphia: Muhlenberg, 1962.

Wright, G. E. "Introduction and Exegesis to Deuteronomy." *The Interpreter's Bible.* Vol 2. New York: Abingdon, 1952. Pp. 311–537.

IV. HISTORICAL BOOKS

20. JOSHUA

Alt, A. "The Settlement of the Israelites in Palestine." *Essays on Old Testament History and Religion*. Garden City: Doubleday, 1967. Pp. 133–169.

Auld, A. G. *Joshua, Judges, and Ruth*. Philadelphia: Westminster, 1985.

_____. *Joshua, Moses and the Land*. Edinburgh: Clark, 1980.

Boice, J. M. *Joshua: We Will Serve the Lord*. Old Tappan, NJ: Revell, 1989.

Boling, R. C. *Joshua. The Anchor Bible*. Vol. 6. Garden City: Doubleday, 1982.

Bright, J. *"Joshua, Introduction and Exegesis." The Interpreter's Bible*. Vol. 2. New York–Nashville: Abingdon, 1953.

Butler, T. C. *Joshua*. Waco: Word, 1983.

Coogan, M. D. "Joshua." *The New Jerome Biblical Commentary*. Ed. by R. Brown, et al. Englewood Cliffs: Prentice Hall, 1990. Pp. 110–31.

Cooke, G. A. *The Book of Joshua. Cambridge Bible*. Cambridge: Cambridge University Press, 1917.

de Geus, C. H. *The Tribes of Israel*. Assen: Van Gorcum, 1976.

Garstang, J. *The Foundations of Bible History; Joshua, Judges*. London: Constable, 1931.

Gottwald, N. K. *The Tribes of Yahweh: A Sociology of the Religion of Liberated Israel, 1250–1050 B.C.E.* Maryknoll: Orbis, 1979.

Gray, J. *Joshua, Judges, Ruth*. Grand Rapids: Eerdmans; Basingstoke: Morgan & Scott, 1986.

Greenspoon, L. J. *Textual Studies in the Book of Joshua.* Chico: Scholars, 1983.

Hamlin, E. J. *Inheriting the Land. A Commentary on the Book of Joshua.* Grand Rapids: Eerdmans; Edinburgh: Handsel, 1984.

Hoppe, L. *Joshua, Judges with an Excursus on Charismatic Leadership in Israel.* Wilmington: Michael Glazier, 1991.

Kaufmann, Y. *The Biblical Account of the Conquest of Palestine.* Jerusalem: Magnes, 1953.

Kenyon, K. M. *The Bible and Recent Archaeology.* Atlanta: John Knox, 1978.

Koopman, W. *Joshua 24 as Poetic Narrative.* Sheffield: JSOT, 1990.

Lapp, P. "The Conquest of Palestine in the Light of Archaeology." *Concordia Theological Monthly* 38 (1967) 283–300.

Lieberman, D. *The Eternal Torah. Part Two: Joshua, Judges, Samuel One, Samuel Two.* New York: Ktav, 1983.

Malamat, A. *Early Israelite Warfare and the Conquest of Canaan.* Oxford: Center for Postgraduate Hebrew Studies, 1976.

Mendenhall, G. E. "The Hebrew Conquest of Canaan." *The Biblical Archaeologist Reader III.* Ed. by G. E. Wright, E. F. Campbell, D. N. Freedman. New York: Doubleday Anchor, 1970.

Miller, J. M. and G. M. Tucker. *The Book of Joshua.* London: Cambridge University Press, 1974.

Polzin, R. *Moses and the Deuteronomist. A Literary Study of the Deuteronomic History Part One: Deuteronomy, Joshua, Judges.* San Francisco: Harper & Row, 1980.

Robinson, H. W. *Deuteronomy and Joshua.* Edinburgh: Jack, 1907; London: Oxford University Press, 1908.

Rowley, H. H. *From Joseph to Joshua.* London: Oxford, 1950.

Smend, R. *Yahweh, War and Tribal Confederation.* Nashville: Abingdon, 1970.

Soggin, J. A. *Joshua: A Commentary.* London: SCM; Philadelphia: Westminster, 1972.

Weippert, M. *The Settlement of the Israelite Tribes in Palestine.* Naperville: Allenson, 1971.

Woudstra, M. H. *The Book of Joshua.* Grand Rapids: Eerdmans, 1981.

Wright, G. E. "Conquest." *Biblical Archaeology.* Rev. ed. Philadelphia: Westminster, 1962.

Wright, G. E. *Shechem: The Biography of a Biblical City.* New York: McGraw Hill, 1965.

Wright, G. E. "The Literary and Historical Problems of Joshua 10 and Judges 1." *Journal of Near Eastern Studies* 5 (1946) 105–114.

21. JUDGES

Auld, A. G. *Joshua, Judges, and Ruth.* Philadelphia: Westminster, 1985.

Baly, M. *Death and Dissymetry: The Politics of Coherence in the Book of Judges.* Chicago: University of Chicago, 1988.

Boling, R. G. *Judges.* Garden City: Doubleday, 1975.

_____. *Judges. Introduction, Translation and Commentary. The Anchor Bible.* Garden City: Doubleday, 1982.

Bright, J. "Isaiah–I." *Peake's Commentary on the Bible.* Ed. by M. Blackwell. London–New York: Nelson, 1962. Pp. 489–515.

Bruce, F. F. *Judges.* London: Inter-Varsity, 1970.

Buarney, C. F. *The Book of Judges.* 2nd ed. London: Rivingtons, 1930.

Calvin, J. *Commentaries on the Book of Joshua,* Grand Rapids: Eerdmans, 1949.

Crenshaw, J. L. *Samson: A Secret Betrayed, A Vow Ignored.* Atlanta: John Knox, 1978.

Cundall, A. E. *Judges and Ruth.* London: Tyndale, 1968.

de Vaux, R. *The Early History of Israel, to the Period of the Judges.* London: Darton, Longman & Todd, 1978.

Garstang, J. *The Foundations of Bible History: Joshua, Judges.* London: Constable, 1931.

Gottwald, N. K. *The Tribes of Yahweh: A Sociology of the Religion of Liberated Israel 1250–1050 B.C.* Maryknoll: Orbis, 1979.

Gray, J. *Joshua, Judges, Ruth.* Grand Rapids: Eerdmans; Basingstoke: Marshall Morgan & Scott, 1986.

Gray, J. *Judges. The New Century Bible Commentary.* Ed. by R. E. Clements and M. Black. Grand Rapids: Eerdmans, 1967.

Hamlin, E. *Judges: At Risk in the Promised Land.* Grand Rapids: Eerdmans, 1990.

Hoppe, L. *Joshua, Judges.* Wilmington: Michael Glazier, 1982.

Kaufman, Y. *The Biblical Account of the Conquest of Palestine.* Jerusalem: Magnes, 1953.

Keil, C. F. and F. Delitzch. *The Book of Judges.* Grand Rapids: Eerdmans, 1973.

Klein, L. R. *The Triumph of Irony in the Book of Judges.* Sheffield: Almond Press, 1988.

Lieberman, D. *The Eternal Torah. Part Two: Joshua, Judges, Samuel One, Samuel Two.* New York: Ktav, 1983.

Limburg, J. *Old Stories for a New Time.* Atlanta: John Knox, 1983.

Lindars, B. "The Israelite Tribes in Judges." *Studies in the Historical Books of the Old Testament.* Leiden: Brill, 1979. Pp. 95–112.

Malamat, A. " The Period of the Judges." *The World History of the Jewish People.* Vol. 3. *Judges.* Tel Aviv: Massada, 1971.

Marcus, D. *Jephthah and his Vow.* Lubbock: Texas Tech Press, 1986.

Martin, J. D. *The Book of Judges.* Cambridge: Cambridge University Press, 1975.

Mayes, A. D. *Israel in the Period of the Judges.* London: SCM; Naperville: Allenson, 1974.

_____. *Judges.* Sheffield: JSOT Press, 1985.

McKenzie, J. L. *The World of the Judges.* Englewood Cliffs: Prentice Hall, 1966.

Moore, G. F. *A Critical and Exegetical Commentary on Judges.* Edinburgh: Clark, 1908.

Morton, J. D. *Judges. The Cambridge Bible Commentary.* Cambridge: Cambridge University Press, 1974.

Myers, J. M. "Judges: Introduction and Exegesis." *The Interpreter's Bible.* Vol. II. New York–Nashville: Abingdon, 1953. Pp. 677–826.

O'Connor, M. "Judges." *The New Jerome Biblical Commentary.* Ed. by R. Brown et al. Englewood Cliffs: Prentice Hall, 1990. Pp. 132–144.

Polzin, R. *Moses and the Deuteronomist. A Literary Study of the Deuteronomic History Part One: Deuteronomy, Joshua, Judges.* San Francisco: Harper & Row, 1980.

Simpson, C. A. *Composition of the Book of Judges.* Oxford: Blackwell, 1957.

Soggin, J. A. *Judges.* Philadelphia: Westminster, 1981.

Webb, B. G. *The Book of Judges: An Integrated Reading.* Sheffield: JSOT Press, 1987.

22. I & II SAMUEL

Ackroyd, P. R. *The First Book of Samuel. The Cambridge Bible Commentary.* Cambridge: The University of Cambridge Press, 1971.

_____. *The Second Book of Samuel.* New York–London: Cambridge University Press, 1977.

Albright, W. F. *Samuel and the Beginnings of the Prophetic Movement.* Cincinnati: Hebrew Union College, 1961.

Anderson, A. *2 Samuel.* Dallas: Word, 1989.

Angnell, I. *Studies in Divine Kingship.* 2nd ed. Oxford: Blackwell, 1967.

Bailey, R. C. *David in Love and War: The Pursuit of Power in 2 Samuel 10–12.* Sheffield: JSOT, 1991.

Baldwin, J. *I and II Samuel. An Introduction and Commentary.* Leicester: Inter-Varsity Press, 1988.

Berlin, A. *Poetics and Interpretation of Biblical Narrative.* Sheffield: Almond Press, 1983.

Birch, B. C. *The Rise of the Israelite Monarchy: The Growth and Development of I Samuel 7-15*. Missoula: Scholars, 1976.

_____. "The Development of the Tradition on the Anointing of Saul in I Sam 9:1–10: 16." *Journal of Biblical Literature* 90 (1971) 55–68.

Brueggemann, W. *David's Truth in Israel's Imagination and Memory.* Philadelphia: Fortress, 1985.

_____. "David and His Theologian." *Catholic Biblical Quarterly* 30 (1968) 156–181.

_____. *First and Second Samuel.* Louisville: Westminster/John Knox, 1990.

_____. "Kingship and Chaos: A Study in Tenth Century Theology." *Catholic Biblical Quarterly* 33 (1971) 317–332.

Caird, G. B. *The First and Second Books of Samuel. The Interpreter's Bible*. Nashville: Abingdon, 1953.

Campbell, A. F. and J. W. Flanagan. "I & II Samuel." *The New Jerome Biblical Commentary.* Ed. by R. Brown et al. Englewood Cliffs: Prentice Hall, 1990. Pp. 145–159.

Carlson, R. A. *David, the Chosen King: A Tradition-Historical Approach to the Second Book of Samuel.* Stockholm: Almqvist & Wiksell, 1964.

Clements, R. E. *Abraham and David.* Naperville: Allenson, 1967.

Conroy, C. *I–II Samuel, I–II Kings, with an Excursus on Davidic Dynasty and Holy City Zion.* Collegeville: Michael Glazier, 1991.

_____. *Absalom Absalom! Narrative and Language in II Samuel 13–20.* Rome: Biblical Institute Press, 1978.

Cross, F. M. "The Ideologies of Kingship in the Era of the Empire: Conditional Covenant and Eternal Decree." *Canaanite Myth and Hebrew Epic: Essays in the History of the Religion of Israel.* Cambridge: Harvard University Press, 1973. Ch. 9.

Driver, S. R. *Notes on the Hebrew Text and the Topography of the Books of Samuel.* Oxford: Clarendon, 1913.

Endres, J. *Temple, Monarchy and Word of God.* Wilmington: Michael Glazier, 1988.

Eslinger, L. M. *Kingship of God in Crisis. A Close Reading of I Samuel 1–12*. Sheffield: JSOT Press, 1985.

Flanagan, J. W. *David's Social Drama: A Hologram of Israel's Early Iron Age*. Sheffield: Almond Press, 1988.

Fokkelman, J. P. *Narrative Art and Poetry in the Books of Samuel: A Full Interpretation Based On Stylistic and Structural Analyses*. Assen: Van Gorcum, 1986.

Foresti, F. *The Rejection of Saul in the Perspective of the Deuteronomistic School*. Rome: Edizioni del Teresianum, 1984.

Frontain, R. J. and J. Wojcik. *The David Myth in Western Literature*. West Lafayette: Purdue University Press, 1980.

Fuller, J. M. *The Bible Commentary, I Samuel-Esther*. Grand Rapids: Baker, 1976.

Garsiel, M. *The First Book of Samuel: A Literary Study of Comparative Structures, Analogies and Parallels*. Ramat-Gan, Israel: Revivim, 1985.

Gehrke, R. D. *I & II Samuel*. Concordia Commentary. St. Louis: Concordia, 1968.

Gerbrandt, G. E. *Kingship According to the Deuteronomistic History*. Atlanta: Scholars, 1960.

Gnuse, R. *The Dream Theophany of Samuel*. New York: University Press of America, 1984.

Goldman, S. *The Books of Samuel. The Soncino Bible*. Bournemouth: Soncino, 1951.

Gordon, R. P. *I & II Samuel*. Sheffield: JSOT Press, 1984.

Gunn, D. M. *The Fate of King Saul. An Interpretation of a Biblical Story*. Sheffield: JSOT Press, 1980.

_____. *The Story of King David: Genre and Interpretation*. Sheffield: The University Press, 1978.

Halpern, B. *The Constitution of the Monarchy in Israel. Harvard Semitic Monographs* 25. Chico: Scholars, 1981.

Hertzberg, H. W. *First and Second Samuel, a Commentary*. Philadelphia: Westminster, 1964.

Ishida, T., ed. *Studies in the Period of David and Solomon and Other Essays.* Winona Lake: Eisenbrauns, 1982.

Kennedy, A. R. *Samuel.* New York: Freude, 1904.

Kirkpatrick, A. F. *The First and Second Books of Samuel.* Cambridge: Cambridge University Press, 1930.

Klein, R. W. *I Samuel.* Waco: Word Books, 1983.

Lewis, J. O. *I and II Samuel, I Chronicles.* Nashville: Broadman, 1980.

Lieberman, D. *The Eternal Torah. Part Two: Joshua, Judges, Samuel One, Samuel Two.* New York: Ktav, 1983.

Long, P. *The Reign and Rejection of King Saul: A Case for Literary and Theological Coherence.* Atlanta: Scholars, 1989.

Mauchline, J. *I & II Samuel,* London: Oliphants, 1971.

McKane, W. *I & II Samuel: The Way to the Throne.* London: SCM 1963.

McCarter, P. K., Jr. *I Samuel.* New York: Doubleday, 1984.

_____. *II Samuel.* New York: Doubleday, 1984.

Miller, P. D. and J. J. Roberts. *The Hand of the Lord: A Reassessment of the Ark Narrative of I Samuel.* Baltimore: Johns Hopkins University Press, 1977.

Miscall, P. *I Samuel, A Literary Reading.* Bloomington: Indiana University Press, 1986.

Newman, M. "The Prophetic Call of Samuel." *Israel's Prophetic Heritage.* M. Newman and W. Harrelson, eds. New York: Harper, 1972. Pp. 86–97.

Newsome, J. D., Jr. *I Samuel, II Samuel.* Atlanta: John Knox, 1982.

Oesterleg, W. *The First Book of Samuel.* Cambridge: 1931.

Payne, D. F. *I & II Samuel.* Philadelphia: Westminster, 1982.

Polzin, R. *Samuel and the Deuteronomist. A Literary Study of the Deuteronomic History: I Samuel.* San Francisco: Harper & Row, 1989.

Provan, I. W. *Hezekiah and the Books of Kings: A Contribution About the Debate and the Composition of the Deuteronomic History.* Berlin–NewYork: de Gruyter, 1988.

Roberts, J. J. "The Davidic Origins of the Zion Tradition." *Journal of Biblical Literature* 92 (1973) 329–344.

Rost, L. *The Succession to the Throne of David.* Sheffield: Almond Press, 1982.

Sternberg, M. *The Poetics of Biblical Narrative.* Bloomington: Indiana University Press, 1985.

Vannoy, R. J. *Covenant Renewal at Gilgal.* Cherry Hill: Mack, 1978.

Whybray, R. N. *The Succession Narrative: A Study of II Samuel 9–20; and I Kings 1 and 2.* London: SCM; Naperville: Allenson, 1968.

23. I & II KINGS

Ahlstrom, G. W. *Royal Administration and National Religion in Ancient Palestine.* Leiden: Brill, 1982.

Auld, A. G. *I & II Kings.* Philadelphia: Westminster, 1986.

Barnes, W. E. *The Two Books of Kings.* Cambridge: At the University Press, 1908.

Bronner, L. *The Stories of Elijah and Elisha.* Leiden: Brill, 1968.

Brueggemann, W. *I Kings.* Atlanta: John Knox, 1982.

_____. *II Kings.* Atlanta: John Knox, 1982.

_____. "II Kings 18–19: The Legitimacy of a Sectarian Hermeneutic." *Horizons in Biblical Theology* 7 (1985) 1–42.

_____. "The Embarrassing Footnote: The Elisha Narrative and Official History." *Theology Today* 44 (1987) 5–14.

Clements, R. E. *Isaiah and the Deliverance of Jerusalem.* Sheffield: JSOT Press, 1980.

Cogan, M. and H. Tadmor. *II Kings: A New Translation with Introduction and Commentary.* Garden City: Doubleday, 1988.

Conroy, C. *I–II Samuel, I–II Kings.* Wilmington: Michael Glazier, 1983.

Cross, F. M. "The Themes of the Book of Kings and the Structure of the Deuteronomistic History." *Canaanite Myth and Hebrew Epic: Essays in the History of the Religion of Israel.* Cambridge: Harvard University Press, 1973. Ch. 10.

de Vries, S. J. *I Kings.* Waco: Word, 1985.

Endres, J. *Temple, Monarchy and Word of God.* Wilmington: Michael Glazier, 1988.

Engnell, I. *Studies in Divine Kingship.* 2nd ed. Oxford: Blackwell, 1967.

Finegan, J. *Handbook of Biblical Chronology.* Princeton: Princeton University Press, 1964.

Frontain, R.-J. and J. Wojcik, eds. *The David Myth in Western Literature.* West Lafayette: Purdue University Press, 1980.

Gottwald, N. K. *All the Kingdoms of the Earth.* New York: Harper & Row, 1964.

Gray, J. *I & II Kings.* Philadelphia: Westminster, 1970, 1980.

Gunn, D. M. *The Story of King David: Genre and Interpretation.* Sheffield: JSOT Press, 1978.

Harrop, G. G. *Elijah Speaks Today: The Long Road into Naboth's Vineyard.* New York: Abingdon, 1975.

Hauser, A. and R. Gregory. *From Carmel to Horeb: Elijah in Crisis.* Sheffield: Almond, 1990.

Hayes, J. H. and P. K. Hooker. *A New Chronology for the Kings of Israel and Judah and its Implications for Biblical History and Literature.* Atlanta: John Knox, 1988.

Heaton, E. W. *Solomon's New Men.* New York: Pica, 1974.

_____. *The Hebrew Kingdoms.* London: Oxford University Press, 1968.

Hobbs, T. R. *II Kings.* Waco: Word, 1985.

_____. *1, 2 Kings.* Dallas: Word, 1989.

Horner, T. *Jonathan Loved David: Homosexuality in Biblical Times.* Philadelphia: Westminster, 1978.

Ishida, T. *The Royal Dynasties in Ancient Israel. A Study on the Formation and Development of Royal–Dynastic Ideology.* Berlin: de Gruyter, 1977.

Jensen, I. L. *I Kings with Chronicles: A Self-Study Guide.* Chicago: Moody, 1968.

Jones, G. H. *I and II Kings, Vol. 1.* Grand Rapids: Eerdmans, 1984.

_____. *I and II Kings, Vol. 2.* Grand Rapids: Eerdmans, 1984.

Long, B. O. *I Kings, with an Introduction to Historical Literature.* Grand Rapids: Eerdmans, 1984.

Malchow, B. "A Manual for Future Monarchs." *Catholic Biblical Quarterly* 47 (1985) 238–45.

Marshall, I. H. *The Book of Kings and Chronicles.* Grand Rapids: Eerdmans, 1967.

Mendenhall, G. E. "The Monarchy." *Interpretation* 29 (1975) 155–170.

Mettinger, T. N. *King and Messiah: The Civil and Sacral Legitimation of the Israelite Kings.* Lund, Sweden: Gleerup, 1976.

Miller, J. M. and J. H. Hayes. *A History of Ancient Israel and Judah.* Philadelphia: Westminster, 1986.

Montgomery, J. A. and H. S. Gehman. *The Books of Kings (International Critical Commentary.)* New York: Scribners, 1951.

Nelson, R. *First and Second Kings.* Atlanta: John Knox, 1987.

Parker, S. B. "Jesebel's Reception of Jehu." *Maarav* 1 (1978–79) 67–78.

Rice, G. *I Kings: Nation Under God.* Grand Rapids: Eerdmans, 1991.

Richards, L. *Edge of Judgment: Pathways to Blessing and Judgment, Studies in I and II Kings, II Chronicles, Prophets of the Divided Kingdoms, Ezekiel, and Jeremiah.* Elgin: Cook, 1977.

Robinson, J. *The Second Book of Kings.* New York–London: Cambridge University Press, 1976.

Robinson, J. *The First Book of Kings.* New York–London: Cambridge University Press, 1972.

Snaith, N. H. *"The First and Second Books of Kings." The Interpreter's Bible.* New York: Abingdon, 1954.

Skinner, J. *Kings.* Edinburgh: Jack; New York: Oxford University Press, 1904.

Speyr, A. *Elijah.* San Francisco: Ignatius, 1990.

Thiele, E. R. *A Chronology of the Hebrew Kings.* Grand Rapids: Zondervan, 1977.

_____. *The Mysterious Numbers of the Hebrew Kings.* Chicago: University of Chicago Press, 1951; 3rd edition, Grand Rapids: Eerdmans, 1983.

van Wyk, W. C., ed. *Studies in the Succession Narrative.* Pretoria: Old Testament Society of South Africa, 1986.

Veer, M. B. *My God is Yahweh: Elijah and Ahab in an Age of Apostacy.* Trans. by T. Plantinga. St. Catherines, Ontario: Paideia, 1980.

Walsh, J. T. and C. T. Begg "I & II Kings." *The New Jerome Biblical Commentary,* ed. by R. Brown et. al. Englewood Cliffs: Prentice Hall, 1990. Pp. 160–185.

Whitcomb, J. C. *Solomon to the Exile; Studies in Kings and Chronicles.* Winona Lake: BMH, 1971.

Whitelam, K. W. *The Just King: Monarchical Judicial Authority in Ancient Israel.* Sheffield: JSOT Press, 1979.

Whybray, R. N. *The Succession Narrative: A Study of II Samuel 9–20; I Kings 1 and 2.* London: SCM; Naperville: Allenson, 1968.

24. I & II CHRONICLES

Ackroyd, P. R. *I & II Chronicles, Ezra, Nehemiah.* London: SCM, 1973.

_____. *I–II Chronicles, Ezra, Nehemiah, Ruth, Jonah, I & II Maccabees.* London: Mowbray, 1970.

_____. *First and Second Chronicles, Ezra, Nehemiah.* London: SCM, 1973.

_____. "History and Theology in the Writings of the Chronicler." *Concordia Theological Monthly* 38 (1967) 501–515.

_____. "The Chronicler as Exegete." *Journal for the Study of the Old Testament* 2 (1977) 2–32.

Allen, L. C. *I, II Chronicles.* Waco: Word, 1987.

Black, R. E. *The Books of Chronicles.* Joplin: College Press, 1973.

Braun, R. L. *I Chronicles.* Waco: Word, 1986.

Castelot, J. J. *The Books of Chronicles.* Collegeville: The Liturgical Press, 1966.

Coggins, R. J. *The First and Second Books of Chronicles.* Cambridge: Cambridge University Press, 1976.

de Vries, S. J. *I and II Chronicles.* Grand Rapids: Eerdmans, 1989.

Dentan, R. C., *The First and Second Books of the Kings: The First and Second Books of the Chronicles.* Richmond: John Knox, 1965.

Dillard, R. B. *II Chronicles.* Waco: Word, 1987.

Endres, J. *Temple, Monarchy, and Word of God.* Wilmington: Michael Glazier, 1988.

Freedman, D. N. "The Chronicler's Purpose." *Catholic Biblical Quarterly* 23 (1961) 436–42.

Graham, M. P. *The Utilization of I and II Chronicles in the Reconstruction of Israelite History of the Nineteenth Century.* Atlanta: Scholars, 1989.

Grindel, J. A. *The Second Book of Chronicles.* New York: Paulist, 1973.

Japhet, S. *Ideology of the Books of Chronicles and Its Place in Biblical Thought.* Jerusalem: Hebrew University, 1973.

Mangan, C. *I–II Chronicles, Ezra, Nehemiah.* Collegeville: Michael Glazier, 1991.

McConville, J. G. *I and II Chronicles.* Philadelphia: Westminster Press, 1984.

Merill, E. H. *I and II Chronicles*. Grand Rapids: Lamplighter Books–Zondervan, 1988.

Myers, J. M. *First and Second Chronicles*. Garden City: Doubleday, 1965.

_____. *I Chronicles, II Chronicles, Ezra, Nehemiah*. Garden City: Doubleday, 1965.

Newsome, J. D. *The Chronicler's View of Prophecy*. Ann Arbor: University Microfilms, 1979.

North, R. J. "The Chronicler: I-II Chronicles, Ezra, Nehemiah." *The New Jerome Biblical Commentary*. Ed. by R. Brown et al. Englewood Cliffs: Prentice Hall, 1990. Pp. 362–398.

Noth, M. *The Chronicler's History*. Sheffield: JSOT Press, 1987.

Petersen, D. L. *Late Israelite Prophecy: Studies in Deutero-Prophetic Literature and in Chronicles*. Missoula: Scholars Press, 1977.

Sailhamer, J. *First and Second Chronicles*. Chicago: Moody Press, 1983.

Throntveit, M. A. *The Significance of the Royal Speeches and Prayers for the Structure and Theology of the Chronicler*. New York: Union Theological Seminary, 1982.

Torrey, C. C. *The Chronicler's History of Israel*. New Haven: Yale University Press, 1954.

Traylor, J. H. *I and II Kings, II Chronicles*. Nashville: Broadman Press, 1981.

Welch, A. C. *The Work of the Chronicler, its Purpose and its Date*. London: Oxford University Press, 1939.

Wilcock, M. *The Message of Chronicles: One Church, One Faith, One Lord*. Leicester–Downers Grove: Inter-Varsity, 1987.

Williamson, H. G. *I and II Chronicles*. Grand Rapids: Eerdmans, London: Marshall, Morgan & Scott, 1982.

_____. *Israel in the Books of Chronicles*. New York: Cambridge University Press, 1977.

Wilson, R. R. *Genealogy and History in the Biblical World*. New Haven: Yale University Press, 1977.

25. EZRA-NEHEMIAH

Ackroyd, P. R. *I & II Chronicles, Ezra, Nehemiah*. London: SCM, 1973.

Batten, L. W. *A Critical and Exegetical Commentary on the Books of Ezra and Nehemiah*. New York: Scribner's, 1913; Edinburgh: Clark, 1949.

Blenkinsopp, J. *Ezra–Nehemiah, A Commentary*. Philadelphia: Westminster Press, 1988.

_____. *Ezra-Nehemiah*. London: SCM, 1989.

_____. *Ezra, Nehemiah, and Esther*. Philadelphia: Westminster, 1988.

Brockington, L. H. *Ezra, Nehemiah, and Esther*. London: Nelson, 1969.

Brug, J. F. *Ezra, Nehemiah, Esther*. Milwaukee: Northwestern, 1985.

Burns, R. J. *Ezra, Nehemiah*. Collegeville: The Liturgical Press, 1985.

Clines, D. J. *Ezra, Nehemiah, Esther*. Grand Rapids: Eerdmans, 1984.

_____. *The Esther Scroll: The Story of the Story*. Sheffield: JSOT Press, 1984.

Coggins, R. J. *The Books of Ezra and Nehemiah*. Cambridge: Cambridge University Press, 1976.

Eskenazi, T. C. *In An Age of Prose: A Literary Approach to Ezra-Nehemiah*. Atlanta: Scholars, 1988.

Fensham, F. C. *The Books of Ezra and Nehemiah*. Grand Rapids: Eerdmans, 1982.

Holmgren, F. C. *Israel Alive Again: A Commentary on the Books of Ezra and Nehemiah*. Grand Rapids: Eerdmans, 1987.

Jensen, I. L. *Ezra, Nehemiah, Esther*. Chicago: Moody, 1970.

Kelly, P. H. *The Book of Ezra; The Book of Nehemiah; The Book of Esther; The Book of Job*. Richmond: John Knox, 1962.

Kidner, D. *Ezra and Nehemiah: An Introduction and Commentary*. Leicester: Downers Grove: Inter-Varsity, 1979.

_____. *Ezra and Nehemiah.* Downers Grove: Inter-Varsity, 1979.

Laney, J. C. *Ezra, Nehemiah.* Chicago: Moody, 1982.

Luck, G. C. *Ezra and Nehemiah.* Chicago: Moody, 1961.

Mangan, C. *I–II Chronicles, Ezra, Nehemiah.* Wilmington: Michael Glazier, 1982.

McConville, J. G. *Ezra, Nehemiah, and Esther.* Philadelphia: Westminster, 1985.

Moriarty, F. L. *The Books of Ezra and Nehemiah.* Collegeville: The Liturgical Press, 1966.

Myers, J. M. *Ezra, Nehemiah. The Anchor Bible.* Garden City: Doubleday, 1965.

Owens, M. F. *Ezra, Nehemiah, Esther, Job.* Nashville: Broadman, 1983.

Ratzlaff, R. *Ezra and Nehemiah; Esther.* Joplin: College Press, 1979.

Rowley, H. H. "Nehemiah's Mission and Its Background." *Bulletin of the John Rylands Library* 37 (1955) 528–61.

Ryle, H. W. *The Books of Ezra and Nehemiah.* Cambridge: University Press, 1893, 1901.

Slotki, J. J. *Daniel, Ezra and Nehemiah.* London: Socino, 1951.

Stone, M. E. *Scriptures, Sects and Visions: A Profile from Ezra to the Jewish Revolts.* Philadelphia: Fortress, 1980.

Torrey, C. C. *The Chronicler's History of Israel.* New Haven: Yale University Press, 1954.

_____. *Ezra Studies.* Chicago: University of Chicago Press, 1910.

Turner, G. A. *Ezra, Nehemiah, Esther, Malachi.* Winona Lake: Light and Life, 1966.

Vos, H. F. *Ezra, Nehemiah, and Esther.* Grand Rapids: Lamplighter–Zondervan, 1987.

Williamson, H. G. *Ezra, Nehemiah.* Waco: Word, 1985.

_____. *Ezra and Nehemiah.* Sheffield: JSOT Press; Sheffield Academic Press, 1987.

_____. *Ezra Nehemiah*. Waco: Word, 1985.

Wright , J. S. *The Date of Ezra's Coming to Jerusalem*. London: Tyndale, 1958.

_____. *Ezra: Nehemiah: Esther: Job*. Grand Rapids: Eerdmans, 1968.

26. RUTH-ESTHER

Anderson, B. W. "The Book of Esther." *The Interpeter's Bible*. Vol. III. New York: Abingdon, 1954. Pp. 821–74.

Atkinson, D. *The Wings of Refuge: The Message of Ruth*. Downers Grove: Inter–Varsity, 1983.

Auld, A. G. *Joshua, Judges, and Ruth*. Philadelphia: Westminster, 1985.

Baldwin, J. *Esther*. Downers Grove: Inter–Varsity, 1984.

Barucof, A. *Judith, Esther*. 2nd ed. Paris: Cerf, 1959.

Beattie, D. R. *Jewish Exegesis of the Book of Ruth*. Sheffield: The University Press, 1977.

Berg, S. B. *The Book of Esther: Motifs, Themes and Structure*. Missoula: Scholars, 1979.

Berlin, A. *Poetics and Interpretation of Biblical Narrative*. Sheffield: Almond Press, 1983.

Bickerman, E. J. *Four Strange Books of the Bible*. New York: Schocken, 1967.

Brockington, L. H. *Ezra, Nehemiah, and Esther*. London: Nelson, 1969.

Campbell, E. F. *Ruth. The Anchor Bible*. Garden City: Doubleday, 1975.

Clines, D. J. *Esther Scroll: The Story of the Story*. Sheffield: JSOT Press, 1984.

_____. *Ezra, Nehemiah, Esther*. Grand Rapids: Eerdmans, 1984.

Craghan, J. *Esther, Judith, Tobit, Jonah, Ruth*. Collegeville: Michael Glazier, 1991.

Cundall, A. E. *Judges and Ruth*. London: Tyndale, 1968.

Fewell, D. and D. Gunn. *Compromising Redemption: Relating Characters in the Book of Ruth.* Louisville: Westminster/John Knox, 1990.

Fischer, J. A. *Song of Songs, Ruth, Lamentations, Ecclesiastes, Esther.* Collegeville: The Liturgical Press, 1986.

Fox, M. *The Redaction of the Books of Esther. On Reading Composite Texts.* Atlanta: Scholars, 1991.

Fuerst, W. J. *The Books of Ruth, Esther, Ecclesiastes, The Song of Songs, Lamentations.* Cambridge: Cambridge University Press, 1975.

Gordis, R. "Love, Marriage, and Business in the Book of Ruth." *A Light unto My Path: Old Testament Studies in Honor of Jacob M. Meyers.* Philadelphia: Temple University Press, 1974. Pp. 241–64.

Gray, J. *Joshua Judges and Ruth. The Century Bible.* London: Nelson, 1967.

_____. *Joshua, Judges, Ruth.* Grand Rapids: Eerdmans; Basingstoke: Marshall Morgan & Scott, 1986.

Halls, R. M. *The Theology of the Book of Ruth.* Philadelphia: Fortress, 1969.

Hubbard, R. L., Jr. *The Book of Ruth.* Grand Rapids: Eerdmans, 1988.

Knight, G. F. *Esther, Song of Songs, Lamentations.* London: Student Christian Movement, 1955.

Knight, G. A. *Ruth and Jonah.* 2nd. ed. London: SCM, 1966.

Laffey, A. L. "Ruth." *The New Jerome Biblical Commentary.* Ed. by R. Brown et al. Englewood Cliffs: Prentice Hall, 1990. Pp. 553–557.

Lattey, C. *The Book of Ruth.* London: Longmans, Green, 1935.

Limburg, J. *Old Stories for a New Time.* Atlanta: John Knox, 1983.

McConville, J. G. *Ezra, Nehemiah, and Esther.* Philadelphia: Westminster, 1985.

Meyers, J. M. *The Linguistic and Literary Form of the Book of Ruth.* Leiden: Brill, 1955.

Montague, G. T. *The Books of Ruth and Tobit.* New York: Paulist, 1973.

Moore, C. A. *Studies In the Book of Esther.* New York: Ktav, 1982.

_____. *Esther.* Garden City: Doubleday, 1971.

_____. *Studies in the Book of Esther.* New York: Ktav, 1982.

Murphy, R. E. *Wisdom Literature: Job, Proverbs, Ruth, Canticles, Ecclesiastes, and Esther.* Grand Rapids: Eerdmans, 1981.

Myers, J. M. *The Linguistic and Literary Form of the Book of Ruth.* Leiden: Brill, 1955.

Sasson, J. M. *Ruth: A New Translation with a Philological Commentary and a Formalistic-Folklorist Interpretation.* Baltimore: Johns Hopkins University Press, 1979.

Sloyan, G. S. *The Books of Ruth and Tobit.* Collegeville: The Liturgical Press, 1968.

Streane, A. W. *The Book of Esther.* Cambridge: Cambridge University Press, 1907.

Zannoni, A. E. "Fact, Folklore, Faith: The Story of Ruth." *The Bible Today* 78 (1975) 391–99.

V. WISDOM LITERATURE

27. GENERAL

Barre, M. L. "Fear of God and the World View of Wisdom." *Biblical Theology Bulletin* 11 (1981) 41–43.

Beaucamp, E. *Man's Destiny in the Book of Wisdom.* New York: Alba House, 1970.

Bentzen, A. *King and Messiah.* Oxford: Blackwell, 1970.

Bergant, D. *What are they Saying About Wisdom Literature?* New York: Paulist, 1984.

_____. "Why Do I Suffer?" *The Bible Today* 20 (1982) 341ff.

Blank, S. H. "Wisdom." *The Interpreter's Dictionary of the Bible.* Vol. IV. New York: Abingdon, 1962. Pp. 852–61.

Blenkinsopp, J. *Wisdom and Law in the Old Testament: The Ordering of Life in Israel and Early Judaism.* Oxford: Oxford University Press, 1983.

Boadt, L. E. *Introduction to Wisdom Literature and Proverbs.* Collegeville: The Liturgical Press, 1986.

Bowes, P. J. "The Structure of Job." *The Bible Today* 20 (1982) 329–333.

Brueggemann, W. "Scripture and an Ecumenical Life Style—A Study of Wisdom Theology." *Interpretation* 24 (1970) 3–60.

_____. "Neglected Sapiential Word Pair." *Zeitschrift für die Alttestamentliche Wissenschaft* 89 (1977) 234–258.

_____. *In Man We Trust: The Neglected Side of Biblical Faith.* Richmond: John Knox, 1973.

Bryce, G. E. *A Legacy of Wisdom: The Egyptian Contribution to the Wisdom of Israel.* Lewisburg: Bucknell University; London: Associated University Press, 1979.

_____. *Israel and the Wisdom of Egypt.* Lewisburg: Bucknell University Press, 1975.

Bullock, C. H. *An Introduction to the Poetic Books of the Old Testament (The Wisdom and Songs of Israel).* Chicago: Moody, 1979.

Clements, R. E. *One Hundred Years of Old Testament Interpretation.* Philadelphia: Westminster, 1976. Pp. 99–117.

_____. *Wisdom for a Changing World: Wisdom in Old Testament Theology.* Berkeley: BIBAL, 1990.

Crenshaw, J. "Wisdom." *Old Testament Form Criticism.* San Antonio: Trinity University Press, 1974. Pp. 225–64.

_____. "Method in Determining Wisdom Influence Upon Historical Literature." *Journal of Biblical Literature* 88 (1969) 129–142.

_____. *Old Testament Wisdom: An Introduction.* Atlanta: John Knox, 1981.

_____. *Studies in Ancient Israelite Wisdom.* New York: Ktav, 1976.

_____. *Theodicy in the Old Testament.* Philadelphia: Fortress, 1983.

Crim, K., ed. "Wisdom." *The Interpreter's Dictionary of the Bible.* Supplementary volume. Nashville: Abingdon, 1976. Pp. 949–960.

Cross, F. M., Jr. and D. N. Freedman. *Studies in Ancient Yahwistic Poetry.* Missoula: Scholars, 1975.

Davidson, R. *Wisdom and Worship.* Philadelphia: Trinity, 1990.

Donald, T. "Semantic Field of Folly in Proverbs, Job, Psalms and Ecclesiastes." *Vetus Testamentum* 13 (1963) 285–292.

Eaton, J. *The Contemplative Face of Old Testament Wisdom in the Context of World Religions.* London—Philadelphia: SMC—Trinity, 1989.

Emerton, J. A. "Wisdom." *Tradition and Interpretation.* Ed. by G. W. Anderson. Oxford: Clarendon, 1979. Pp. 214–237.

Gaebelein, F. E., ed. *Expositor's Bible Commentary*. Vol. 5. Grand Rapids: Zondervan, 1990.

Gaiser, F. *Psalms*. Minneapolis: Augsburg–Fortress, 1988.

Gammie, J. G., W. A. Brueggemann, W. L. Humphreys and J. M. Ward, eds. *Israelite Wisdom: Theological and Literary Essays in Honor of Samuel Terrien*. Missoula: Scholars, for Union Theological Seminary, New York, 1978.

_____. "Spacial and Ethical Dualism in Jewish Wisdom and Apocalyptic Literature." *Journal of Biblical Literature* 93 (1974) 356–385.

_____ and L. Perdue, eds. *The Sage in Israel and the Ancient Near East*. Winona Lake: Eisenbrauns, 1990.

Harvey, J. "Wisdom Literature and Biblical Theology." *Biblical Theology Bulletin* 1 (1971) 308–319.

Herbert, A. S. "Wisdom." *Dictionary of the Bible*, J. Hastings, ed. New York: Scribner's, 1963. Pp. 1039–40.

Hoglund, K. G., et al., eds. *The Listening Heart. Essays in Wisdom and the Psalms in honor of Roland E. Murphy*. Sheffield: JSOT Press, 1987.

Imschoot, V. "Wisdom." *Encyclopedic Dictionary of the Bible*. New York: McGraw-Hill, 1963. Pp. 2583–91.

Irving, W. A. "The Wisdom Literature." *The Interpreter's Bible*. Vol 1. Nashville: Abingdon-Cokesbury, 1952. Pp. 212–219.

Jarvis, F. W. *Prophets, Poets, Priests and Kings*. New York: Seabury, 1974.

Kalugila, L. *The Wise King, Studies in Royal Wisdom as Divine Revelation in the Old Testament and its Environment*. Lund: Gleerup, 1980.

Kugel, J. L. *The Idea of Biblical Poetry. Parallelism and its History*. New Haven: Yale University Press, 1981.

Kraus, H. J. *Psalms 60–150: A Commentary*. Trans. by H. C. Oswald. Minneapolis: Augsburg, 1989.

Lambert, W. G. *Babylonian Wisdom Literature.* Oxford: Clarendon, 1960.

Malchow, B. "Social Justice in the Wisdom Literature." *Biblical Theology Bulletin* 12 (October, 1982) 120–123.

_____. "The Roots of Israel's Wisdom in Sacral Kingship." Ph.D. dissertation, Marquette University. Ann Arbor: University Microfilms, 1973.

_____. "The Wisdom of the Anointed." *The Lutheran Quarterly* 28 (1976) 70–82.

_____. "The Wise as a Model for Ministry." *Schola* 4 (1981) 7–43.

_____. "Wisdom"s Contribution to Dialogue." *Biblical Theology Bulletin* 13 (1983), 111–15.

McDonald, D. B. *The Hebrew Philosophical Genius.* Princeton: Princeton University Press, 1936.

McKenzie, J. L. "Reflections on Wisdom." *Journal of Biblical Literature* 86 (1967) 1–9.

_____. "Wisdom, Wisdom Literature." *Dictionary of the Bible.* Milwaukee: Bruce, 1965. Pp. 929–33.

Miller, M. S. and J. L. Miller, eds. "Wisdom." *Harper's Bible Dictionary.* New York: Harper & Row, 1973. Pp. 817–819.

Monroe, M. T. *Enjoying the Wisdom Books.* London: Longmans, 1964.

Montgomery, J. W. "Wisdom as Gift: The Wisdom Concept in Relation to Biblical Messianism." *Interpretation* 16 (1967) 43–57.

Morgan, D. F. *Wisdom in the Old Testament Traditions.* Atlanta: John Knox, 1981.

Murphy, R. E. "Form Criticism and Wisdom Literature." *Catholic Biblical Quarterly* 31 (1969) 475–483.

_____. "Assumptions and Problems in Old Testament Wisdom Research." *Catholic Biblical Quarterly* 29 (1967) 407–418.

_____. "The Hebrew Sage and Openess to the World." Villanova University Symposium (unpublished).

_____. *Introduction to the Wisdom Literature of the Old Testament.* Collegeville: The Liturgical Press, 1965.

_____. "Introduction to Wisdom Literature." *The Jerome Biblical Commentary.* Ed by R. Brown et al. Englewood Cliffs: Prentice Hall, 1968. Pp. 487–94.

_____. "Introduction To Wisdom Literature." *The New Jerome Biblical Commentary.* Ed. by R. Brown et al. Englewood Cliffs: Prentice Hall, 1990. Pp. 447–452.

_____. *Seven Books of Wisdom.* Milwaukee: Bruce, 1960.

_____. *The Tree of Life: An Exploration of Biblical Wisdom Literature.* New York: Doubleday, 1990.

_____. *Wisdom Literature & Psalms.* Nashville: Abingdon, 1983.

_____. *Wisdom Literature: Job, Proverbs, Ruth, Canticles, Ecclesiastes, Esther.* Grand Rapids: Eerdmans, 1981.

Noth, M. and W. D. Thomas, eds. *Wisdom in Israel and in the Near East.* Leiden: Brill, 1955.

O'Connor, K. M. *The Wisdom Literature.* Collegeville: Michael Glazier, 1991.

O'Grady, J. F. "Wisdom and the Wiseman." *The Bible Today* 18 (1980) 143–148.

Oesterley, W. O. *The Wisdom of Egypt and the Old Testament.* New York: Macmillan, 1927.

Paterson, J. *The Wisdom of Israel.* London–Nashville: Lutterworth–Abingdon, 1961.

Perdue, L. G. *Wisdom and Cult.* Missoula: Scholars, 1977.

Priest, J. F. "Where Is Wisdom to Be Placed?" *Journal of Bible and Religion* 31 (1963) 275–282.

Rankin, O. S. *Israel's Wisdom Literature.* Edinburgh: T. & T. Clark, 1964.

Ranston, H. *The Old Testament Wisdom Books and Their Teaching.* London: Epworth: Press, 1930.

Reese, J. M. "Sharing Biblical Wisdom." *The Bible Today* 18 (1980) 149–153.

_____. *Hellenistic Influence on the Book of Wisdom and its Consequences.* Rome: Biblical Institute Press, 1970.

_____. "In Praise of Wisdom." *The Bible Today* 18 (1980) 160–165.

Rylaarsdam, J. C. *Revelation in Jewish Wisdom Literature.* Chicago: University of Chicago Press, 1946.

_____. "Hebrew Wisdom." *Peake's Commentary.* London–New York: T. Nelson, 1962. Pp. 386–90.

Scott, R. B. *The Way of Wisdom in the Old Testament.* New York: MacMillan, 1971.

Sheppard, G. T. *Wisdom as a Hermeneutical Construct. A Study in the Sapientializing of the Old Testament.* Berlin–New York: de Gruyter, 1980.

Skehan, P. W. *Studies in Israelite Poetry and Wisdom.* Washington, D.C.: The Catholic Biblical Association, 1971.

Snell, P. "A Journey of Faith." *The Bible Today* 20 (1982) 329–33.

Steinmueller, J. E. "Wisdom in the Ancient Near East" and "Wisdom in the Old Testament." *Interpreter's Dictionary of the Bible.* Supplementary Volume. New York: Abingdon, 1976. Pp. 949–956.

Steinmueller, J. E., and K. Sullivan, ed. "Wisdom." *Catholic Biblical Encyclopedia–Old Testament.* New York: Wagner, 1959. Pp. 113–43.

Thomas, D. W., ed. *Wisdom in Israel and the Ancient Near East.* Leiden: Brill, 1960.

Tucker, B. D. "Wisdom of God and Wisdom of Man." *The Japan Christian Quarterly.* 37 (1971) 242–249.

Urbach, E. E. *The Sages: Their Concepts and Beliefs.* Volumes 1 and 2. Jerusalem: Magnes, 1975.

Vawter, B. *The Path of Wisdom: Biblical Investigations.* Wilmington: Michael Glazier, 1986.

von Rad, G. "Wisdom and Law in the Old Testament Wisdom Literature." *Concordia Theological Monthly* 43 (1972) 600–610.

_____. *Wisdom in Israel.* Nashville: Abingdon, 1974.

Whedbee, J. W. *Isaiah and Wisdom.* Nashville: Abingdon, 1971.

Whybray, R. N. *The Intellectual Tradition in the Old Testament.* Berlin–New York: de Gruyter, 1974.

Wilken, R. L., ed. *Aspects of Wisdom in Judaism and Early Christianity.* Notre Dame: University of Notre Dame Press, 1975.

Wilkens, U. "Sophia." *Theological Dictionary of the New Testament.* Volume VII. Grand Rapids: Eerdmans, 1985. Pp. 515–19.

Wood, J. *Wisdom Literature.* London: Duckworth, 1967.

Xavier, L. D. "Wisdom." *Dictionary of Biblical Theology.* New York: Desclée, 1967. Pp. 577–79.

Zannoni, A. E. "Five Disconcerting Theological Reflections from Old Testament Wisdom Literature." *St Luke's Journal of Theology* 19, 4 (1976) 286–298.

_____. "The Hebrew Sage: A Model for Lay Campus Ministry." *Process. The Journal of the Catholic Campus Ministry Association* IV, 2 (1978) 9–12.

Zimmerli, W. "Place and Limit of Wisdom in the Framework of Old Testament Theology." *Scottish Journal of Theology* 17 (1964) 146–158.

28. PSALMS

Ackroyd, P. R. *Doors of Perception: A Guide to Reading the Psalms.* Leighton Buzzard: Faith, 1978.

Allen, L. C. *Psalms 101–150. Word Biblical Commentary.* Waco: Word, 1983.

Alonso-Schökel, L. *A Manual of Hebrew Poetics.* Rome: Pontifical Biblical Institute, 1988.

Alonso-Schökel, L. "The Poetic Structure of Psalm 42–43." London. *Journal for the Society of the Study of the Old Testament* 1 (1976) 4–11.

Anderson, A. A. *Psalms 1–72.* Grand Rapids: Eerdmans, 1972.

_____. *Psalms 73–150.* Grand Rapids: Eerdmans, 1972.

_____. *The Book of Psalms. New Century Bible Series.* London: Oliphants, 1972.

Anderson, B. W. *Out of the Depths: The Psalms Speak For Us Today.* Philadelphia: Westminster, 1983.

Auffret, P. *The Literary Structure of Psalm 2.* Sheffield: The University Press, 1977.

Barth, C. F. *Introduction To The Psalms.* New York: Scribners, Oxford: Blackwell; New York: Scribner's, 1966.

Beaucamp, E. *Le Psautier. Sources Bibliques.* 2 vols. Paris: Gabalta, 1976.

Bellinger, W. H. *Psalmody and Prophecy.* Sheffield: JSOT Press, 1984.

Berlin, A. *Poetics and Interpretation of Biblical Narrative.* Sheffield: Almond Press, 1983.

Berrigan, D. *Uncommon Prayer: A Book of Psalms.* New York: Seabury, 1978.

Binnie, W. *The Psalms: Their History, Teaching, and Use.* London: Hodder & Stoughton, 1886.

Bird, T. E. *A Commentary On The Psalms.* London: Burns & Oates, 1927.

Bonhoeffer, D. *Meditating on the Word.* Cambridge: Cowley, 1986.

_____. *Psalms: The Prayer Book of the Bible.* Minneapolis: Augsburg, 1970.

Botz, P. *Runways To God: The Psalms As Prayer.* Collegeville: The Liturgical Press, 1979.

Briggs, C. A. and E. G. Briggs. *A Critical and Exegetical Commentary on the Book of Psalms.* 2 vols. Edinburgh: T & T Clark, 1906.

Brillet, G. *Meditations on the Old Testament, The Psalms.* New York: Desclée, 1960.

Broyles, C. C. *The Conflict of Faith and Experience in the Psalms.* Sheffield: JSOT Press, 1989.

Brueggemann, W. *Israel's Praise: Doxology Against Idolatry and Ideology.* Philadelphia: Fortress, 1988.

_____. *Praying the Psalms*. Winona: St. Mary's, 1982.

_____. *The Message of the Psalms: A Theological Commentary*. Minneapolis: Augsburg, 1984.

_____. "Psalm 100 *(Expository Article)*." *Interpretation* 39 (1985) 65–69.

_____. "Psalm 109: Three Times 'Steadfast Love'." *Word & World: Theology for Christian Ministry* 5 (1985) 144–154.

_____. "Psalms and the Life of Faith: A Suggested Typology of Function." *Journal for the Study of the Old Testament* 17 (1980) 3–32.

_____. "The costly Loss of Lament." *Journal for the Study of the Old Testament* 36 (1986) 57–71.

_____. "Formfulness of Grief." *Interpretation* 31 (1977) 263–275.

Buber, M. *Right and Wrong: An Interpretation of Some Psalms*. London: SCM, 1952.

Bullock, C. H. *An Introduction to the Old Testament Poetic Books*. Chicago: Moody, 1979.

Calvin, J. *Commentary on the book of Psalms*. Grand Rapids: Eerdmans, 1949.

Chase, M. E. *The Psalms for the Common Reader*. New York: Norton, 1962.

Clifford, R. J. *Psalms 1–72. (Commentary)*. Collegeville: The Liturgical Press, 1986.

_____. *Psalms 73–150. (Commentary)*. Collegeville: The Liturgical Press, 1986.

Craghan, J. F. *The Psalms: Prayers For The Ups, Downs and In-Betweens of Life*. Wilmington: Michael Glazier, 1985.

Craigie, P. C. and N. H. Ridderbos. "Psalms." *The International Standard Bible Encyclopedia*. Volume 3. G. W. Bromiley, ed. Grand Rapids: Eerdmans, 1986. Pp. 1029–40.

_____. *Psalms 1–50. Word Biblical Commentary*. Waco: Word, 1983.

Craven, T. *Psalms*. Wilmington: Michael Glazier, 1987.

Croft, S. J. *The Identity of the Individual In The Psalms. Journal for the Study of the Old Testament*. Supplement 44. Sheffield: JSOT Press, 1987.

Cross, F. M., Jr. and D. N. Freedman. *Studies in Ancient Yahwistic Poetry*. Missoula: Scholars, 1975.

Culley, R. C. *Oral Formulaic Language in the Biblical Psalms*. Toronto: University of Toronto Press, 1967.

Dahood, M. *Psalms. The Anchor Bible*. 3 vols. Garden City: Doubleday, 1966, 1968, 1970.

_____. *Psalms*. 3 volumes. Garden City: Doubleday, 1965, 1968, 1970.

Dalglish, E. R. *Psalm Fifty-One in Light of Ancient Near Eastern Paternism*. Leiden: Brill, 1962.

Drijvers, P. *The Psalms Their Structure and Meaning*. New York: Herder and Herder, 1965.

Dunlop, L. *Patterns of Prayer in the Psalms*. New York: Seabury, 1982.

Eaton, J. H. *Psalms: Introduction and Commentary*. London: SCM, 1967.

_____. "The Psalms and Israelite Worship." *Tradition and Interpretation*. G.W. Anderson, ed. Oxford: Clarendon, 1979.

_____. *Kingship and the Psalms*. Naperville: Alec R. Allenson, 1976.

_____. *Kingship and the Psalms,* 2nd. ed. Sheffield: JSOT Press, 1986.

Fishbane, M. *Text and Texture*. New York: Schocken, 1979.

Fisher, J. A. *The Psalms. I Will Be Their God and They Shall Be My People*. Canfield: Alba House, 1974.

Fitzgerald, A. "Hebrew Poetry." *The New Jerome Biblical Commentary*. Ed. by R. Brown et al. Englewood Cliffs: Prentice Hall, 1990. Pp. 201–208.

_____. "Hebrew Poetry." *The Jerome Biblical Commentary*. Ed. by R. Brown et al. Englewood Cliffs: Prentice Hall, 1968. Part 1, Pp. 242–43.

Follis, E. R. *Directions in Biblical Hebrew Poetry*. Sheffield: JSOT Press, 1987.

Freedman, D. N. *Pottery, Poetry, and Prophecy: Studies in Early Hebrew Poetry*. Winona Lake: Eisenbrauns, 1980.

Garrone, G. M. *How to Pray the Psalms*. Notre Dame: Fides, 1965.

Geller, S. A. *Parallelism in Early Biblical Poetry*. Missoula: Scholars, 1979.

Gestenberger, E. *Psalms, Part 1, with an Introduction to Cultic Poetry*. Grand Rapids: Eerdmans, 1987.

_____. "Psalms." *Old Testament Form Criticism*. San Antonio: Trinity University Press, 1974. Pp. 179–224.

Gevirtz, S. *Patterns in the Early Poetry of Israel*. Chicago: University of Chicago Press, 1964.

Goldinday, J. *Songs From a Strange Land: Psalms 42–51*. Downers Grove: Inter-Varsity, 1978.

Goulder, M. D. *The Psalms of the Sons of Korah*. Sheffield: JSOT Press, 1983.

Gray, G. B. *The Forms of Hebrew Poetry*. New York: Ktav, 1970.

Guardini, R. *The Wisdom of the Psalms*. Chicago: H. Regnery, 1968.

Gunkel, H. *The Psalms: A Form Critical Introduction*. Philadelphia: Fortress, 1967.

Guthrie, H. H. *Israel's Sacred Songs: A Study of Dominant Themes*. New York: Seabury, 1978.

Haglund, E. *Historical Motifs in the Psalms*. Uppsala: Gleerup, 1984.

Hayes, J. H. *Understanding The Psalms*. Valley Forge: Judson, 1976.

Hempel, J. "Psalms, Book of." *Interpreter's Dictionary of the Bible*. Vol. 3. G. A. Buttrick, ed. New York: Abingdon, 1962. Pp. 942–58.

Herzog, A. "Psalms, Book of." *Encyclopedia Judaica* 13. Jerusalem: Keter, 1972. Columns 1303–33.

Hoglund, K. G. et al., eds. *The Listening Heart: Essays in Wisdom and the Psalms in Honor of Roland E. Murphy (Journal For The*

Study of the Old Testament Supplement 58). Sheffield: JSOT, 1987.

Holman, J. "The Structure of Psalm CXXXIX." *Vetus Testamentum* 21 (1971) 298–310.

Hopkins, D. D. "New Directions In Psalms Research: Good News For Theology and Church." *St. Luke's Journal of Theology* 29 (1986) 271–83.

Inch, M. A. *Psychology in the Psalms: A Portrait of Man in God's World.* Waco: Word, 1969.

Johnson, A. R. *Sacred Kingship In Ancient Israel.* Cardiff, Wales: University Press, 1967.

Keel-Leu, O. *The Symbolism of the Biblical World: Ancient Near Eastern Iconography and the Book of Psalms.* New York: Seabury, 1978.

Kenik, H. A. "Code of Conduct for a King: Psalm 101." *Journal of Biblical Literature* 95 (1976) 391–403.

Kidner, D. *Psalms 1-72.* London: Inter-Varsity, 1973.

_____. "Psalms 1–72." *Tyndale Old Testament Commentaries.* Vol. 1. Downers Grove: Inter-Varsity, 1973.

_____. *Psalms 73–150.* London: Inter-Varsity, 1975.

Kirkpatrick, A. F. *The Book of Psalms.* Grand Rapids: Baker, 1982.

Kissane, E. J. *The Book of Psalms.* Westminster: Newman, 1953.

Knight, G. A. *Psalms.* 2 volumes. *The Daily Bible Study Series.* Philadelphia: Westminster, 1982.

Knight, J. and L. Sinclair, eds. *The Psalms and Other Studies on the Old Testament.* Nashotah: Nashotah House Seminary, 1990.

Kodell, J. "The Poetry of the Psalms." *The Bible Today* 65 (1973) 1108–13.

Kraus, H. J. *Theology of the Psalms.* Minneapolis: Augsburg, 1986.

_____. *Psalms 1–59: A Commentary.* Minneapolis: Augsburg, 1988.

_____. *Psalms 60–150: A Commentary.* Minneapolis: Augsburg, 1989.

_____. *Theology of the Psalms.* Minneapolis: Augsburg, 1986.

Kselman, J. S. and M. L. Barré. "Psalms." *The New Jerome Biblical Commentary.* Ed. by R. Brown, et al. Englewood Cliffs: Prentice Hall, 1990. Pp. 523–552.

Kugel, J. L. *The Idea of Biblical Poetry.* New Haven: Yale University Press, 1981.

Leslie, E. A. *The Psalms, Translated in the Light of Hebrew Life and Worship.* New York–Nashville: Abingdon, 1949.

Leupold, H. C. *Exposition of the Psalms.* Columbus: Wartburg, 1959.

Lewis, C. S. *Reflections On The Psalms.* London: Bless, 1958.

Limburg, J. *Psalms for Sojourners.* Minneapolis: Augsburg, 1986.

_____. "A Psalms for Sojourners." *Word and World* 5 (1985) 180–197.

MacKenzie, R. A. *The Psalms: A Selection.* Collegeville: The Liturgical Press, 1967.

Malchow, B. "God or King in Psalm 146." *The Bible Today* 89 (1977) 1166–70.

Mays, J. L. "The David of the Psalms." *Interpretation* 40 (1986) 143–155.

McCandless, J. B. "Enfleshing the Psalms." *Religious Education* 81, 3 (1986) 372–90.

McConville, J. G. "Statement of Assurance in Psalms of Lament." *Irish Biblical Studies* 8 (1986) 64–75.

McKenzie, J. L. "Psalms." *Dictionary of the Bible.* Milwaukee: Bruce, 1965. Pp. 702–706.

Merton, T. *Bread In The Wilderness.* New York: New Directions, 1953.

_____. *Praying The Psalms.* Collegeville: The Liturgical Press, 1956.

Miller, P. D. *Interpreting The Psalms.* Philadelphia: Fortress, 1986.

Mowbray, T. L. "The Function in Ministry of Psalms Dealing With Anger." *Journal of Pastoral Counseling* 21 (1986) 34–39.

Mowinckel, S. *The Psalms In Israel's Worship.* New York: Abingdon; Oxford: Blackwell, 1962.

Murphy, R. E. "Israel's Psalms: Contribution to Today's Prayer Style." *Review For Religious* 34 (1975) 113–20.

_____. "Psalms." *The Jerome Biblical Commentary.* Ed. by R. Brown et al. Englewood Cliffs: Prentice Hall, 1968. Pp. 569–602.

_____. "The Faith of the Psalmist." *Interpretation* 34 (1980) 229–239.

_____. "The Psalms in Modern Life." *The Bible Today* 25 (1987) 231–39.

_____. *The Psalms, Job.* Philadelphia: Fortress, 1977.

_____. *Wisdom Literature and Psalms.* Nashville: Abingdon, 1983.

Nasuti, H. P. *Tradition History and the Psalms of Asaph.* Atlanta: Scholars, 1988.

Nordlund, R. T. *Sunday Afternoon in the Psalms.* New York: Vantage, 1973.

Oesterley, W. O. *A New Approach to the Psalms.* New York: Scribner's, 1937.

_____. *The Psalms: Translated With Text-Critical and Exegetical Notes.* New York: Macmillan, 1939, 1953, 1959.

Peifer, C. J. "Sing For Us The Songs of Zion: The Jerusalem Psalms." *The Bible Today* 97 (1978) 1690–6.

Peterson, E. H. *Answering God: the Psalms as Tools for Prayer.* San Francisco: Harper & Row.

_____. *A Year with the Psalms: 365 Meditations and Prayers.* Waco: Word, 1979.

Pierik, M. *The Psalter in the Temple and the Church.* Washington, D.C.: Catholic University of America Press, 1957.

Pietersma, A. *Two Manuscripts of the Greek Psalter in the Chester Beatty Library Dublin.* Rome: Biblical Institute Press, 1978.

Quesson, N. *The Spirit of the Psalms.* Marie-France Curtin, trans. Mahwah: Paulist, 1991.

Richard, D. A. *The Drama of the Psalms.* Valley Forge: Judson, 1970.

Ringgren, H. *The Faith of the Psalmists.* London: SCM Press, 1963; Philadelphia: Fortress, 1974.

Rogerson, J. W. and J. W. McKay. *Psalms. The Cambridge Bible Commentary on the New English Bible.* 3 vols. New York: Cambridge University Press, 1977.

Routley, E. *Exploring the Psalms.* Philadelphia: Westminster, 1975.

Ryan, M. P. *Key to the Psalms.* Chicago: Fides, 1957.

Sabourin, L. *The Psalms: Their Origin and Meaning.* Staten Island: Alba House, 1969.

Sanders, J. A. *The Dead Sea Psalms Scroll.* Ithaca: Cornell University Press, 1967.

Seybold, K. *Introducing the Psalms.* Edinburgh: T & T Clark. 1990.

Shepherd, M. *The Psalms in Christian Worship: A Practical Guide.* Minneapolis: Augsburg, 1976.

Singer, S. F. "The Psalter at a Glance." *Bible Review* 2 (1986) 32–33.

Skehan, P. W. *Studies In Israelite Poetry and Wisdom.* Washington, D.C.: Catholic Biblical Association of America, 1971.

Smith, M. S. "Seeing God in the Psalms: The Background to the Beatific Vision in the Hebrew Bible." *Catholic Biblical Quarterly* 50 (1988) 171–83.

_____. *Psalms: The Divine Journey.* New York–Mahwah: Paulist, 1987.

Stuart, D. K. *Studies in Early Hebrew Meter.* Missoula: Scholars, 1976.

Stuhlmueller, C. *Psalms.* 2 vols. Collegeville: Michael Glazier, 1991.

Tate, M. E. "The Interpretation of the Psalms." *Review and Expositor* 81 (1984) 363–375.

Terrien, S. L. *The Psalms and Their Meaning For Today.* Indianapolis: Bobbs-Merrill, 1952.

Timko, P. "The Psalms: An Introduction to Their Historical and Literary Character." *The Bible Today* 65 (March, 1973) 1095–9.

Tombs, L. E. "The Book of Psalms." *Wisdom Literature and Poetry.* Charles M. Laymon, ed. Nashville: Abingdon, 1983.

Treves, M. *The Dates of the Psalms.* Pisa: Giardini Stampatori, 1988.

Troeger, T. H. *Rage! Reflect! Rejoice! Praying with the Psalmists.* Philadelphia: Westminster, 1977.

Tsevat, M. "A Study of the Language of the Biblical Psalms." *Journal of Biblical Literature Monograph Series* IX. Philadelphia: 1955.

VanGemeren, W. A. "Psalms." *Expositor's Bible Commentary.* Vol. 5. Grand Rapids: Zondervan, 1989.

Vogel, D. W. *Psalms For Worship Today.* St. Louis: Concordia, 1974.

Watson, W. G. *Classical Hebrew Poetry: A Guide to Its Techniques.* Sheffield: JSOT Press, 1986.

Watters, W. R. *Formula Criticism and the Poetry of the Old Testament.* Berlin–New York: de Gruyter, 1976.

Weiser, A. *The Psalms.* London: SCM; Philadelphia: Westminster, 1962.

Welch, A. C. *The Psalter in Life, Worship and History.* Oxford: Clarendon, 1926.

Westermann, C. *Praise and Lament In The Psalms.* Atlanta: John Knox, 1981.

_____. "Psalms, Book of." *The Interpreter's Dictionary of the Bible.* Supplementary volume. Keith Crim, ed. Nashville: Abingdon, 1976. Pp. 705–710.

_____. *The Living Psalms.* Grand Rapids: Eerdmans, 1989.

_____. *The Praise of God in the Psalms.* Richmond: John Knox, 1965.

_____. *The Psalms, Structure, Content and Message.* Minneapolis: Augsburg, 1980.

White, R. E. *A Christian Handbook to the Psalms.* Grand Rapids, Michigan: Eerdmans, 1984.

Williams, D. *Psalms 72–150.* Dallas: Word, 1989.

Wilson, G. H. *The Editing of the Hebrew Psalter.* Chico: Scholars, 1985.

Worden, T. *The Psalms Are Christian Prayer.* New York: Sheed & Ward, 1961.

Zannoni, A. E. "Praying The Psalms." *St. Luke's Journal of Theology* 19 (1976), 203–208.

29. JOB

Albertson, R. G. "Job and the Ancient Near Eastern Wisdom Literature." *Scripture in Context II.* W. Hall, J. Meyer, and L. Purdue, eds. Winona Lake: Eisenbrauns, 1983.

Anderson, F. I. *Job: An Introduction and Commentary.* London–Downers Grove: Inter-Varsity Press, 1976.

Bachar, S. "Concerning the Date of the Book of Job." *Beth Mikra* 24 (1978) 75–76.

Barre, M. L. "A Note on Job XIX 25." *Vetus Testamentum* 29 (1979) 107–110.

Bergant, D. *Job, Ecclesiastes.* Collegeville: Michael Glazier, 1991.

Bernard, C. W. "Hymn to Wisdom: Exegesis of Job 28:20-28." *Duke Divinity Review* 39 (1974) 105–126.

Besserman, L. L. *The Legend of Job in the Middle Ages.* Cambridge: Harvard University Press, 1979.

Blommerde, A. C. *Northwest Semitic Grammar and Job.* Rome: Biblical Institute Press, 1969.

Bourke, M. *The Book of Job.* 2 volumes. New York: Paulist, 1962.

Ceresko, A. R. *Job 29–31 in the Light of Northwest Semitic.* Rome: Biblical Institute Press, 1980.

Clines, D. J. *Job 1–20.* Dallas: Word, 1989.

Cook, A. S. *The Root of the Thing: A Study of Job and Song of Songs.* Bloomington: Indiana University Press, 1968.

Cox, D. *The Triumph of Impotence: Job and the Tradition of the Absurd.* Rome: Gregorian University Press, 1978.

Craigie, P. C. "Job and Ugaritic Studies." *Studies in the Book of Job.* W. Aufrecht, ed. Waterloo, Ontario: Laurier University Press, 1985.

Crenshaw, J. L., ed. *Theodicy in the Old Testament.* Philadelphia: Fortress, 1983.

Damico, A., trans. *Thomas Aquinas: Literal Exposition on Job.* Atlanta: Scholars, 1989.

Davidson, A. B. *The Book of Job.* Cambridge: University Press, 1961.

Day, P. *An Adversary in Heaven. Satan in the Hebrew Bible.* Atlanta: Scholars, 1989.

Dhorme, E. P. *A Commentary and the Book of Job.* London: Nelson, 1967; Nashville: T. Nelson, 1984.

Dick, M. B. "Job 31, The Oath of Innocence, and The Sage." *Zeitschrift für die Alttestamentliche Wissenschaft* 95 (1983) 31–51.

_____. "The Legal Metaphor in Job 31." *Catholic Biblical Quarterly* 41 (1979) 37–50.

Driver, S. R. and G. B. Gray. *The Book of Job.* Edinburgh: T. & T. Clark, 1921.

Eaton, J. H. *Job.* Sheffield: JSOT Press, 1985, 1987.

Ewing, W. *Job: A Vision of God.* New York: Seabury, 1976.

Freehof, S. B. *Book of Job: A Commentary.* New York: Union of American Hebrew Congregations, 1958.

Frost, G. E. *The Color of the Night: Reflections on the Book of Job.* Minneapolis: Augsburg, 1977.

Gibson, J. C. *Job.* Philadelphia: Westminster, 1985.

Glatzer, N. M. *The Dimensions of Job.* New York: Schocken, 1969.

Glazner, A. "Introduction to the Book of Job." *Beth Mikra* 23 (1978) 189–202.

Good, E. M. *In Turns of Tempest: A Reading of Job.* Stanford: Stanford University Press, 1990.

Gordis, R. *The Book of God and Man.* Chicago: University of Chicago Press, 1965.

_____. *The Book of Job: Commentary, New Translation and Special Studies.* New York: Jewish Theological Seminary of America, 1978.

Grabbe, L. L. *Comparative Philology and the Text of Job: A Study in Methodology.* Missoula: Scholars, 1977.

Gramlich, M. "Job Before and After." *The Bible Today* 94 (1978) 1492–1502.

Greenberg, M. J., C. Greenfield and N. M. Sarna. *The Book of Job. A New Translation According to the Traditional Hebrew Text.* Philadelphia: Jewish Publication Society, 1980.

Guinan, M. D. *Job.* Collegeville: The Liturgical Press, 1986.

Habel, N. "Only the Jackal is My Friend: On Friends and Redeemers in Job." *Interpretation* 31 (1977) 227–236.

Habel, N. C. *Job.* Atlanta: John Knox, 1981.

_____. *The Book of Job.* London: Cambridge University Press, 1975.

_____. *The Book of Job.* Philadelphia: Westminster, 1985.

Halpern, B. "Yhwh's Summary of Justice in Job XIV:20." *Vetus Testamentum* 28, (1978) 167–171.

Hartley, J. E. *The Book of Job.* Grand Rapids: Eerdmans, 1988.

Heater, H., Jr. *A Septuagint Translation Technique in the Book of Job.* Washington, D.C.: The Catholic Biblical Association, 1982.

Janzen, J. G. *Job. Interpretation: A Bible Commentary for Teaching and Preaching.* Atlanta: John Knox, 1985.

Jones, E. *The Triumph of Job.* London: SCM, 1966.

Jung, C. G. *Answer to Job.* Cleveland–New York: World, 1970.

Kahn, J. H. *Job's Illness: Loss, Grief, and Integration.* Oxford–New York: Pergamon, 1975.

Kissane, E. J. *The Book of Job.* New York: Sheed and Ward, 1946.

MacKenzie, R. A. "The Transformation of Job." *Biblical Theology Bulletin* 9 (1979) 51–57.

MacKenzie, R.A. and R. E. Murphy. "Job." *The New Jerome Biblical Commentary.* Ed. by R. Brown et al. Englewood Cliffs: Prentice Hall, 1990. Pp. 366–488.

MacKenzie, R. A. "Job." *The Jerome Biblical Commentary.* Ed. by R. Brown et al. Englewood Cliffs: Prentice Hall, 1968.

Macleish, A. *J.B.: A Play in Verse.* Cambridge, MA: Riverside, Sentry Edition, 1961.

Malchow, B. "Nature from God's Perspective: Job 38–39." *Dialog* 21 (1982) 130–33.

Michel, W. L. *Job in the Light of Northwest Semitic.* Vol. 1. Rome: Biblical Institute Press, 1987.

Mitchell, S. *Into the Whirlwind: A Translation of the Book of Job.* Garden City: Doubleday, 1979.

Murphy, R. E. *The Psalms, Job.* Philadelphia: Fortress, 1977.

_____. *Wisdom Literature: Job, Proverbs, Ruth, Canticles, Ecclesiastes, and Esther.* Grand Rapids: Eerdmans, 1981.

Patrick, D. "Job's Address of God." *Zeitschrift für die Alttestamentliche Wissenschaft.* 91 (1979) 268–282.

Peake, A. S. *Job.* Edinburgh: T. C. & E. C. Jack, 1905.

Penchansky, D. *The Betrayal of God: Ideological Conflict in Job.* Louisville: Westminster/John Knox, 1990.

Polzin, R. and D. Robertson, eds. *Studies in the Book of Job. Semeia* 7. Missoula: Scholars, 1977.

Pope, M. H. *Job.* Garden City: Doubleday, 1973.

Rignell, L. G. "Comments on Some Cruces Interpretum in the Book of Job." *Annual of the Swedish Theological Institute* 2 (1977) 111–118.

Roberts, J. J. "Job and the Israelite Religious Tradition." *Zeitschrift für die Alttestamentliche Wissenschaft* 89 (1977) 107–114.

Robinson, H. W. *The Cross in the Old Testament.* Philadelphia: Westminster, 1955.

Robinson, T. H. *Job and His Friends.* London: SCM, 1954.

Rodd, C. *The Book of Job*. Philadephia: Trinity, 1990.

Rowley, H. H. *Job*. London: Thomas Nelson, 1970; Grand Rapids: Eerdmans, 1980.

_____. *The Book of Job*. Grand Rapids: Eerdmans, 1981.

_____. "The Book of Job and Its Meaning." *Bulletin of the John Rylands Library* 41 (1958) 167–207.

Sanders, P. S. *Twentieth Century Interpretations of the Book of Job*. Englewood Cliffs: Prentice Hall, 1955, 1968.

Sawicki, M. "What Did Job See?" *The Bible Today* 91 (1977) 1304–10.

Scaffela, F. "A Reading of Job." *Journal for the Study of the Old Testament* 14 (1979) 63–67.

Snaith, N. A. *The Book of Job: Its Origins and Purpose*. Naperville: Alex Allenson, 1968.

Terrien, S. "Introduction to the Exegesis of Job." *The Interpreter's Bible*. New York: Abingdon, 1954.

_____. *Job: Poet of Existence*. Indianapolis: Bobbs-Merrill, 1957.

The Book of Job. A New Translation According to the Traditional Hebrew Text. Intros. by M. Greenberg, J. C. Greenfield, and N. M. Sarna. Philadelphia: Jewish Publication Society, 1980.

Tsevat, M. *The Meaning of the Book of Job and other Biblical Studies*. New York: Ktav, 1981.

Van Selms, A. *Job*. Grand Rapids: Eerdmans, 1985.

Vawter, B. *Job and Jonah: Questioning the Hidden God*. New York: Paulist, 1983.

Vellanickal, M. "The Problem of Suffering in the Book of Job." *Beblebhashyam* 4 (1978) 292, 311.

Vinton, P. "Radical Aloneness: Job and Jeremiah." *The Bible Today* 99 (1978) 1843–49.

Weiss, M. *The Story of Job's Beginning*. Jerusalem: Magnes, 1983.

Westermann, C. *The Structure of the Book of Job*. Philadelphia: Fortress, 1981.

Wilcox, J. *The Bitterness of Job: A Philosophical Reading*. Ann Arbor: The University of Michigan Press, 1990.

Williams, J. G. "Deciphering the Unspoken: The Theophany of Job." *Hebrew Union College Annual* 49 (1978) 59–72.

Zerafa, P. P. *The Wisdom of God in the Book of Job*. Rome: Herder, 1978.

30. PROVERBS

Aitken, K. T. *Proverbs*. Philadelphia: Westminster, 1986.

Alden, R. L. *Proverbs. A Commentary on an Ancient Book of Timeless Advice*. Grand Rapids: Baker, 1983.

Andrew, M. E. "Variety of Expression in Proverbs XXIII: 29-35." *Vetus Testamentum*. 28 (1978) 102–103.

Böstrom, L. *The God of the Sages: The Portrayal of God in the Book of Proverbs*. Stockhom: Almqvist & Wiksell, 1990.

Bryce, G. D. "Another Wisdom Book in Proverbs." *Journal of Biblical Literature* 91 (1972) 145–157.

_____. "Omen-Wisdom in Ancient Israel." *Journal of Biblical Literature* 94 (1975) 19–37.

Camp, C. V. *Wisdom and the Feminine in the Book of Proverbs*. Sheffield: Almond Press, 1985.

Collins, J. J. *Proverbs/Ecclesiastes*. Atlanta: John Knox, 1980.

Cox, D. *Proverbs, with an Introduction to Sapiential Books*. Collegeville: Michael Glazier, 1991.

Dahood, M. J. *Proverbs and Northwest Semitic Philology*. Rome: Pontifical Biblical Institute, 1963.

Drane, J. W. *Old Testament Faith*. New York: Harper, 1986.

Elmslie W. A. *Studies in Life From Jewish Proverbs*. London: J. Clark, 1917.

Emerton, J. A. "A Note On Proverbs II." *Journal of Theological Studies* 30 (1979) 153–158.

Farmer, K. *Proverbs and Ecclesiastes: Who Knows What Is Good?* Grand Rapids: Eerdmans, 1991.

Fontaine, C. R. *Traditional Sayings in the Old Testament: A Contextual Study. Bible and Literature*, 5. Sheffield: Almond Press, 1982.

Forestell, J. T. *The Book of Proverbs.* New York: Paulist, 1960.

Goldingway, J. E. "Proverbs V and IX." *Revue Biblique* 84 (1977) 80–93.

Greenstone, J. H. *Proverbs, with Commentary.* Philadelphia: Jewish Publication Society of America, 1950.

Habel, N. C. "Symbolism of Wisdom in Proverbs 1–9." *Interpretation* 26 (1972) 131–157.

Jones, E. D. *Proverbs and Ecclesiastes; Introduction and Commentary.* New York: MacMillan, 1961.

Kelly, B. "The Book of Proverbs." *Interpretation* 2 (1948) 342–355.

Kidner, D. *The Proverbs: An Introduction and Commentary.* London: Tyndale, 1964.

_____. *The Wisdom of Proverbs, Job and Ecclesiates.* Downers Grove: Inter-Varsity, 1985.

Lang, B. *Wisdom and the Book of Proverbs.* New York: Pilgrim, 1986.

McCreesh, T. P. "Proverbs." *The New Jerome Biblical Commentary.* Ed. by R. Brown et al. Englewood Cliffs: Prentice Hall, 1990. Pp. 453–461.

McKane, W. "Functions of Language and Objectives of Discourse According to Proverbs, 10–30." *La Sagesse de l'Ancien Testament.* M. Gilbert et al., eds. Leuven: University Press, 1979.

_____. *Proverbs: A New Approach.* Philadelphia: Westminster, 1970.

Murphy, R. E. *Wisdom Literature: Job, Proverbs, Ruth, Canticles, Ecclesiastes, and Esther.* Grand Rapids: Eerdmans, 1981.

_____. "Kerygma of the Book of Proverbs." *Interpretation* 29 (1966) 3–14.

Nel, P. J. *The Structure and Ethos of the Wisdom Admonitions in Proverbs.* Berlin–New York: de Gruyter, 1982.

Nel, P. "Authority in the Wisdom Admonitions." *Zeitschrift für die Alttestamentliche Wissenschaft* 93 (1981) 418–426.

Oesterly, W. O. *The Book of Proverbs*. London: Methuen & Co., 1929.

Ogden, G. S. "The Better Proverb (Tob-Spruch), Rhetorical Criticism and Qoheleth." *Journal of Biblical Literature* 96 (1977) 489–505.

Paran, M. "The Uniqueness of the A Fortiori Pattern in the Book of Proverbs." *Beth Mikra* 23 (1978) 221–223.

Plaut, W. G. *The Book of Proverbs: A Commentary*. New York: Union of American Hebrew Congregations, 1961.

Ross, A. P. "*Proverbs*." *Expositor's Bible Commentary*. Vol. 5. Grand Rapids: Zondervan, 1989.

Scott, R. B. *Proverbs and Ecclesiastes*. Garden City: Doubleday, 1965.

Simpson, W. K., ed. *The Literature of Ancient Egypt: An Anthology of Stories, Instructions and Poetry*. New Haven: Yale University Press, 1973.

Skehan, P. W. "A Single Editor for the Whole Book of Proverbs." *Catholic Biblical Quarterly* 10 (1948) 115–130.

_____. "Structure in Poems on Wisdom: Proverbs 8 and Sirach 24." *Catholic Biblical Quarterly* 4 (1979) 365–379.

_____. "The Seven Columns of Wisdom's House in Proverbs 1–9." *Catholic Biblical Quarterly* 4 (1947) 190–198.

Waltke, B. K. "The Book of Proverbs and Ancient Wisdom Literature." *Bibliotheca Sacra* 136 (1979) 221–238.

Whybray, R. N. *The Book of Proverbs*. Cambridge: Cambridge University Press, 1972.

_____. *Ecclesiastes: Based on the Revised Standard Version*. Grand Rapids: Eerdmans, 1989.

_____. *Wealth and Poverty in the Book of Proverbs*. Sheffield, JSOT, 1990.

_____. *Wisdom in Proverbs*. London: SCM, 1965.

Williams, J. G. *Those Who Ponder Proverbs: Aphoristic Thinking and Biblical Literature*. Sheffield: Almond Press, 1981.

Wright, A. G. "Ecclesiastes (Qoheleth)." *The New Jerome Biblical Commentary.* Ed. by R. Brown et al. Englewood Cliffs: Prentice Hall, 1990. Pp. 489–495.

31. ECCLESIASTES (QOHELETH)

Bickerman, E. J. *Four Strange Books of the Bible.* New York: Schocken, 1967.

Collins, J. J. *Proverbs/Ecclesiastes.* Atlanta: John Knox, 1980.

Crenshaw, J. *Ecclesiastes, A Commentary. Old Testament Library.* Philadelphia: Westminster, 1987.

Davidson, R. *Ecclesiastes and the Song of Solomon.* Philadelphia: Westminster, 1986.

Eaton, M. E. *Ecclesiastes.* Downers Grove: Inter–Varsity, 1983.

Ellul, J. *Reason for Being: A Meditation on Ecclesiastes.* Grand Rapids: Eerdmans, 1991.

Fischer, J. A. *Song of Songs, Ruth, Lamentations, Ecclesiastes, Esther.* Collegeville: The Liturgical Press, 1986.

Fox, M. V. *Qohelet and His Contradictions.* Sheffield: Almond Press, 1989.

Fox, M. V. and B. Porten. "Unsought Discoveries: Qoheleth 7:23–8:1a." *Hebrew Studies* 19 (1978) 26–38.

Fredericks, D. C. *Qoheleth's Language: Re-evaluating Its Nature and Date.* Lewiston: Mellen, 1988.

Fuerst, W. J. *The Books of Ruth, Esther, Ecclesiastes, The Song of Songs, Lamentations.* Cambridge: Cambridge University Press, 1975.

Ginsberg, H. L. *Studies in Kohelet.* New York: Jewish Theological Seminary of America, 1950.

Glatzer, N. *Koheleth: The Man and His World.* New York: Jewish Theological Seminary of America, 1951, 1955, 1963; New York: Schocken, 1951, 1968.

Gordis, R. *Koheleth.* New York: Jewish Theological Seminary, 1951.

_____. *Koheleth: The Man and His World.* New York: Schocken, 1968.

_____. *The Wisdom of Ecclesiastes.* New York: Behrman, 1945.

Horton, E. H. "Koheleth's Concept of Opposites Compared to Samples of Greek Philosophy and Near and Far East Wisdom Classics." *Numen-International Review for the History of Religion* 19 (1972) 11-21.

Hubbard, D. A. *Beyond Futility. Messages of Hope from the Book of Ecclesiastes.* Grand Rapids: Eerdmans, 1976.

Jones, E. D. *Proverbs and Ecclesiastes: Introduction and Commentary.* New York: MacMillan, 1961.

Kidner, D. *A Time to Mourn and a Time to Dance: Ecclesiastes and the Way of the World.* London–Downers Grove: Inter-Varsity, 1976.

Loader, J. A. *Ecclesiastes.* Grand Rapids: Eerdmans, 1986.

_____. *Polar Structures in the Book of Qoheleth.* Berlin: de Gruyter, 1979.

Matthew, J. "Terrestrial Realities in Qoheleth's Teaching." *Jeevadhara* 8 (1978) 6–20.

Murphy, R. E. "Qoheleth's Quarrel with the Fathers." *From Faith to Faith.* G. Y. Hadidian, ed. Pittsburg: Pickwick, 1979. Pp. 235–45.

_____. "Form Critical Studies in the Song of Songs." *Interpretation* 27 (1973) 413–22.

_____. *The Book of Ecclesiastes and Canticle of Canticles.* New York: Paulist, 1961.

_____. *Wisdom Literature: Job, Proverbs, Ruth, Canticles, Ecclesiastes, and Esther.* Grand Rapids: Eerdmans, 1981.

Rankin, O. S. "The Book of Ecclesiastes." *The Interpreter's Bible.* Vol. 5. New York: Abingdon, 1956.

Salters, R. B. "A Note on the Exegesis of Ecclesiastes 3:15b." *Zeitschrift für die Alttestamentliche Wissenschaft* 88 (1976) 419–422.

_____. "Notes on the Hebrew History of the Interpretation of Koh. 5:5." *Zeitschrift für die Alttestamentliche Wissenschaft* 89 (1977) 423–426.

Scott, R. B. *Proverbs, Ecclesiastes*. Garden City: Doubleday, 1965.

Sheppard, G. T. "The Epilogue to Qoheleth as Theological Commentary." *Catholic Biblical Quarterly* 39 (1977) 182–189.

Walsh, J. T. "Despair as a Theological Virtue in the Spirituality of Ecclesiastes." *Biblical Theology Bulletin* 12 (1982) 46–49.

Whitely, C. F. *Koheleth, His Language and Thought*. Berlin–New York: de Gruyter, 1979.

_____. *Koheleth*. Berlin: de Gruyter, 1979.

Whybray, R. N. *Ecclesiastes*. Grand Rapids: Eerdmans, 1989.

_____. *Ecclesiastes: Based on the Revised Standard Version*. Grand Rapids: Eerdmans; London: Marshall, Morgan & Scott, 1989.

Wilson, R. R. "Qoheleth's Use of the 'Nothing is Better' Form." *Journal of Biblical Literature* 98 (1979) 339–350.

Wright, A. "The Riddle of the Sphinx: The Structure of the Book of Qoheleth." *Catholic Biblical Quarterly* 30 (1968) 313–334.

Wright, J. S. "Ecclesiastes." *The Expositor's Bible Commentary*. Vol. 5. Grand Rapids: Zondervan, 1989.

Zimmermann, F. *The Inner World of Qohelet*. New York: Ktav, 1973.

32. SONG OF SONGS (SONG OF SOLOMON, "CANTICLE OF CANTICLES")

Brenner, A. *The Song of Songs*. Sheffield: JSOT, 1989.

Carr, G. L. *The Song of Solomon*. Downers Grove: Inter-Varsity, 1984.

_____. "Is the Song of Songs a Sacred Marriage Drama?" *Journal of the Evangelical Theological Society* 22 (1979) 103–114.

Cook, A. S. *The Root of The Thing: A Study of Job and Song of Songs*. Bloomington: Indiana University Press, 1968.

Davidson, R. *Ecclesiastes and the Song of Solomon*. Philadelphia: Westminster, 1968.

Dryburgh, B. *Lessons for Lovers in the Song of Solomon*. New Canaan: Keats, 1975.

Falk, M. *Love Lyrics from the Bible. A Translation and Literary Study of the Song of Songs*. Sheffield: Almond Press, 1982.

_____. *The Song of Songs*. San Francisco: Harper, 1990.

Fischer, J. A. *Song of Songs, Ruth, Lamentations, Ecclesiastes, Esther*. Collegeville: The Liturgical Press, 1968.

Fox, M. V. *The Song of Songs and Ancient Egyptian Love Songs*. Madison: University of Wisconsin Press, 1988.

Fuerst, W. J. *The Books of Ruth, Esther, Ecclesiastes, The Song of Songs, Lamentations*. Cambridge: Cambridge University Press, 1975.

Ginsburg, C. D. *The Song of Songs and Coheleth*. New York: Ktav, 1970.

Gordis, R. *The Song of Songs and Lamentations*. New York: Ktav, 1974.

Goulder, M. D. *The Song of Fourteen Songs*. Sheffield: The University Press, 1986.

Guthrie, H. *Israel's Sacred Songs*. New York: Seabury, 1966.

Heidt, W. G. *The Canticle of Canticles: The Book of Wisdom*. Collegeville: Human Life Center, 1979.

Jastrow, M. Jr. *The Song of Songs, Being a Collection of Love Lyrics of Ancient Palestine*. Philadelphia: J. P. Lippincott, 1921.

Kinlaw, D. F. *"Song of Songs." The Expositor's Bible Commentary*. Vol. 5 Grand Rapids: Zondervan, 1989.

Knight, G. A. and F. W. Golka. *Revelation of God: A Commentary on the Song of Songs and Jonah*. Edinburgh: Handsel; Grand Rapids: Eerdmans, 1988.

Landy, F. *Paradoxes of Paradise: Identity and Difference in the Song of Songs*. Sheffield: Almond Press, 1983.

Mariaselvam, A. *The Song of Songs and Ancient Tamil Love Poems: Poetry and Symbolism*. Rome: Biblical Institute Press, 1988.

Meek, T. V. "Introduction and Exegesis to the Song of Solomon." *The Interpreter's Bible*. Vol. 5. New York: Abingdon, 1956. Pp. 91–97.

Morris, L. *Testaments of Love. A Study of Love in the Bible*. Grand Rapids: Eerdmans, 1981.

Murphy, R. E. "Form Critical Studies in the Song of Songs." *Interpretation* 27 (1973) 413–422.

_____. "Interpreting the Song of Songs." *Biblical Theology Bulletin* 9 (1979) 99–105.

_____. "Canticle of Canticles." *The New Jerome Biblical Commentary*. Ed. by R. Brown et al. Englewood Cliffs: Prentice Hall, 1990. Pp. 462–465.

_____. *The Song of Songs: A Commentary on the Book of Canticles of the Song of Songs*. Minneapolis: Fortress, 1990.

_____. *The Song of Songs*. Philadelphia: Fortress, 1989.

_____. *Wisdom Literature: Job, Proverbs, Ruth, Canticles, Ecclesiastes, and Esther*. Grand Rapids: Eerdmans, 1981.

Paul, S. M. "An Unrecognized Medical Idiom in Canticles 6:12 and Job 9:21." *Biblica* 59 (1978) 545–47.

Pope, M. H. *Song of Songs*. Garden City: Doubleday, 1977.

Reese, J. M. *The Book of Wisdom, Song of Songs*. Wilmington: Michael Glazier, 1983.

Rowley, H. H. "The Interpretation of the Song of Songs." *The Servant of the Lord and Other Essays on the Old Testament*. 2nd ed. Oxford: Blackwell, 1965. Pp. 195–245.

Sasson, J. "Unlocking the Poetry of Love in the Song of Songs." *Bible Review*. Vol. 1 (1985) 11–19.

Schonfield, H. J. *The Song of Songs.* New York: New American Library, 1959.

Tournay, R. *Word of God, Song of Love: A Commentary on the Song of Songs.* Mahwah: Paulist, 1988.

Trible, P. *God and the Rhetoric of Sexuality.* Philadelphia: Fortress, 1978.

White, J. B. *A Study of the Language of Love in the Song of Songs and Ancient Egyptian Poetry.* Missoula: Scholars, 1978.

Winston, D. *The Wisdom of Solomon.* Garden City: Doubleday, 1979.

VI. PROPHETS

33. GENERAL WORKS ON THE PROPHETIC LITERATURE

Allis, O. T. *Prophecy and the Church.* Philadelphia: Presbyterian & Reformed Press, 1945.

Amerding, C. E. and W. W. Gasque, eds. *Dreams, Visions and Oracles: the Layman's Guide to Biblical Prophecy.* Grand Rapids: Baker, 1977.

Ackroyd, P. *Exile and Restoration.* London: SCM; Philadelphia: Westminster, 1968.

Anderson, B. W. *The Eighth Century Prophets.* Philadelphia: Fortress, 1978.

Anderson, B. W. and W. Harrelson, eds. *Israel's Prophetic Heritage.* New York: Harper & Row, 1962.

Barton, J. *Oracles of God: Perceptions of Ancient Prophecy in Israel after the Exile.* New York: Oxford University Press, 1988.

Beck, M. H. and L. Williamson, Jr. *Mastering Old Testament Facts. Book 4: Prophetic Writings.* Atlanta: John Knox, 1981.

Beecher, W. J. *The Prophets and the Promise.* Grand Rapids: Baker, 1963.

Bellinger, W. H., Jr. *Psalmody and Prophecy.* Sheffield: JSOT Press, 1984.

Bergen, R. V. *The Prophets and the Law.* Cincinnati: Hebrew Union College–Jewish Institute of Religion, 1974.

Blank, S. "The Prophetic Paradigm." *Essays in Old Testament Ethics.* James L. Crenshaw and John T. Willis, eds. New York: Ktav, 1974.

Blank, S. H. *Understanding the Prophets.* New York: Union of American Hebrew Congregations, 1969.

Blenkinsopp, J. *A History of Prophecy in Israel.* Philadelphia: Westminster, 1983.

_____. "The Prophetic Reproach." *Journal of Biblical Literature* 90 (1971) 267–78.

_____. *A History of Prophecy in Israel: from the Settlement in the Land to the Hellenistic Period.* Philadelphia: Westminster, 1983.

_____. *Prophecy and Canon.* Notre Dame: University of Notre Dame Press, 1977.

Brandt, L. F. *Prophets Now.* St. Louis: Concordia, 1979.

Bright, J. "The Prophets of Israel: Some Preliminary Remarks." *Jeremiah. The Anchor Bible.* Garden City: Doubleday, 1965.

Brueggemann, W. *Hopeful Imagination: Prophetic Voices in Exile.* Philadelphia: Fortress, 1986.

_____. *The Prophetic Imagination.* Philadelphia: Fortress, 1978.

_____. *Hope Within History.* Atlanta: John Knox, 1987.

Buber, M. *The Prophetic Faith.* New York: Macmillan, 1949; Harper, 1960.

Bullock, C. H. *An Introduction to the Old Testament Prophetic Books.* Chicago: Moody, 1986.

Carroll, R. *When Prophecy Failed. Cognitive Dissonance in the Prophetic Traditions of the Old Testament.* New York: Seabury, 1979.

Cassirer, H. W. *Grace and Law. St. Paul, Kant, and the Hebrew Prophets.* Grand Rapids: Eerdmans, 1988.

Chisholm, R. B. *Interpreting the Minor Prophets.* Grand Rapids: Zondervan, 1990.

Clements, R. E. *Isaiah and the Deliverance of Jerusalem: A Study of the Interpretations of Prophecy in the Old Testament.* Sheffield: JSOT Press, 1980.

_____. *One Hundred Years of Old Testament Interpretation.* Philadelphia: Westminster, 1976.

_____. *Prophecy and Covenant.* Naperville: Alec R. Allenson, 1965.

_____. *Prophecy and Tradition.* Atlanta: John Knox, 1975.

Coggins, R., A. Phillips and M. Knibb, eds. *Israel's Prophetic Tradition: Essays in Honour of Peter Ackroyd.* London: Cambridge University Press, 1982.

Cohen, B. D. *God's Angry Men.* New York: Bloch, 1961.

Collins, T. *Line–forms in Hebrew Poetry: A Grammatical Approach to the Stylistic Study of The Hebrew Prophets.* Rome: Biblical Institute Press, 1978.

Craghan, J. F. "Mari and Its Prophets." *Biblical Theology Bulletin* 5 (1975) 32–55.

Craigie, P. C. *Twelve Prophets.* Volume 1. Philadelphia: Westminster, 1984.

_____. *Twelve Prophets.* Volume 2. Philadelphia: Westminster, 1985.

Crenshaw, J. L. *Prophetic Conflict and its Effects Upon Israelite Religion.* New York: de Gruyter, 1971.

Davies, E. W. *Prophecy and Ethics; Isaiah and the Ethical Traditions of Israel. Journal for the Study of the Old Testament Supplement Series*, 16. Sheffield: University of Sheffield, Department of Biblical Studies, 1981.

DeVries, S. J. *Prophet Against Prophet.* Grand Rapids: Eerdmans, 1978.

Drane, J. W. *Old Testament Faith.* New York: Harper, 1986.

Efird, J. M. *The Old Testament Prophets: Then and Now.* Valley Forge: Judson, 1982.

Ellis, E. E. *Prophecy and Hermeneutic in Early Christianity.* Tübingen: Mohr, 1978.

Epstein, L. *Social Justice in the Ancient Near East and the People of the Bible.* London: SCM, 1986.

Fosbroke, H. E. "The Prophetic Literature." *The Interpereter's Bible.* Vol. 1. New York: Abingdon, 1952. Pp. 201–211.

Freeman, H. E. *An Introduction to the Old Testament Prophets.* Chicago: Moody, 1968.

Glover, W. B. *Biblical Origins of Modern Secular Culture.* Macon: Mercer University Press, 1984.

Gottwald, N. K. *All the Kingdoms of the Earth. Israelite Prophecy and International Relations in the Ancient Near East.* New York: Harper & Row, 1964.

Gowan, D. E. *Bridge Between the Testaments. A Reappraisal of Judaism from the Exile to the Birth of Christianity.* Pittsburgh: Pickwick, 1976.

Graffy, A. *A Prophet Confronts His People: The Disputation Speech in the Prophets.* Rome: Biblical Institute Press, 1984.

Heaton, E. W. *The Old Testament Prophets.* Atlanta: John Knox, 1977.

Heschel, A. *The Prophets.* 2 vols. New York: Harper & Row, 1962, 1969, 1975.

Hillers, D. R. *Treaty Curses and the Old Testament Prophets.* Rome: Pontifical Biblical Institute, 1964.

Jarvis, F. W. *Prophets, Poets, Priests, and Kings.* New York: Seabury, 1974.

Jaspers, K. *The Origins and Goal of History.* New Haven–London: Yale University Press, 1953.

Johnson, A. R. *The Cultic Prophet and Israel's Psalmody.* Cardiff: University of Wales Press, 1979.

_____. *The Cultic Prophet in Ancient Israel.* Cardiff: University of Wales Press, 1962.

Keil, C. F. *Minor Prophets.* Grand Rapids: Eerdmans, 1978.

Knight, D. A. and G. Tucker, eds. "Prophecy and the Prophetic Literature." *The Hebrew Bible and its Modern Interpreters.* Philadelphia: Fortress, 1985. Pp. 325–368.

Koch, K. *The Prophets: The Assyrian Period.* Philadelphia: Fortress, 1983.

_____. *The Prophets: The Babylonian and Persian Periods.* Philadelphia: Fortress, 1984.

_____. *The Prophets: Volume One: The Assyrian Age.* Philadelphia: Fortress, 1982.

_____. *The Prophets: Volume Two: The Babylonian and Persian Periods.* Philadelphia: Fortress, 1984.

Kraeling, E. G. *Commentary on the Prophets.* 2 vols. Camden: Nelson, 1966.

Kuhl, C. *The Prophets of Israel.* Richmond: John Knox, 1977.

Lang, B. *Monotheism and the Prophetic Minority.* Sheffield: Almond Press, 1983.

Limburg, J. *The Prophets and the Powerless.* Atlanta: John Knox, 1977.

_____. "The Prophets in Recent Study: 1967–1977." *Interpretation* 32 (1978) 56–68.

Lindblom, J. *Prophecy in Ancient Israel.* Philadelphia: Fortress, 1962.

Loewe, M. and C. Blacker, eds. *Oracles and Divination.* Boulder: Shambhala, 1981.

Malchow, B. "The Prophetic Contribution to Dialogue," *Biblical Theology Bulletin* 16 (1986), 127–31.

March, W. E. "Prophecy." *Old Testament Form Criticism.* San Antonio: Trinity University Press, 1974. Pp. 164–69.

Mays, J. and P. Achtemeier, eds. *Interpreting the Prophets.* Philadelphia: Fortress, 1987.

McCarthy, D. J. *Kings and Prophets.* Milwaukee: Bruce, 1968.

McKane, W. *Prophets and Wise Men.* Naperville: Alec R. Allenson, 1965.

McKay, J. *Religion in Judah Under the Assyrians.* Naperville: A. R. Allenson, 1975.

Miller, J. W. *Meet the Prophets.* New York: Paulist, 1987.

Miller, P. D., Jr. *Sin and Judgment in the Prophets.* Chico: Scholars, 1982.

Mowinckel, S. *Prophecy and Tradition.* Oslo: Jacob Dybwas, 1946.

Mowley, H. *Guide to Old Testament Prophecy.* Atlanta: John Knox, 1979.

_____. *Reading the Old Testament Prophets.* Atlanta: John Knox, 1979.

Napier, B. D. "Prophet, Prophetism." *The Interpreter's Bible.* Vol. 3. New York: Abingdon Press, 1965. Pp. 896–919.

Newsome, J. D., Jr. *The Hebrew Prophets.* Atlanta: John Knox, 1984.

Nielsen, K. *Yahweh as Prosecutor and Judge: An Investigation of the Prophetic Lawsuit.* Sheffield: JSOT Press, 1979.

Norquist, M. *How to Read and Pray the Prophets.* Liguori: Liguori Publications, 1980.

Noth, M. "History and Word of God in the Old Testament." *Laws in the Pentateuch and Other Studies.* Philadelphia: Fortress, 1967. Pp. 179–193.

Olan, L. A. *Prophetic Faith and The Secular World.* New York: Ktav; Dallas: Institute for Jewish Studies, 1982.

Orlinsky, H. M., ed. *Interpreting the Prophetic Tradition.* Cincinnati: Hebrew Union College Press, 1969.

Overholt, T. W. *Channels of Prophecy The Social Dynamics of Prophetic Activity.* Philadelphia: Fortress, 1989.

_____. *Prophecy in Cross-Cultural Perspective: A Sourcebook for Biblical Researchers.* Atlanta: Scholars, 1986.

_____. "Prophecy: The Problem of Cross-Cultural Comparison." *Semeia* 21 (1981) 55–78.

Perdue, L. G. and B. W. Kovacs, eds. *A Prophet to the Nations.* Winona Lake: Eisenbrauns, 1984.

Peterson, D. L. *Late Israelite Prophecy: Studies in Deutero-Prophetic Literature and in Chronicles.* Missoula: Scholars, 1977.

_____. *Prophecy in Israel. Search for an Identity.* Philadelphia: Fortress; London: S.P.C.K., 1987.

_____. *The Roles of Israel's Prophets.* Sheffield: JSOT Press, 1981.

Pusey, E. B. *The Minor Prophets.* 2 vols. Grand Rapids: Baker, 1950.

Reid, D. P. *What Are They Saying About the Prophets?* New York: Paulist, 1980.

Roberts, W. P. *The Prophets Speak Today.* Cincinnati: St. Anthony Messenger, 1981.

Ross, J. "Prophecy in Hamath, Israel, and Mari." *Harvard Theological Review* 43 (1970) 1–28.

_____. "The Prophecy as Yahweh's Messenger." *Israel's Prophetic Heritage.* Ed. by B.W. Anderson and W. Harrelson. New York: Harper & Row, 1962. Pp. 98–107.

Rowley, H. H. "Elijah on Mount Carmel." *Bulletin of the John Rylands Library* 43 (1960–61) 190–210.

_____. *Prophecy and Religion in Ancient China and Israel.* New York: Harper & Brothers, 1956.

_____. *Studies in Old Testament Prophecy.* Edinburgh: Clark; New York: Scribner, 1950.

Sanders, R. N. *Radical Voices in the Wilderness.* Waco: Word, 1970.

Sawyer, J. F. *Prophecy and the Prophets of the Old Testament.* New York: Oxford University Press, 1987.

Schuller, E. *Post-Exilic Prophets.* Wilmington: Michael Glazier, 1988.

Scott, R. B. *The Relevance of the Prophets.* New York: Macmillan, 1969.

Seilhamer, F. H. *Prophets and Prophecy.* Philadelphia: Fortress, 1977.

Skilba, R. J. *Pre-Exilic Prophecy.* Collegeville: The Liturgical Press/ Michael Glazier, 1991.

Skinner, J. *Prophecy and Religion.* Cambridge: Cambridge University Press, 1922.

_____. *Pre-Exilic Prophets.* Collegeville: The Liturgical Press/ Michael Glazier, 1990.

Smith, G. A. *The Book of the Twelve Prophets.* New York: Harper & Row, 1940.

Stuhlmueller, C. *The Prophets and the Word of God.* Notre Dame: Fides, 1964.

Taylor, J. B. *The Minor Prophets.* Grand Rapids: Eerdmans, 1970.

Van Gemeren, W. A. *Interpreting the Prophetic Word.* Grand Rapids: Zondervan, 1990.

Vawter, B. "Introduction to the Prophetic Literature." *The Jerome Biblical Commentary.* Ed. by R. Brown et al. Englewood Cliffs: Prentice Hall, 1968. Pp. 223–237.

_____. "Introduction to the Prophetic Literature." *The New Jerome Biblical Commentary.* Ed. by R. Brown et al. Englewood Cliffs: Prentice Hall, 1990. Pp. 196–200.

_____. *The Conscience of Israel.* New York: Sheed and Ward, 1961.

Voegelin, E. *Order and History, Israel and Revelation.* Vol. 1. Baton Rouge: Louisiana State University Press, 1956.

von Rad, G. *Old Testament Theology.* Vol. 2. New York: Harper & Row, 1965.

_____. *The Message of the Prophets.* New York: Harper & Row, 1967, 1972.

_____. *The Prophetic Message.* London: SCM, 1968.

_____. *The Prophets. Old Testament Theology.* Vol. 2. San Francisco: Harper & Row, 1966.

Ward, J. M. *The Prophets.* Nashville: Abingdon, 1982.

_____. *Amos–Hosea.* John Knox, 1981.

_____. *Thus Says The Lord: The Message of the Prophets.* Nashville: Abingdon, 1991.

Welch, A. C. *Kings and Prophets of Israel.* London: Lutterworth; New York: Philosophical Library, 1952.

Westermann, C. *Basic Forms of Prophetic Speech.* Philadelphia: Westminster, 1967.

_____. *Elements of Old Testament Theology.* Trans. by D. W. Scott. Atlanta: John Knox, 1982.

_____. "The Prophets." *A Thousand Years and a Day,* Chapter VI. Philadelphia: Muhlenberg, 1962.

_____. *What does the Old Testament Say About God?* F. W. Golka, ed. Atlanta: John Knox, 1979.

Whitely, C. F. *The Prophetic Achievement.* Leiden: Brill, 1963.

Wilson, R. R. *Prophecy and Society in Ancient Israel.* Philadelphia: Fortress, 1980.

Winward, S. *A Guide to the Prophets.* Atlanta: John Knox, 1969, 1976.

Wolff, H. W. *Confrontations with Prophets.* Philadelphia: Fortress, 1983.

Wood, L. J. *The Prophets of Israel.* Grand Rapids: Baker, 1979.

Zimmerli, W. "Prophetic Proclamation and Reinterpretation." *Tradition and Theology in the Old Testament.* Douglas Knight, ed. Philadelphia: Fortress, 1977. Pp. 69–100.

Zimmerli, W. *The Law and the Prophets.* Oxford: Blackwell, 1965.

34. MAJOR PROPHETS

a. Isaiah 1–39

Blank, S. *Prophetic Faith in Isaiah.* New York: Harper, 1958.

Brueggemann, W. "Unity and Dynamic in the Isaiah Tradition." *Journal for the Study of the Old Testament* 29 (1984) 89–107.

Childs, B. S. *Isaiah and the Assyrian Crisis.* London: SCM; Naperville: Alec R. Allenson, 1967.

_____. "Isaiah." *Introduction to the Old Testament as Scripture.* Ch. 17. Philadelphia: Fortress, 1979.

Clements, R. E. *Isaiah 1–39.* Grand Rapid: Eerdmans, 1980.

Clements, R. E. *Isaiah and the Deliverance of Jerusalem: A Study of the Interpretation of Prophecy in the Old Testament.* Sheffield: JSOT Press, 1980.

Davies, E. W. *Prophecy and Ethics: Isaiah and the Ethical Traditions of Israel.* Sheffield: JSOT Press, 1981.

Delitzche, F. *Isaiah. Commentary on the Old Testament.* 2 vols. Grand Rapids: Eerdmans, 1980.

Dreyer, H. J. and J. J. Gluck, eds. *Semitics*. Vol. 6. Pretoria: University of South Africa, 1978.

Engnell, I. *The Call of Isaiah*. Uppsala: A.B. Lundequistka; Leipzig: Otto Harrassowitz, 1959.

Evans, C. A. *To See and Not Perceive: Isaiah 6: 9-10 in Early Jewish and Christian Interpretation*. Sheffield: JSOT Press, 1989.

Hammershaim, E. *Some Aspects of Old Testament Prophecy from Isaiah to Malachi*. Copenhagen: Rosenkilde og Bagger, 1966.

Hayes, J. H. and S. A. Irvine. *Isaiah the Eighth-Century Prophet: His Time and His Preaching*. Nashville: Abingdon, 1987.

Herbert, A. S. *The Book of the Prophet Isaiah, Chapters 1–39*. Cambridge: University Press, 1973.

Holladay, W. L. *Isaiah: Scroll of a Prophetic Heritage*. Grand Rapids: Eerdmans, 1978.

Hunter, A. V. *Seek the Lord! A Study of the Meaning and Function of the Exhortation in Amos, Hosea, Isaiah, Micah, and Zephaniah*. Baltimore: St. Mary's Seminary & University, 1982.

Irwin, W. H. *Isaiah 28–33. Translation with Philological Notes. Biblica et Orientalia* 30. Rome: Biblical Institute Press, 1977.

Jensen, J. *Isaiah 1–39*. Collegeville: Michael Glazier, 1991.

_____. "The Age of Immanuel." *Catholic Biblical Quarterly* 41 (1979) 220–239.

_____. *The Use of Torah by Isaiah*. Washington, D.C.: Catholic Biblical Association of America, 1973.

_____ and W. H. Irwin. "Isaiah 1–39." *The New Jerome Biblical Commentary*. Ed. by R. Brown et al. Englewood Cliffs: Prentice Hall, 1990. Pp. 229–248.

Johnson, D. G. *From Chaos to Restoration: An Integrative Reading of Isaiah 24–27*. Sheffield: JSOT Press, 1988.

Kaiser, O. *Isaiah 1–12*. Philadelphia: Westminster, 1972, 1983.

_____. *Isaiah 13–39*. Philadelphia: Westminster, 1974.

Kissane, E. J. *The Book of Isaiah*. Dublin: Brown and Nolan, 1960.

Leslie, E. A. *Isaiah; Chronologically Arranged, Translated, and Interpreted.* New York: Abingdon, 1963.

Macintosh, A. A. *Isaiah XXI. A Palimpsest.* New York: Cambridge University Press, 1980.

Miller, W. R. *Isaiah 24–27 and the Origin of Apocalyptic.* Missoula: Scholars, 1976.

Nielsen, K. *There is Hope for a Tree: The Tree as Metaphor in Isaiah.* Sheffield: JSOT Press, 1989.

Olley, J. W. *"Righteousness" in the Septuagint of Isaiah: A Contextual Study.* Missoula: Scholars Press, 1979.

Oswalt, J. *The Book of Isaiah, Chapters 1–39.* Grand Rapids: Eerdmans, 1986.

Ridderbos, J. *Isaiah.* Grand Rapids: Zondervan, 1985.

Roberts, J. J. *Isaiah 1–39. Interpretation Series.* Atlanta: John Knox, 1989.

Sawyer, J. F. *Isaiah.* Volume 1. Philadelphia: Westminster, 1984.

Schmitt, J. J. *Isaiah and His Interpreters.* New York–Mahwah: Paulist, 1986.

Scott, R. B. "Introduction and Exegesis to Isaiah 1–39." *The Interpreter's Bible.* Vol. 5. New York: Abingdon, 1956. Pp. 151–164.

Seitz, C. R., ed. *Reading and Preaching the Book of Isaiah.* Philadelphia: Fortress, 1988.

Smith, G. A. *The Book of Isaiah.* London: Hodder & Stoughton, 1927.

Stansell, G. *Micah and Isaiah: A Form and Tradition Historical Comparison.* Atlanta: Scholars, 1988.

van Wyk, W. C., ed. *Studies in Isaiah.* Pretoria: NHW, 1981.

Vriezen, T. C. "Essentials of the Theology of Isaiah." *Israel's Prophetic Heritage.* New York: Harper & Row, 1962. Pp. 128–146.

Ward, J. M. *Amos and Isaiah: Prophets of the Word of God.* Nashville: Abingdon, 1969.

Watts, J. *Isaiah.* Dallas: Word, 1989.

_____. *Isaiah 1–33.* Waco: Word, 1985.

_____. *Isaiah 34–66.* Waco: Word, 1987.

Whedbee, J. W. *Isaiah and Wisdom.* Nashville: Abingdon, 1971.

Whybray, R. N. *The Second Isaiah.* Sheffield: JSOT Press, 1983.

Widyapranawa, S. H. *Isaiah 1–39.* Grand Rapids: Eerdmans, 1989.

_____. *The Lord Is Savior: Faith in National Crisis: A Commentary on the Book of Isaiah 1–39. International Theological Commentary.* Grand Rapids: Eerdmans, 1990.

Wiklander, B. *Prophecy as Literature: A Text-Linguistic and Rhetorical Approach to Isaiah 2–4.* Stockholm: Liber Tryck, 1984.

Wilson, R. A., trans. *Isaiah 13–39: A Commentary.* Philadelphia: Westminster, 1974.

Wolf, H. M. "A Solution to the Immanuel Prophecy in Isaiah 7:14–8:22." *Journal of Biblical Literature* 91 (1972) 449–56.

Wright, G. E. *The Book of Isaiah.* Richmond: John Knox, 1964.

Young, E. J. *The Book of Isaiah: The English Text, with Introduction, Exposition, and Notes.* Grand Rapids: Eerdmans, 1965.

b. Second Isaiah 40–55

Anderson, B. W. "Exodus Typology in Second Isaiah." *Israel's Prophetic Heritage.* New York: Harper & Row, 1962. Pp. 177–195.

_____. "Exodus and Covenant in Second Isaiah and Prophetic Tradition." *Magnalia Dei, The Mighty Acts of God*; Essays on the Bible and Archaeology in memory of G. Ernest Wright, ed. by Frank Moore Cross, Werner E. Lemke and Patrick D. Miller, Jr. Garden City: Doubleday, 1976. Pp. 339–360.

Birch, B. *Singing the Lord's Song: A Study of Isaiah 40–55.* Nashville, Abingdon, 1990.

Clements, R. E. *Isaiah and the Deliverance of Jerusalem: A Study of the Interpretation of Prophecy in the Old Testament.* Sheffield: JSOT Press, 1980.

Clifford, R. J. *Fair Spoken and Persuading, An Interpretation of Second Isaiah.* New York: Paulist Press, 1984.

Clines, D. J. *I, He, We, and They: A Literary Approach to Isaiah 53.* Sheffield: The University Press, 1976.

Conrad, E. W. "Second Isaiah and the Priestly Oracle of Salvation." *Zeitschrift für die Alttestamentliche Wissenschaft* 93 (1981) 234–246.

Conrad, E. W. "The 'Fear Not' Oracles in Second Isaiah." *Vetus Testamentum* 34 (1984) 129–152.

de Boer, P. A. *Second Isaiah's Message.* Leiden: Brill, 1956.

Gitay, Y. *Prophecy and Persuasion. A Study of Isaiah 40–48.* Bonn: Linguistica Biblica, 1981.

Goldingay, J. *God's Prophet, God's Servant: A Study in Jeremiah and Isaiah 40–55.* Exeter: Paternoster, 1984.

Harner, P. B. *Grace and Law in Second Isaiah: "I Am the Lord."* Lewiston–Queenston, Ontario: Mellen, 1988.

Herbert, A. S. *The Book of the Prophet Isaiah, Chapters 40–66.* Cambridge: Cambridge University Press, 1975.

Kaufmann, Y. *History of the Religion of Israel. Vol. IV: From the Babylonian Captivity to the End of Prophecy.* New York: Ktav, 1977.

Knight, G. A. *Deutero-Isaiah: A Theological Commentary on Isaiah 40–55.* New York: Abingdon, 1965.

_____. *Isaiah 40–55: Servant Theology.* Grand Rapids: Eerdmans, 1984.

Mays, J. *Ezekiel, Second Isaiah.* Philadelphia: Fortress, 1978.

McKenzie, J. L. *Second Isaiah. Anchor Bible.* Garden City: Doubleday, 1968.

Melugin, R. F. *The Formation of Isaiah 40–55. Beiheift zur Zeitschrift für die Alttestamentliche Wissenschaft* 141. Berlin: de Gruyter, 1976.

Mettinger, T. N. *A Farewell to the Servant Songs. A Critical Examination of an Exegetical Axiom.* Lund: Gleerup, 1983.

Muilenburg, J. "Introduction and Exegesis to Isaiah 40–66." *The Interpreter's Bible, V.* New York: Abingdon, 1956. Pp. 381–418.

North, C. R. *Isaiah 40–55.* New York: Macmillan, 1964.

_____. *The Second Isaiah. Introduction, Translation and Commentary to Chapters XL – LV.* Oxford: Clarendon, 1964.

_____. *The Suffering Servant in Deutero-Isaiah.* New York: Oxford, 1956.

Robertson, E. H. *Jeremiah, Lamentations, Ezekiel, Isaiah 40–66.* London: Mowbray, 1970.

Rowley, H. H. *The Servant of the Lord and Other Essays on the Old Testament.* London: Lutterworth, 1952; New York: Oxford, 1956.

Sawyer, J. F. *Isaiah.* Vol. 2. Philadelphia: Westminster, 1986.

Scullion, J. *Isaiah 40–66.* Collegeville: Michael Glazier, 1991.

Smart, J. D. *History and Theology in Second Isaiah: A Commentary on Isaiah 35, 40–66.* Philadelphia: Westminster, 1965.

Staeker, D. M., trans. *Isaiah 40–66: A Commentary.* Philadelphia: Westminster, 1969.

Stuhlmueller, C. *Creative Redemption in Deutero-Isaiah.* Rome: Biblical Institute Press, 1970.

_____. "Deutero–Isaiah and Trito–Isaiah." *The New Jerome Biblical Commentary.* Ed. by R. Brown et al. Englewood Cliffs: Prentice Hall, 1990. Pp. 329–348.

von Waldow, H. E. "The Message of Deutero–Isaiah." *Interpretation* 21 (1968) 259–287.

Watts, J. D. *Isaiah 34–66.* Waco: Word Books, 1987.

Westermann, C. *Isaiah 40-66.* Philadelphia: Westminster, 1969.

Whybray, R. N. *Isaiah 40–66. The New Century Bible.* London: Oliphants; Grenwood: Attic, 1975.

_____. *Isaiah 40–66. The New Century Bible Commentary.* Grand Rapids: Eerdmans, 1981.

_____. *Thanksgiving for a Liberated Prophet: An Interpretation of Isaiah Chapter 53*. Sheffield: The University, 1978.

_____. *The Second Isaiah*. Sheffield: JSOT Press, 1983.

Wilson, A. *The Nation in Deutero Isaiah: A Study on Composition and Structure*. Lewiston: Mellen, 1986.

Zimmerli, W. and J. Jeremiah. *The Servant of God*. Naperville: Allenson, 1957.

Zimmerli, W. "The Message of the Prophet Ezekiel." *Interpretation* 23 (1969) 131–157.

c. Third Isaiah 56–66

Achtemeier, E. R. *The Community and Message of Isaiah 56–66: A Theological Commentary*. Minneapolis: Augsburg, 1982.

Hamlin, E. J. *Comfort My People: A Guide to Isaiah 40–66*. Atlanta: John Knox, 1979.

Jones, D. R. *Isaiah fifty-six to sixty-six and Joel, Introduction and Commentary*. London: SCM, 1964.

Knight, G. A. *Isaiah 56–66*. Grand Rapids: Eerdmans, 1985.

_____. *The New Israel: A Commentary on the Book of Isaiah 56–66*. Grand Rapids: Eerdmans, 1985.

Mouw, R. J. *When the Kings Come Marching In*. Grand Rapids: Eerdmans, 1983.

Odeberg, H. *Trito-Isaiah: Isaiah fifty-six to sixty-six; a Literary and Linguistic Analysis*. Uppsala: Lundequistaska, 1931.

Polan, G. *In the Ways of Justice Toward Salvation: A Rhetorical Analysis of Isaiah 56–59*. New York: Peter Lang, 1986.

d. Ezekiel

Boadt, L. *Ezekiel's Oracles Against Egypt: A Literary and Philological Study of Ezekiel 29–32*. Rome: Biblical Institute Press, 1980.

_____. "Ezekiel." *The New Jerome Biblical Commentary*. Ed. by R. Brown et al. Englewood Cliffs, NJ: Prentice Hall, 1990. Pp. 305–328.

Brownlee, W. H. *Ezekiel 1–19.* Waco: Word, 1986.

Carley, K. W. *Ezekiel Among the Prophets: A Study of Ezekiel's Place in the Prophetic Tradition,* Naperville: Alec R. Allenson, 1974.

_____. *The Book of the Prophet Ezekiel.* Cambridge: Cambridge University Press, 1974.

Cody, A. *Ezekiel with an Excursus on Old Testament Priesthood.* Collegeville: Michael Glazier, 1991.

Cooke, G. A. *A Critical and Exegetical Commentary on the Book of Ezekiel.* New York: Scribner's, 1937.

Craigie, P. C. *Ezekiel.* Philadelphia: Westminster, 1983.

Davis, E. F. *Swallowing the Scroll: Textuality and the Dynamics of Discourse in Ezekiel's Prophecy.* Sheffield: Almond Press, 1989.

Eichrodt, W. *Ezekiel: A Commentary.* London: SCM; Philadelphia: Westminster, 1970.

Greenberg, M. *Ezekiel 1–20. The Anchor Bible,* 22. Garden City: Doubleday, 1983.

Hals, R. M. *Ezekiel.* Grand Rapids: Eerdmans, 1989.

Howie, C. G. *"Ezekiel-Daniel." Layman's Bible Commentary.* Vol. 13. Richmond: John Knox, 1961.

Joyce, P. *Divine Initiative and Human Response in Ezekiel.* Sheffield: JSOT Press, 1989.

Keil, C. F. *Ezekiel, Daniel.* Grand Rapids: Eerdmans, 1973.

Klein, R. *Ezekiel: The Prophet and His Message.* Columbia: University of South Carolina, 1988.

Levenson, J. D. *Theology of the Program of Restoration of Ezekiel 40–48.* Missoula: Scholars, 1976.

Lust, J., ed. *Ezekiel and His Book. Textual and Literary Criticism and their Interrelation.* Leuven: Leuven University Press, 1986.

May, H. G. "Introduction and Exegesis to Ezekiel." *The Interpreter's Bible, VI.* New York: Abingdon, 1956. Pp. 41–66.

Mays, J. L. *Ezekiel, Second Isaiah: Proclamation Commentaries.* Philadelphia: Fortress, 1978.

Raitt, T. M. *A Theology of Exile. Judgment/Deliverance in Jeremiah and Ezekiel.* Philadelphia: Fortress, 1977.

Robertson, E. H. *Jeremiah, Lamentations, Ezekiel, Isaiah 40–66.* London: Mobray, 1970.

Rooker, M. *Biblical Hebrew in Transition: The Language of the Book of Ezekiel.* JSOT Supplement. Sheffield: JSOT, 1990.

Rowley, H. H. *The Book of Ezekiel in Modern Study.* Manchester: John Rylands Library, 1953.

Smith, J. *The Book of the Prophet Ezekiel.* London: S.P.C.K.; New York: MacMillan, 1931.

Stalker, D. M. *Ezekiel.* London: SCM, 1968.

Stuart, D. *Ezekiel.* Dallas: Word, 1989.

Taylor, J. B. *Ezekiel.* Downers Grove: Inter–Varsity, 1969.

Torrey, C. C. *Pseudo-Ezekiel and the Original Prophecy.* New Haven: Yale University Press, 1930.

van Dijk, H. J. *Ezekiel's Prophecy on Tyre:* A New Approach. Rome: Biblical Institute Press, 1967.

Vawter, B. and L. Hoppe. *Ezekiel: A New Heart.* Grand Rapids: Eerdmans, 1991.

Wevers, J. W. *Ezekiel.* London: Nelson, 1969; Grand Rapids: Eerdmans, 1982.

Zimmerli, W. *Ezekiel.* (*Hermeneia.*) 2 vols. Philadelphia: Fortress, 1979, 1983.

_____. *I am Yahweh.* Trans. by D. W. Scott. Atlanta: John Knox, 1982.

e. Jeremiah

Achtemeier, E. *Deuteronomy, Jeremiah.* Philadelphia: Fortress Press, 1978.

Althann, R. *A Philological Analysis of Jeremiah 4–6 in the Light of Northwest Semitic.* Rome: Biblical Institute Press, 1983.

Baumgartner, W. *Jeremiah's Poem's of Lament.* Sheffield: Almond Press, 1988.

Berridge, J. M. *Prophet, People, and the Word of Yahweh: An Examination of Form and Content in the Proclamation of the Prophet Jeremiah.* Zurich: EVX, 1970.

Blank, S. *Jeremiah: Man and Prophet.* Cincinnati: Hebrew Union College, 1961.

Boadt, L. *Jeremiah 1–25.* Collegeville: Michael Glazier, 1991.

_____. *Jeremiah 26–52, Habakkuk, Zephaniah, Nahum.* Wilmington: Michael Glazier, 1982.

Bright, J. *Jeremiah. The Anchor Bible.* Garden City: Doubleday, 1965.

_____. "The Date of the Prose Sermons of Jeremiah." *Journal of Biblical Literature* 70 (1952) 15–35.

Brueggemann, W. *Jeremiah 1–25: To Pluck Up, to Tear Down.* Grand Rapids: Eerdmans, 1988.

_____. "The Book of Jeremiah: Portrait of a Prophet." *Interpretation* 37 (1983) 130–145.

_____. "Making History: Jeremiah's guide for Christians who know how to blush." *The Other Side* 22 (1986) 21–25.

_____. "Israel's Sense of Place in Jeremiah." *Rhetorical Criticism: Essays in Honor of James Muilenburg.* Ed. by J. Jacksom and M. Kessler. Allison Park: Pickwick, 1974. Pp. 130–145.

_____. "'Is there no Balm in Gilead': The Hope and Despair of Jeremiah." *Sojourners* 14(1985) 26–29.

_____. *Jeremiah 26–52.* Grand Rapids: Eerdmans, 1991.

_____. "A Second Reading of Jeremiah after the Dismantling (Jer. 24)." *Ex Auditu: An Annual of the Frederick Neumann Symposium on Theological Interpretation of Scripture* 1 (1985) 156–168.

_____. "The Epistemological Crisis of Israel's Two Histories (Jer. 9: 22-23)." *Israelite Wisdom: Theological Essays in Honor of*

Samuel Terrien. Ed. by J. G. Gammie et al. Missoula: Scholars, 1978. Pp. 85–104.

_____. "'The 'Uncared For' Now Cared For (Jer. 30: 12-17): A Methodological Consideration." *Journal of Biblical Literature* 104 (1983) 419–428.

_____. *To Pluck Up, to Tear Down.* Grand Rapids: Eerdmans, 1988.

Carroll, R. P. *From Chaos to Covenant: Prophecy in the Book of Jeremiah.* New York: Crossroads, 1981.

_____. *Jeremiah.* Sheffield: JSOT Press, 1989.

_____. *Jeremiah, A Commentary.* Philadelphia: Westminster Press, 1986.

_____. "Prophecy, Dissonance, and Jer. 26." *A Prophet to the Nations.* Ed. by Perdue and Kovacs. Winona Lake: Eisenbrauns, 1984. Pp. 381–391.

Couturier, G. P. "Jeremiah." *The New Jerome Biblical Commentary.* Ed. by R. Brown et al. Englewood Cliffs: Prentice Hall, 1990. Pp. 265–297.

Davidson, R. *Jeremiah.* Volume 1. Philadelphia: Westminster, 1983.

_____. *Jeremiah and Lamentations.* Volume 2. Philadelphia: Westminster, 1985.

Diamond, A. R. *The Confession of Jeremiah in Context: Scenes of Prophetic Drama.* Sheffield: JSOT Press, 1987.

Feinberg, C. L. *Jeremiah: A Commentary.* Grand Rapids: Zondervan, 1982.

Gottwald, N. K. *All the Kingdoms of the Earth.* New York: Harper & Row, 1964.

Hable, N. C. *Are You Joking Jeremiah?* St. Louis: Herder & Herder, 1969.

_____. *Concordia Commentary: Jeremiah, Lamentation.* St. Louis: Concordia, 1968.

Holladay, W. *Jeremiah.* Vol. I. Philadelphia: Fortress, 1986.

_____. *Jeremiah: A Fresh Reading*. New York: Pilgrim, 1990.

_____. *Jeremiah: Spokesman Out of Time*. Philadelphia: United Church, 1974.

_____. *The Architecture of Jeremiah 1–20*. Lewisburg: Bucknell University, 1976.

Hyatt, J. P. "Introduction and Exegesis to Jeremiah." *The Interpreter's Bible,* V. New York: Abingdon, 1956.

_____. "Jeremiah." *The Interpreter's Bible.* Vol. 5. New York: Abingdon, 1958. Pp. 779ff.

_____. *Jeremiah, Prophet of Courage and Hope*. New York: Abingdon, 1958.

Janzen, J. G. *Studies in the Text of Jeremiah.* Cambridge: Harvard University Press, 1973.

Keil, C. F. *Jeremiah, Lamentations.* Grand Rapids: Eerdmans, 1973.

Kidner, D. *The Message of Jeremiah: Against the Tide.* Downers Grove: Inter-Varsity, 1987.

Leslie, E. A. *Jeremiah; Chronologically Arranged, Translated and Interpreted.* Nashville: Abingdon, 1964.

Lundblom, J. R. *Jeremiah: A Study in Ancient Hebrew Rhetoric.* Missoula: Scholars, 1975.

Martens, E. *Jeremiah.* Scottdale: Herald Press, 1986.

McKane, W. *Jeremiah-I.* Edinburgh: T. & T. Clark, 1986.

Mottu, H. "Jeremiah Versus Hannaniah: Ideology and Truth in Old Testament Prophecy." *The Bible and Liberation: Political and Social Hermeneutics.* Norman K. Gottwald, ed. Maryknoll: Orbis, 1983. Pp. 235–51.

Muilenburg, J. "The Terminology of Adversity in Jeremiah." *Translating and Understanding the Old Testament.* H. T. Frank & W. L. Reed, eds. New York: Abingdon, 1970. Pp. 42–63.

Nicholson, E. W. *Preaching to the Exiles: A Study in the Prose Tradition in the Book of Jeremiah.* Oxford: Basil Blackwell, 1970.

_____. *The Book of the Prophet Jeremiah 1–25.* Cambridge: Cambridge University Press, 1973.

_____. *The Book of the Prophet Jeremiah 26–52*. Cambridge: Cambridge University Press, 1975.

O'Connor, K. *The Confessions of Jeremiah. Their Interpretation and Their Role in Chapters 1–25*. Atlanta: Scholars, 1989.

Overholt, T. W. *The Threat of Falsehood: A Study in the Theology of the Book of Jeremiah*. Naperville: Alec R. Allenson, 1970.

Perdue, L. G., and B. W. Kovacs, eds. *A Prophet to the Nations: Essays in Jeremiah Studies*. Winona Lake: Eisenbrauns, 1984.

Polk, T. *The Prophetic Persona. Jeremiah and the Language of Self*. Sheffield: JSOT Press, 1984.

Raitt, T. M. *A Theology of Exile: Judgment/Deliverance in Jeremiah and Ezekiel*. Philadelphia: Fortress, 1977.

Robertson, E. H. *Jeremiah, Lamentations, Ezekiel, Isaiah 40–66*. London: Mowbray, 1970.

Rowley, H. H. "The Early Prophecies of Jeremiah in their Setting." *A Prophet to the Nations*. L. G. Perdue and B. W. Kovacs, eds. Winona Lake: Eisenbrauns, 1984.

_____. "The Prophet Jeremiah and the Book of Deuteronomy." *Studies in Old Testament Prophecy*. Edinburgh: Clark, 1950. Pp. 157–174.

Skinner, J. *Prophecy and Religion. Studies in the Life of Jeremiah*. Cambridge: Cambridge University Press, 1922.

Smith, M. *The Laments of Jeremiah and Their Contexts. A Literary and Redactional Study of Jeremiah 11–20*. Atlanta: Scholars, 1991.

Soderlund, S. *The Greek Text of Jeremiah: A Revised Hypothesis*. Sheffield: JSOT Press, 1985.

Streame, A. W. *The Book of the Prophet Jeremiah, Together with Lamentations*. Cambridge: Cambridge University Press, 1913.

Stuhlman, L. *The Prose Sermons of the Book of Jeremiah*. Atlanta: Scholars, 1986.

Thompson, J. A. *The Book of Jeremiah*. Grand Rapids: Eerdmans, 1979.

Unterman, J. *From Repentance to Redemption: Jeremiah's Thought in Transition.* Sheffield: JSOT Press, 1987.

Welch, A. C. *Jeremiah, His Time and His Work.* Oxford: Blackwell, 1951.

Zlotowitz, B. M. *The Septuagint Translation of the Hebrew Terms in Relation to God in the Book of Jeremiah.* New York: Ktav, 1981.

f. Daniel

Baldwin, J. C. *Daniel. Tyndale Old Testament Commentaries.* Downers Grove: Inter-Varsity, 1978.

Braverman, J. *Jerome's* Commentary on Daniel: *A Study of Comparative Jewish and Christian Interpretations of the Hebrew Bible.* Washington D. C.: Catholic Biblical Association, 1978.

Casey, M. *Son of Man. The Interpretation and Influence of Daniel 7.* London: S.P.C.K., 1979.

Clifford, R. *The Book of Daniel.* Chicago: Franciscan Herald, 1980.

Collins, J. J. *Daniel with an Introduction to Apocalyptic Literature.* Grand Rapids: Eerdmans, 1984.

_____. *Daniel, First Maccabees, Second Maccabees with an Excursus on the Apocalyptic Genre.* Collegeville: Michael Glazier, 1991.

_____. *The Apocalyptic Imagination.* NewYork: Crossroad, 1984.

_____. *The Apocalyptic Vision of the Book of Daniel.* Chico: Scholars; Missoula: Scholars, 1977.

Davies, P. R. *Daniel.* Sheffield: JSOT Press, 1985.

Driver, S. R. *The Book of Daniel.* Cambridge: University Press, 1905.

Feech, A. J. *The Son of Man in Daniel Seven.* Berrien Springs: Andrews University, 1979.

Fewell, D. N. *Circle of Sovereignty. A Story of Stories in Daniel 1–6.* Sheffield: Almond Press, 1988.

Ginsberg, H. L. *Studies in Daniel.* New York: Jewish Theological Seminary of America, 1948.

Goldingay, J. E. *Daniel. Word Biblical Commentary.* Dallas: Word, 1989.

Hammer, R. *The Book of Daniel.* New York & London: Cambridge University Press, 1976.

Hanson, P. D. *The Dawn of Apocalyptic: The Historical and Sociological Roots of Jewish Apocalyptic Eschatology.* Philadelphia: Fortress, 1975.

_____, ed. *Visionaries and their Apocalypses.* Philadelphia: Fortress, 1983.

Harrison, R. K. *Jeremiah and Lamentations.* Downers Grove: Inter–Varsity, 1973.

Hartmann, L. F. and A. A. Di Lella. *The Book of Daniel.* Garden City: Doubleday, 1978.

_____. "Daniel." *The New Jerome Biblical Commentary.* Ed. by R. Brown et al. Englewood Cliffs: Prentice Hall, 1990. Pp. 406–420.

Heaton, W. W. *The Book of Daniel: Introduction and Commentary.* London: SCM, 1956.

Jeansonne, S. P. *The Old Greek Translation of Daniel 7–12.* Washington, D.C.: The Catholic Biblical Association of America, 1988.

Keil, C. F. *Ezekiel, Daniel.* Grand Rapids: Eerdmans, 1973.

Koch, K. et al. *Daniel.* Neukirchen-Vluyn: Verlag des Erziehungsvereins, 1986.

Lacocque, A. *Daniel in His Time.* Columbia: University of South Carolina, 1988.

_____. *The Book of Daniel.* Atlanta: John Knox, 1979.

Moore, C. *Daniel, Esther and Jeremiah: The Additions. The Anchor Bible* Series. Garden City: Doubleday, 1977.

Porteous, N. *Daniel.* Old Testament Library. Philadelphia: Westminster, 1965.

Reid, S. *Enoch and Daniel: A Form Critical and Sociological Study of the Historical Apocalypses.* Berkeley: BIBAL, 1989.

Russell, D. S. *Apocalyptic: Ancient and Modern.* Philadelphia: Fortress, 1978.

_____. *Daniel.* Edinburgh: St. Andrew; Philadelphia: Westminster, 1981.

_____. *Daniel: An Active Volcano.* Louisville: Westminster/John Knox, 1989.

_____. *The Method and Message of Jewish Apocalyptic.* Philadelphia: Westminster, 1964.

Schmithals, W. *The Apocalyptic Movement.* Nashville: Abingdon, 1975.

Seitz, C. R., ed. *Reading and Preaching the Book of Daniel.* Philadelphia: Fortress, 1988.

Slotki, J. J., ed. *Daniel, Ezra and Nehemiah; Hebrew text and English Translation with an Introduction and Commentary.* London: Soncino, 1951.

Towner, W. S. *Daniel, Interpretation: Biblical Commentary.* Atlanta: John Knox, 1984.

Wallace R. S. *The Lord is King: The Message of Daniel.* Downers Grove: Inter–Varsity, 1979.

Wilson, R. D. *Studies in the Book of Daniel. A Classic Defense of the Historicity and Integrity of Daniel's Prophecy.* Grand Rapids: Baker, 1979.

35. MINOR PROPHETS

a. Lamentations

Albrektson, B. *Studies In the Text and Theology of the Book of Lamentations. Studia Theologica Ludensia* 21. Lund, Sweden: Gleerup, 1963.

Ash, A. L. *Jeremiah and Lamentations.* Abilene: Abeline Christian University Press, 1987.

Cheyne, T. K. *Jeremiah and Lamentations.* New York: Funk & Wagnalls, 1913.

Davidson, R. *Jeremiah, Vol. 2. Lamentations.* Philadelphia: Westminster, 1985.

Erdman, C. R. *The Book of Jeremiah and Lamentations, An Exposition.* Westwood: Revell, 1955.

Fischer, J. A. *Song of Songs, Ruth, Lamentations, Ecclesiastes, Esther.* Collegeville: The Liturgical Press, 1986.

Fuerst, W. J. *The Books of Ruth, Esther, Ecclesiastes, The Song of Songs, Lamentations.* Cambridge: Cambridge University Press, 1975.

Gordis, R. *The Song of Songs and Lamentations.* New York: Ktav, 1974.

Gottwald, N. K. *Studies in the Book of Lamentations.* London: SCM; Chicago: Alec R. Allenson, 1954.

_____. *Studies in the Book of Lamentations. Studies in Biblical Theology,* 14. Rev. ed. London: SCM Press, 1962.

Guinan, M. D. "Lamentations." *The New Jerome Biblical Commentary.* Ed. by R. Brown et al. Englewood Cliffs: Prentice Hall, 1990. Pp. 558–562.

Harrison, R. K. *Jeremiah and Lamentations; An Introduction and Commentary.* Downers Grove: Inter-Varsity, 1973.

Hillers, D. *Lamentations. The Anchor Bible.* Garden City: Doubleday, 1972.

Horbel, N. C. *Concordia Commentary: Jeremiah, Lamentations.* St. Louis: Concordia, 1968.

Keil, C. F. *Jeremiah, Lamentations.* Grand Rapids: Eerdmans, 1973.

Knight, G. A. *Esther, Song of Songs, Lamentations: Introduction and Commentary.* London: SCM, 1955.

Kodell, J. *Lamentations, Haggai, Zechariah, Malachi, Obadiah, Joel, Second Zechariah, Baruch.* Collegeville: Michael Glazier, 1991.

Meek, T. J. and W. P. Merrill. "The Book of Lamentations." *The Interpreter's Bible.* Vol. VI. Nashville: Abingdon, 1956. Pp. 1–38.

Provan, I. *Lamentations.* Grand Rapids: Eerdmans, 1991.

Robertson, E. H. *Jeremiah, Lamentations, Ezekiel, Isaiah 40–66.* London: Mobray, 1970.

Smith, J. E. *Jeremiah and Lamentations.* Joplin: College, 1972.

Tigay, J. H. "Lamentations, Book of." *Encycopedia Judaica*. Vol. 10, cols. 1368–75.

Widengren, G. *The Accadian and Songs of Lamentation*. Uppsala: Almquist & Wiksell, 1936.

b. Hosea

Anderson, F. I. and D. N. Freedman. *Hosea. The Anchor Bible*. New York: Doubleday, 1980.

Beeby, H. D. *Grace Abounding: a Commentary on the Book of Hosea. International Theological Commentary*. Grand Rapids: Eerdmans, 1989.

Brueggemann, W. *Tradition for Crisis: A Study in Hosea*. Richmond: John Knox, 1968.

Buss, M. J. *The Prophetic Word of Hosea. A Morphological Study*. Berlin: Alfred Topelmann, 1969.

Cohen, G. G. and H. R. Vandermey. *Hosea–Amos*. Chicago: Moody, 1981.

Craigie, P. C. *Twelve Prophets, Vol. 1. (Hosea–Jonah)* Philadelphia: Westminster, 1984.

Daniels, D. *Hosea and Salvation History: The Early Traditions of Israel in the Prophecy of Hosea*. New York: de Gruyter, 1990.

Doorly, W. *Prophet of Love: Understanding the Book of Hosea*. Mahwah: Paulist Press, 1991.

Ellison, H. L. *The Prophets of Israel, From Elijah to Hosea*. Exeter: Paternoster, 1969.

Emmerson, G. I. *Hosea: An Israelite Prophet in Judean Perspective*. Sheffield: JSOT Press, 1984.

Gelston, A. *Kingship in the Book of Hosea*. Leiden: Brill, 1974.

Harper, W. R. *A Critical and Exegetical Commentary on Amos and Hosea*. New York: Scribner's, 1905.

Hubbard, D. *Hosea: An Introduction and Commentary*. Downers Grove: Inter-Varsity, 1989.

Hunter, A. V. *Seek the Lord! A Study of the Meaning and Function of the Exhortation in Amos, Hosea, Isaiah, Micah and Zephaniah.* Baltimore: St. Mary's Seminary and University, 1982.

Kidner, D. *Love to the Loveless: The Message of Hosea.* Downers Grove: Inter–Varsity, 1981.

King, P. J. *Amos, Hosea, Micah–An Archaeological Commentary.* Philadelphia: Westminster, 1988.

Knight, G. A. *Hosea. God's Love.* London: SCM, 1960.

_____. *Hosea: Introduction and Commentary.* London: SCM, 1969.

Limburg, J. *Hosea–Micah.* Atlanta: John Knox, 1988.

Mays, J. L. *Hosea.* Philadelphia: Westminster, 1969, 1975.

Mc Carthy, D. J. and R. E. Murphy. "Hosea." *The New Jerome Biblical Commentary.* Ed. by R. Brown et al. Englewood Cliffs: Prentice Hall, 1990. Pp. 265–297.

Mc Keating, H. *The Books of Amos, Hosea and Micah.* Cambridge: Cambridge University Press. 1971.

Robinson, H. W. *The Cross of Hosea.* Philadelphia: Westminster, 1949.

Rowley, H. H. "The Marriage of Hosea." *Bulletin of John Rylands Library 39* (1956) 220–233.

Smith, B. K. *Hosea, Joel, Amos, Obadiah, Jonah.* Nashville: Broadman, 1982.

Snaith, N. H. *Mercy and Sacrifice: A Study of the Book of Hosea.* London: SCM, 1953.

Stuart, D. K. *Hosea–Jonah.* Waco: Word, 1987.

Vawter, B. *Amos, Hosea, Micah, with an Introduction to Classical Prophecy.* Wilmington: Michael Glazier; Dublin: Gill & Macmillan, 1981.

Ward, J. M. *Hosea: A Theological Commentary.* New York: Harper & Row, 1966.

Wolff, H. W. *Hosea. Hermeneia.* Philadelphia: Fortress, 1974.

Yee, G. A. *Composition and Tradition In The Book of Hosea, A Redaction Critical Investigation.* Atlanta: Scholars, 1987.

c. Joel

Ahlström, G. *Joel and the Temple Cult of Jerusalem.* Supplements to *Vetus Testamentum* 21. Leiden: Brill, 1971.

Allen, L. C. *The Books of Joel, Obadiah, Jonah, and Micah.* Grand Rapids: Eerdmans, 1976.

Emmerson, G. I. *Hosea: An Israelite Prophet in Judean Perspective.* Sheffield: JSOT Press, 1984.

Gaebelin, A. C. *The Prophet Joel: An Exposition.* New York: Our Hope, 1909.

Hubbard, D. A. *Joel and Amos.* Downers Grove: Inter–Varsity, 1989.

Kapelrud, A. S. *Joel Studies.* Uppsala: Lundequistska–Almqvist & Wiksells, 1948.

Kodell, J. *Lamentations, Haggai, Zechariah, Malachi, Obadiah, Joel, Second Zechariah, Baruch.* Wilmington: Michael Glazier, 1982.

Mallon, E. D. "Joel–Obadiah." *The New Jerome Biblical Commentary.* Ed. by R. Brown et al. Englewood Cliffs: Prentice Hall, 1990. Pp. 399–405.

Ogden, G. S. and Richard R. Deutsch. *A Promise of Hope–A Call to Obedience: A Commentary on the Books of Joel and Malachi.* Grand Rapids: Eerdmans, 1987.

Prinsloo, W. *The Theology of Joel.* Berlin: de Gruyter, 1985.

Rand, H. B. *Joel's Prophetic Message and Warning.* Haverhill: Anglo–Saxon Federation of America, 1930.

Smith, B. K. *Hosea, Joel, Amos, Obadiah, Jonah.* Nashville: Broadman, 1982.

Smith, J. M., W. H. Ward and J. A. Bewer. *A Critical and Exegetical Commentary on Micah, Zephaniah, Nahum, Habakkuk, Obadiah, and Joel.* Edinburgh: T. & T. Clark, 1948.

Wade, G. W. *Books of the Prophets Michah, Obadiah, Joel and Jonah with Introduction and Notes.* London: Methuen, 1925.

Watts, J. D. *The Books of Joel, Obadiah, Jonah, Nahum, Habakkuk and Zephaniah.* Cambridge: Cambridge University Press, 1975.

Wolff, H. W. *Joel and Amos.* Philadelphia: Fortress, 1977.

d. Amos

Auld, A. G. *Amos.* Sheffield: JSOT Press, 1986.

Barré, M. L. "Amos." *The New Jerome Biblical Commentary.* Ed. by R. Brown et al. Englewood Cliffs: Prentice Hall, 1990. Pp. 209–216.

Barstad, H. M. *The Religious Polemic in Amos.* Leiden: Brill, 1984.

Barton, J. *Amos's Oracles Against the Nations: A Study of Amos 1:3–2:5.* London–New York: Cambridge University Press, 1980.

Cohen, G. G. and H. Ronald Vandermey. *Hosea–Amos.* Chicago: Moody, 1981.

Coote, R. B. *Amos Among the Prophets: Composition and Theology.* Philadelphia: Fortress Press, 1981.

Doorly, W. J. *Prophet of Justice: Understanding The Book of Amos.* New York: Paulist Press, 1989.

Hammershaimb, E. *The Book of Amos. A Commentary.* Oxford: Basil Blackwell; New York: Schocken, 1970.

Hunter, A. V. *Seek the Lord! A Study of the Meaning and Function of the Exhortation in Amos, Hosea, Isaiah, Micah and Zephaniah.* Baltimore: St. Mary's Seminary and University, 1982.

Isabell, C. D. "Another Look at Amos 5:26." *Journal of Biblical Literature* 97 (1978) 97–99.

Joyce, P. *Divine Initiative and Human Response in Ezekiel.* Sheffield: JSOT, 1989.

Kapelrud, A. S. *Central Ideas in Amos.* Oslo: Oslo University Press, 1956, 1961, 1971.

Kapelrud, A. S. "New Ideas in Amos." Supplements to *Vetus Testamentum* 15 (1965) 193–206.

King, P. J. *Amos, Hosea, Micah–An Archaeological Commentary.* Philadelphia: Westminster, 1988.

Limburg, J. "Amos 7:4: A Judgment with Fire?" *Catholic Biblical Quarterly* 35 (1973) 346–49.

_____. "Sevenfold Structures in the Book of Amos." *The Journal of Biblical Literature* 106 (1987) 207–22.

Martin-Achard, R. *God's People in Crisis: A Commentary on the Book of Amos.* Grand Rapids: Eerdmans, 1984.

Mays, J. L. *Amos.* Philadelphia: Westminster, 1969, 1976.

Motyer, J. A. *The Day of the Lion: The Message of Amos.* Downers Grove: Inter–Varsity, 1974.

Overholt, T. W. "Commanding the Prophets; Amos and the Problem of Prophetic Authority." *Catholic Biblical Quarterly* 41 (1979) 517–532.

Paul, S. *Amos.* Minneapolis: Fortress, 1991.

_____. "Fishing Imagery in Amos 4:2" *Journal of Biblical Literature* 97 (1978) 183–90.

Polley, M. *Amos and the Davidic Empire: A Socio-Historical Approach.* New York: Oxford University Press, 1989.

Rosenbaum, S. *Amos of Israel: A New Interpretation.* Macon: Mercer, 1990.

Rowley, H. H. "Was Amos a Nabi?" *Festschrift Otto Eisefeldt.* Halls: Niemeyer, 1947.

Smith, B. K. *Hosea, Joel, Amos, Obadiah, Jonah.* Nashville: Broadman, 1982.

Soggin, J. A. *The Prophet Amos.* London: SCM, 1987.

Stuhlmueller, C. *Amos, Hosea, Micah, Nahum, Zephaniah, Habakkuk.* Collegeville: The Liturgical Press, 1986.

Vawter, B. *Amos, Hosea, Micah, with an Introduction to Classical Prophecy.* Collegeville: Michael Glazier, 1991.

Ward, J. M. *Amos and Isaiah: Prophets of the Word of God.* New York: Abingdon, 1969.

Watts, J. D. *Vision and Prophecy in Amos.* Leiden: Brill; Grand Rapids: Eerdmans, 1958.

Wolff, H. W. *Amos the Prophet: The Man and His Background.* Philadelphia: Fortress, 1973.

_____. *Joel and Amos. Hermeneia.* Philadelphia: Fortress, 1977.

e. Obadiah

Allen, L. C. *The Books of Joel, Obadiah, Jonah, and Micah.* Grand Rapids: Eerdmans, 1976.

Baker, D. W., T. D. Alexander and B. K. Waltke. *Obadiah, Jonah and Micah.* Leicester–Downers Grove: Inter-Varsity, 1988.

Beyer, B. *Obadiah, Jonah.* Grand Rapids: Lamplighter Books, Zondervan, 1982, 1988.

Coggins, R. J. and S. Paul Reémi. *Nahum, Obadiah, Esther.* Grand Rapids: Eerdmans,   1985.

Coggins, R. J. *Israel Among the Nations: A Commentary on the Books of Nahum and Obadiah.* Grand Rapids: Eerdmans, 1985.

Eaton, J. H. *Obadiah, Nahum, Habakkuk and Zephaniah; Introduction and Commentary.* Londom: SCM, 1961.

Gaebelin, F. E. *Four Minor Prophets: Obadiah, Jonah, Habakkuk, and Haggai; Their Message for Today.* Chicago: Moody, 1970.

_____. *The Servant and the Dove; Obadiah and Jonah, Their Messages and Their Work.* New York: Our Hope, 1946.

Hillis, D. W. *The Books of Obadiah.* Grand Rapids: Baker, 1968.

Holladay, W. *Jeremiah: A Fresh Reading.* New York: Pilgrim, 1990.

Kodell, J. *Lamentations, Haggai, Zechariah, Malachi, Obadiah, Joel, Second Zechariah, Baruch.* Wilmington: Michael Glazier, 1982.

Lanchester, H. C. *Obadiah and Jonah in the Revised Version with Introduction and Notes.* Cambridge: University Press, 1918.

Marbury, E. *Obadiah and Habakkuk.* Minneapolis: Klock & Klock, 1979, 1965.

Smith, B. K. *Hosea, Joel, Amos, Obadiah, Jonah.* Nashville:Broadman, 1982.

Smith, J. M., W. H. Ward and J. A. Bewer. *A Critical and Exegetical Commentary on Micah, Zephaniah, Nahum, Habakkuk, Obadiah, and Joel.* Edinburgh: T. & T. Clark, 1948.

Thompson, J. A. *The Book of Jeremiah.* Grand Rapids: Eerdmans, 1979.

Wade, G. W. *Books of the Prophets Michah, Obadiah, Joel and Jonah with Introduction and Notes.* London: Methuen, 1925.

Watts, J. D. *Obadiah: A Critical Exegetical Commentary.* Grand Rapids: Eerdmans, 1969.

_____. *The Books of Joel, Obadiah, Jonah, Nahum, Habakkuk and Zephaniah.* Cambridge: Cambridge University Press, 1975.

Wolff, H. *Obadiah and Jonah.* Minneapolis: Augsburg, 1986.

f. Jonah

Aalders, G. C. *The Problem of the Book of Jonah.* London: Tyndale, 1958.

Alexander, T. D. *Jonah: Introduction and Commentary.* Leicester: Inter–Varsity, 1988.

Allen, L. C. *The Books of Joel, Obadiah, Jonah, and Micah.* Grand Rapids: Eerdmans, 1976.

Baker, D. W., T. D. Alexander and B. K. Waltke. *Obadiah, Jonah and Micah.* Leicester: Inter-Varsity, 1988.

Bickermann, E. *Four Strange Books of the Bible.* New York: Schocken, 1967.

Bowers, R. H. *The Legend of Jonah.* The Hague: Martinus Nijhoff, 1971.

Bull, G. T. *The City and the Sign: An Interpretation of the Book of Jonah.* London: Hodder & Stoughton, 1970.

Ceresko, A. R. "Jonah." *The New Jerome Biblical Commentary.* Ed. by R. Brown et al. Englewood Cliffs: Prentice Hall, 1990. Pp. 580–584.

Craghan, J. *Esther, Judith, Tobit, Jonah, Ruth.* Wilmington: Michael Glazier, 1982.

Craigie, P. C. *Twelve Prophets. Vol. 1. Hosea–Jonah.* Philadelphia: Westminster, 1984.

Ellul, J. *The Judgment of Jonah.* Grand Rapids: Eerdmans, 1971.

Fretheim, T. E. *The Message of Jonah.* Minneapolis: Augsburg, 1977.

Ginn, R. *Jonah, The Spirituality of a Runaway Prophet.* Locust Valley: Living Flame, 1978.

Knight, G. A. and F. W. Golka. *Revelation of God: A Commentary on the Song of Songs and Jonah.* Edinburgh: Handsel; Grand Rapids: Eerdmans, 1988.

Lacocque, A. and P. E. Lacocque. *Jonah: A Psycho-Religious Approach to the Prophet.* Columbia: University of South Carolina, 1990.

_____. *The Jonah Complex.* Atlanta: John Knox, 1981.

Landes, G. "Jonah, Book of." *The Interpreter's Dictionary of the Bible.* Supplementary Volume. Nashville: Abingdon, 1976. Pp. 488–491.

Limburg, J. *Old Stories for a New Time.* Atlanta: John Knox, 1983.

Magonet, J. *Form and Meaning: Studies in Literary Techniques in the Book of Jonah.* Sheffield: Almond Press, 1983.

Nowell, I. *Jonah, Tobit, Judith.* Collegeville: The Liturgical Press, 1986.

Sasson, J. *Jonah: A New Translation with Introduction, Commentary, and Interpretation.* New York: Doubleday, 1990.

Smith, B. K. *Hosea, Joel, Amos, Obadiah, Jonah.* Nashville: Broadman, 1982.

Stuart, D. K. *Hosea–Jonah.* Waco: Word, 1987.

Vawter, B. *Job and Jonah.* New York: Paulist, 1983.

Wade, G. W. *Books of the Prophets Michah, Obadiah, Joel and Jonah with Introduction and Notes.* London: Methuen, 1925.

Watts, J. D. *The Books of Joel, Obadiah, Jonah, Nahum, Habakkuk and Zephaniah.* Cambridge: Cambridge University Press, 1975.

Wolff, H. *Jonah: Church in Revolt.* St. Louis: Clayton, 1978.

_____. *Obadiah and Jonah.* Minneapolis: Augsburg, 1986.

g. Micah

Alfaro, J. I. *Justice and Loyalty: a Commentary on the Book of Micah. International Theological Commentary.* Grand Rapids: Eerdmans, 1988.

Allen, L. C. *The Books of Joel, Obadiah, Jonah, and Micah.* Grand Rapids: Eerdmans, 1976.

Baker, D. W., T. D. Alexander and B. K. Waltke. *Obadiah, Jonah and Micah.* Leicester: Inter-Varsity, 1988.

Brueggemann, N. W. *To Act Justly, Love Tenderly, Walk Humbly: An Agenda For Ministers.* New York: Paulist, 1986.

Hagstrom, D. G. *The Coherence of the Book of Micah. A Literary Analysis.* Atlanta: Scholars, 1988.

Hillers, D. R. *Micah.* Philadelphia: Fortress, 1984.

Hunter, A. V. *Seek the Lord! A Study of the Meaning and Function of the Exhortation in Amos, Hosea, Isaiah, Micah and Zephaniah.* Baltimore: St. Mary's Seminary and University, 1982.

King, P. J. *Amos, Hosea, Micah–An Archaeological Commentary.* Philadelphia: Westminster, 1988.

Laberge, L. "Micah." *The New Jerome Biblical Commentary.* Ed. by R. Brown et al. Englewood Cliffs: Prentice Hall, 1990. Pp. 249–254.

Malchow, B. "The Rural Prophet: Micah." *Currents in Theology and Mission* 7 (1980) 48–52.

Mays, J. L. *Micah: A Commentary.* Philadelphia: Westminster, 1976.

Mc Keating, H. *The Books of Amos, Hosea and Micah.* Cambridge: Cambridge University Press, 1971.

Smith, J. M., W. H. Ward and J. A. Bewer. *A Critical and Exegetical Commentary on Micah, Zephaniah, Nahum, Habakkuk, Obadiah, and Joel.* Edinburgh: T. & T. Clark, 1948.

Smith, R. L. *Micah–Malachi.* Waco: Word, 1984.

Stansell, G. *Micah and Isaiah: A Form and Tradition Historical Comparison.* Atlanta: Scholars, 1988.

Van Der Wal, A. *Micah: A Classified Bibliography*. Amsterdam: Free University Press, 1990.

Vawter, B. *Amos, Hosea, Micah, with an Introduction to Classical Prophecy*. Wilmington: Glazier; Dublin: Gill and MacMillan, 1981.

Wade, G. W. *Books of the Prophets Michah, Obadiah, Joel and Jonah with Introduction and Notes*. London: Methuen, 1925.

Waltke, B. *Micah: Introduction and Commentary*. Leicester: Inter–Varsity, 1988.

Wolff, H. W. *Micah the Prophet*. Philadelphia: Fortress, 1981.

h. Nahum

Achtemeier, E. R. *Nahum–Malachi*. Atlanta: John Knox, 1986.

Baker, D. W. *Nahum, Habakkuk and Zephaniah*. Leicester: Inter-Varsity, 1988.

Boadt, L. *Jeremiah 26–52, Habakkuk, Zephaniah, Nahum*. Wilmington: Michael Glazier, 1982.

Cathcart, K. J. *Nahum in Light of Northwest Semitic*. Rome: Biblical Institute Press, 1973.

Christensen, D. L. *Tranformations of the War Oracle in Old Testament Prophecy: Studies in the Oracles Against the Nations*. Missoula: Scholars, 1975.

Clark, D. and H. Hatton. *A Translator's Handbook on the Books of Nahum, Habakkuk, and Zephaniah*. New York: United Bible Societies, 1989.

Coggins, R. J. and S. P. Reémi. *Nahum, Obadiah, Esther*. Grand Rapids: Eerdmans, 1985.

Coggins, R. J. *Israel Among the Nations: A Commentary on the Books of Nahum and Obadiah*. Grand Rapids: Eerdmans, 1985.

Haldar, A. *Studies in the Book of Nahum*. Uppsala: Lundequistska, 1947.

Maier, W. A. *The Book of Nahum*. St. Louis: Concordia, 1959; Grand Rapids: Baker, 1980.

Mendenhall, G. E. *The Tenth Generation.* Baltimore: John Hopkins University Press, 1973. Pp. 69–104.

Robertson, O. Palmer. *The Books of Nahum, Habakkuk, and Zephaniah. New International Commentary on the Old Testament.* Grand Rapids: Eerdmans, 1990.

Smith, J. M., W. H. Ward and J. A. Bewer. *A Critical and Exegetical Commentary on Micah, Zephaniah, Nahum, Habakkuk, Obadiah, and Joel.* Edinburgh: T. & T. Clark, 1948.

Watts, J. D. *The Books of Joel, Obadiah, Jonah, Nahum, Habakkuk and Zephaniah.* Cambridge: Cambridge University Press, 1975.

i. Habakkuk

Achtemeier, E. *Nahum-Malachi.* Atlanta: John Knox, 1986.

Albright, W. F. "The Psalm of Habakkuk." *Studies in Old Testament Prophecy.* Ed. by H. H. Rowely. New York: Scribners, 1950. Pp. 1–18.

Baker, D. W. *Nahum, Habakkuk and Zephaniah.* Leicester: Inter-Varsity, 1988.

Barber, C. J. *Habakkuk and Zephaniah.* Chicago: Moody, 1985.

Boadt, L. *Jeremiah 26–52, Habakkuk, Zephaniah, Nahum.* Wilmington: Michael Glazier, 1982.

Brownlee, W. H. *The Text of Habakkuk in the Ancient Commentary from Qumran.* Philadelphia: Society of Biblical Literature, 1959.

Davidson, A. B. *The Books of Nahum, Habakkuk and Zephaniah.* Cambridge: University Press, 1920.

Eaton, J. H. *Obadiah, Nahum, Habakkuk and Zephaniah; Introduction and Commentary.* London: SCM, 1961.

Eszenyei Széles, M. *Wrath and Mercy: A Commentary on the Books of Habakkuk and Zephaniah.* Grand Rapids: Eerdmans; Edinburgh: Handsel, 1987.

Fuerbringer, L. E. *The Eternal Why: the Prophet Habakkuk Answers a Timeless Question.* St. Louis: Concordia, 1947.

Gaebelin, F. E. *Four Minor Prophets: Obadiah, Jonah, Habakkuk, and Haggai; Their Message for Today.* Chicago: Moody, 1970.

Gowan, D. E. *The Triumph of Faith in Habakkuk.* Atlanta: John Knox, 1976.

Lloyd–Jones, D. M. *From Fear to Faith; Studies in the Book of Habakkuk.* London: Inter–Varsity, 1953.

Robertson, O. P. *The Books of Nahum, Habakkuk, and Zephaniah.* Grand Rapids: Eerdmans, 1989.

Smith, J. M., W. H. Ward and J. A. Bewer. *A Critical and Exegetical Commentary on Micah, Zephaniah, Nahum, Habakkuk, Obadiah, and Joel.* Edinburgh: T. & T. Clark, 1948.

Stoll, J. H. *The Book of Habakkuk; a Study Manual.* Grand Rapids: Baker, 1972.

Taylor, C. L., Jr. "Introduction and Exegesis of Habakkuk." *The Interpreter's Bible.* Vol. 6. Nashville: Abingdon, 1956. Pp. 973–1003.

Watts, J. D. *The Books of Joel, Obadiah, Jonah, Nahum, Habakkuk and Zephaniah.* Cambridge: Cambridge University Press, 1975.

j. Zephaniah

Baker, D. W. *Nahum, Habakkuk and Zephaniah.* Leicester: Inter-Varsity, 1988.

Boadt, L. *Jeremiah 26–52, Habakkuk, Zephaniah, Nahum.* Wilmington: Michael Glazier, 1982.

Eaton, J. H. *Obadiah, Nahum, Habakkuk, and Zephaniah.* London: SCM, 1961.

Eszenyei, Széles M. *Wrath and Mercy: A Commentary on the Books of Habakkuk and Zephaniah.* Grand Rapids: Eerdmans, 1987.

House, P. R. *Zephaniah: a Prophetic Drama.* Decatur: Almond, 1988.

Hunter, A. V. *Seek the Lord! A Study of the Meaning and Function of the Exhortation in Amos, Hosea, Isaiah, Micah and Zephaniah.* Baltimore: St. Mary's Seminary and University, 1982.

Kapelrud, A. S. *The Message of the Prophet Zephaniah.* Oslo: Universitetsforlaget, 1975.

Robertson, O. P. *The Books of Nahum, Habakkuk, and Zephaniah.* Grand Rapids: Eerdmans, 1989.

Smith, J. M., W. H. Ward, and J. A. Bewer. *A Critical and Exegetical Commentary on Micah, Zephaniah, Nahum, Habakkuk, Obadiah, and Joel.* Edinburgh: T. & T. Clark, 1948.

Taylor, C. L. "The Book of Zephaniah." *The Interpreter's Bible.* Vol. 6. Nashville: Abingdon, 1956. Pp. 1005–1034.

Wahl, T. P., I. Nowell and A. R. Ceresko. "Zephaniah, Nahum, Habakkuk." *The New Jerome Biblical Commentary.* Ed. by R. Brown et al. Englewood Cliffs: Prentice Hall, 1990. Pp. 255–264.

Watts, J. D. *The Books of Joel, Obadiah, Jonah, Nahum, Habakkuk and Zephaniah.* Cambridge: Cambridge University Press, 1975.

k. Haggai

Ackroyd, P. "Haggai." *Peake's Commentary on the Bible.* M. Black and H. H. Rowley, eds. New York: Nelson, 1962. Pp. 643–45.

_____. "Studies in the Book of Haggai and Zechariah 1–8." *Journal of Jewish Studies* 3 (1952) 151–156.

_____. "Studies in the Book of Haggai." *Journal of Jewish Studies* 3 (1952) 163–176.

Baldwin, J. G. *Haggai, Zechariah, Malachi.* London: Tyndale; Downers Grove: Inter-Varsity, 1972.

Cody, A. "Haggai, Zechariah, Malachi." *The New Jerome Biblical Commentary.* Ed. by R. Brown et al. Englewood Cliffs: Prentice Hall, 1990. Pp. 349–361.

Coggins, R. J. *Haggai, Zechariah, Malachi.* Sheffield: JSOT Press, 1987.

Dods, M. *The Post–Exilian Prophets: Haggai, Zechariah, Malachi.* Edinburgh: T. & T. Clark.

Jones, D. R. *Haggai, Zechariah and Malachi: Introduction and Commentary.* London: SCM, 1962.

Kodell, J. *Lamentations, Haggai, Zechariah, Malachi, Obadiah, Joel, Second Zechariah, Baruch.* Wilmington: Michael Glazier, 1982.

Mason, R. *The Books of Haggai, Zechariah and Malachi.* Cambridge: Cambridge University Press, 1977.

Meyers, C. and E. Meyers. *Haggai, Zechariah 1–8. The Anchor Bible.* Garden City: Doubleday, 1987.

Petersen, D. *Haggai and Zechariah 1–8.* Philadelphia: Westminster, 1984.

Stuhlmueller, C. *Rebuilding With Hope: A Commentary on the Books of Haggai and Zechariah.* Grand Rapids: Eerdmans, 1988.

Verhoef, P. A. *The Books of Haggai and Malachi.* Grand Rapids: Eerdmans, 1987.

Wolff, H. W. *Haggai.* Minneapolis: Augsburg, 1988.

l. Zechariah

Alexander, L. W. *Zechariah: His Visions and Warnings.* London: James Nisbet , 1885.

Baldwin, J. G. *Haggai, Zechariah, Malachi.* London: Tyndale; Downers Grove: Inter-Varsity Press, 1972.

Chambers, T. W. *The Book of Zechariah.* New York: Scribner & Armstrong, 1875.

Coates, C. A. *An Outline of the Prophets Haggai and Zechariah; Substance of Bible Readings.* Kingston–on–Thames: Stow Hill Bible and Tract Depot, 1944.

Coggins, R. J. *Haggai, Zechariah, Malachi.* Sheffield: JSOT Press, 1987.

Dods, M. *The Post–Exilian Prophets: Haggai, Zechariah, Malachi.* Edinburgh: T. & T. Clark, 1983.

Feinberg, C. L. *God Remembers; a Study of the Book of Zechariah.* Wheaton: Van Kampen Press, 1950.

Hanson, P. D. *The Dawn of Apocalyptic.* Philadelphia: Fortress, 1979.

Kodell, J. *Lamentations, Haggai, Zechariah, Malachi, Obadiah, Joel, Second Zechariah, Baruch.* Wilmington: Michael Glazier, 1982.

Laney, C. *Zechariah.* Chicago: Moody, 1984.

Leupold, H. C. *Exposition of Zechariah.* Columbus: Wartburg, 1956.

Luck, G. C. *Zechariah, A Study of the Prophetic Visions of Zechariah.* Chicago: Moody, 1969.

Mason, R. *The Books of Haggai, Zechariah and Malachi.* Cambridge: Cambridge University Press, 1977.

Meyer, F. B. *The Prophet of Hope: Studies in Zechariah.* Chicago: F. H. Revell, 1900.

Meyers, C. and E. Meyers. *Haggai, Zechariah 1–8: A New Translation with Introduction and Commentary.* Garden City: Doubleday, 1987.

Perowne, T. T. *Haggai and Zechariah.* Cambridge: University Press, 1890, 1886.

Petersen, D. *Haggai and Zechariah 1–8.* Philadelphia: Westminster, 1985.

Smith, J. M., W. H. Ward and J. A. Bewer. *A Critical and Exegetical Commentary on Haggai, Zechariah, Malachi and Jonah.* Edinburgh: T. & T. Clark, 1912.

Stuhlmueller, C. *Rebuilding With Hope: A Commentary on the Books of Haggai and Zechariah.* Grand Rapids: Eerdmans, 1988.

m. Malachi

Baldwin, J. G. *Haggai, Zechariah, Malachi.* London: Tyndale; Downers Grove: Inter-Varsity Press, 1972.

Coggins, R. J. *Haggai, Zechariah, Malachi.* Sheffield: JSOT Press, 1987.

Dentan, R. C. "The Book of Malachi, Introduction and Exegesis." *The Interpreter's Bible.* Vol. 6. Nashville: Abingdon, 1956. Pp. 1117–44.

Dods, M. *The Post–Exilian Prophets: Haggai, Zechariah, Malachi.* Edinburgh: T. & T. Clark, 1983.

Glazier-MacDonald, B. *Malachi, The Divine Messenger.* Atlanta: Scholars, 1987.

Hammershaimb, E. *Some Aspects of Old Testament Prophecy from Isaiah to Malachi.* Copenhagen: Rosenkilde og Bagger, 1966.

Hanson, P. D. *The People Called: The Growth of Community in the Bible*. San Francisco: Harper & Row, 1986.

Kaiser, W. C. *Malachi: God's Unchanging Love*. Grand Rapids: Baker, 1984.

Kodell, J. *Lamentations, Haggai, Zechariah, Malachi, Obadiah, Joel, Second Zechariah, Baruch*. Wilmington: Michael Glazier, 1982.

Malchow, B. "The Messenger of the Covenant in Mal 3:1." *Journal of Biblical Literature* 103 (1984), 252–255.

Mason, R. *The Books of Haggai, Zechariah and Malachi*. Cambridge: Cambridge University Press, 1977.

Ogden, G. S. and R. R. Deutsch. *A Promise of Hope–A Call to Obedience: A Commentary on the Books of Joel and Malachi*. Grand Rapids: Eerdmans, 1987.

Smith, R. L. *Micah–Malachi*. Waco: Word, 1984.

Verhoef, P. A. *The Books of Haggai and Malachi*. Grand Rapids: Eerdmans, 1987.

VII. OLD TESTAMENT APOCALYPTIC LITERATURE

Beale, G. K. *The Use of Daniel in Jewish Apocalyptic and in the Revelation of St. John.* Lanham: University Press of America, 1984.

Brown, R. E. *The Semitic Background of the Term "Mystery" in the New Testament.* Philadelphia: Fortress, 1968.

Burkitt, F. C. *Jewish and Christian Apocalypses.* London: Published for the British Academy by H. Milford, 1914.

Collins, J. J. *The Apocalyptic Vision of the Book of Daniel.* Missoula: Scholars, 1977.

_____. *Daniel, First Maccabees, Second Maccabees, with an excursus on the Apocalyptic Genre.* Wilmington: Michael Glazier, 1981.

_____. *Daniel, with an Introduction to Apocalyptic Literature.* Grand Rapids: Eerdmans, 1984.

_____, ed. *Apocalypse: The Morphology of a Genre.* Missoula: Scholars, 1979.

_____. "Old Testament Apocalypticism and Eschatology." *The New Jerome Biblical Commentary.* Ed. by R. Brown et al. Englewood Cliffs: Prentice Hall, 1990. Pp. 298–304.

_____. *The Apocalyptic Imagination: An Introduction to the Jewish Matrix of Christianity.* New York: Crossroads, 1984.

Cross, F. M. "The Early History of the Apocalyptic Community at Qumran." *Canaanite Myth and Hebrew Epic.* Cambridge: Harvard University Press, 1973. Ch. 12.

Ferch, A. J. *The Apocalyptic "Son of Man" in Daniel 7.* Ann Arbor: University Microfilms, 1979.

Ferrar, J. *From Daniel to Saint John the Divine; A Study in Apocalypse.* London: S.P.C.K.; New York: Macmillan, 1930.

Frost, S. B. *Old Testament Apocalyptic: Its Origins and Growth.* London: Epworth, 1952.

_____. "Apocalyptic and History." *The Bible in Modern Scholarship.* J. P. Hyatt, ed. New York: Abingdon, 1963.

Funk, R. W. *Apocalypticism.* New York: Herder, 1969.

Hanson, P. D. "Apocalypse Genre; "Apocalypticism." *The Interpreter's Dictionary of the Bible.* Supplementary volume. Nashville: Abingdon, 1976. Pp. 27–34.

_____. "Apocalyptic Seers and Priests in Conflict, and the Development of the Visionary/Pragmatic Polarity." *The Diversity of Scripture: A Theological Interpretation.* Philadelphia: Fortress, 1982.

_____. *Jewish Apocalyptic against its Near Eastern Environment. Revue Biblique* 78 (1971) 31–58.

_____. *Old Testament Apocalyptic.* Nashville: Abingdon, 1987.

_____. *The Dawn of Apocalyptic.* Philadelphia: Fortress 1975.

_____, ed. *Visionaries and their Apocalypses.* London: S.P.C.K.; Philadelphia: Fortress, 1983.

_____. "Old Testament Apocalyptic Reexamined." *Interpretation* 25 (1971) 454–79.

Hellholm, D., ed. *Apocalypticism in the Mediterranean World and The Near East.* Tübingen: Mohr, 1983.

Himmelfarb, M. *Tours of Hell: An Apocalyptic Form in Jewish and Christian Literature.* Philadelphia: Fortress, 1983.

Knibb, M. A. "Prophecy and the Emergence of the Jewish Apocalypses." *Israel's Prophetic Tradition.* New York: Cambridge University Press, 1982. Pp. 155–80.

Koch, K. *The Rediscovery of Apocalyptic.* London: SCM, 1972.

Kvanvig, H. S. *Roots of the Apocalyptic: The Mesopotamian Background of the Enoch Figure and the Son of Man.* Neukirchen–Vluyn: Neukirchen, 1988.

Lamber, W. G. *The Background of Jewish Apocalyptic.* London: Athalone Press, University of London, 1978.

Millar, W. R. *Isaiah 24–27 and The Origin of Apocalyptic.* Missoula: Scholars, 1976.

Morris, L. *Apocalyptic.* 2nd ed. Grand Rapids: Eerdmans, 1974, 1972.

Mowinckel, S. *He That Cometh.* New York: Abingdon, 1956.

Nicholson, E. W. "Apocalyptic." *Tradition and Interpretation.* G. W. Anderson, ed. Oxford: Clarendon, 1979. Pp. 189–213.

Porter, F. C. *The Messages of the Apocalyptical Writers.* New York: Scribner, 1905.

Rowland, C. *The Open Heaven: A Study of Apocalyptic in Judaism and Christianity.* New York: Crossroad, 1982.

Rowley, H. H. *Jewish Apocalyptic and the Dead Sea Scrolls.* London: Athalone Press, University of London, 1957.

_____. *The Relevance of Apocalyptic.* London–Redhill: Lutterworth, 1947, 1980.

Rudman, S. S., trans. *Theocracy and Eschatology.* Oxford: Blackwell, 1968.

Russell, D. S. *Between the Testaments.* Philadelphia: Muhlenburg, 1960.

_____. *The Method and Message of Jewish Apocalyptic.* Philadelphia, Westminster, 1964.

_____. *Apocalyptic: Ancient and Modern.* Philadelphia, Fortress, 1978.

Schmithals, W. *The Apocalyptic Movement. Introduction and Interpretation.* Trans. by J. E. Steely. Nashville: Abingdon, 1975.

Sneen, D. *Visions of Hope: Apocalyptic Themes from Biblical Times.* Minneapolis: Augsburg, 1978.

Steely, J. E. *The Apocalyptic Movement.* Nashville: Abingdon, 1975.

Stone, M. E., ed. *Jewish Writings of the Second Temple Period.* Philadelphia: Fortress; Assen: Van Gorcum, 1984.

Van Wyk, W. C. *Old Testament Essays: Aspects of Apocalypticism.* Pretoria, South Africa: unknown, 1984.

Welch, A. C. *Visions of the End; a Study in Daniel and Revelation.* London: Clarke, 1958, 1922.

Wicks, H. J. *The Doctrine of God in the Jewish Apocryphal and Apocalyptic Literature.* New York: Ktav, 1971.

VIII. DEUTEROCANONICAL BOOKS

36. JUDITH

Alonzo-Schökel, L. *Ruth, Tobias, Judith, Esther. Los Libros Sagrados* VIII 99–163. Madrid: Ediciones Christiandad, 1973.

_____. "Narrative Structure In the Book of Judith." *Protocol Series of the Colloquies of the Center for Hermeneutical Studies in Hellenistic and Modern Culture* XII 17 (March, 1974).

Burns, E. J. "The Genealogy of Judith." *Catholic Biblical Quarterly* 18 (1956) 19–22.

Craghan, J. *Esther, Judith, Tobit, Jonah, Ruth.* Wilmington: Michael Glazier, 1982.

Craven T. "Artistry and Faith in the Book of Judith." *Semeia* 8 (1977) 75–101.

_____. *Artistry and Faith in the Book of Judith.* Chico: Scholars, 1983.

Dancy, J. C. *The Shorter Books of the Apocrypha: Tobit, Judith, Rest of Esther, Baruch, Letter of Jeremiah, additions to Daniel and Prayer of Manasseh.* Cambridge: University Press, 1972.

Enslin, M. S. *The Book of Judith.* Leiden: Brill, 1972.

Gaster, M. "Judith, The Book of." *Encyclopedia Biblica.* T. K. Cheyne and J.S. Black, eds. III, cols. 2642–46. New York: Macmillan, 1914.

Grintz, Y. M. "Judith, Book of." *Encyclopedia Judaica,* X. Jerusalem: Keter, 1971. Pp. 451–59.

McNeil, B. "Reflections on the Book of Judith." *The Downside Review* 96 (1978) 199–207.

Montague, G. T. *The Books of Esther and Judith.* New York: Paulist, 1973.

Moore, C. A. *Judith.* New York: Doubleday, 1985.

Nowell, I. *Jonah, Tobit, Judith.* Collegeville: The Liturgical Press, 1986.

_____, T. Craven and D. Dumm. "Tobit, Judith, Esther." *The New Jerome Biblical Commentary.* Ed. by R. Brown et al. Englewood Cliffs: Prentice Hall, 1990. Pp. 568–579.

Purdie, E. *The Story of Judith in German and English Literature.* Paris: Honoré Champien, 1927.

Wahl, T. P. *The Books of Judith and Esther.* Collegeville: The Liturgical Press, 1971.

37. TOBIT

Craghan, J. *Esther, Judith, Tobit, Jonah, Ruth.* Wilmington: Michael Glazier, 1982.

Dancy, J. C. *The Shorter Books of the Apocrypha: Tobit, Ruth, Rest of Esther, Baruch, Letter of Jeremiah, Additions to Daniel and Prayer of Manasseh.* Cambridge: University Press, 1972.

Doran, R. "Narrative Literature." *Early Judaism and Its Modern Interpreters.* R.A. Kraft and G. W. Nickelsburg, eds. Philadelphia: Fortress; Atlanta: Scholars, 1986. Pp. 287–310.

Hanhart, R., ed. *Tobit.* Gottingen: Vandenhoeck & Ruprecht, 1983.

Held, J. S. *Rembrandt and the Book of Tobit.* Northampton: Gehenna, 1964.

Montague, G. T. *The Books of Ruth and Tobit.* New York: Paulist, 1973.

Nickelsburg, G. W. *Resurrection, Immortality and Eternal Life in Intertestamental Judaism.* Cambridge: Harvard University Press, 1972.

Nowell, I. *Jonah, Tobit, Judith.* Collegeville: The Liturgical Press, 1986.

Petersen, N. R. "Tobit." *The Books of the Bible.* B. W. Anderson, ed New York: Scribner, 1949.

Sayce, A. H. *Tobit and the Babylonian Apocryphal Writings.* London Dent; Philadelphia: Lippincott, 1903.

Sloyan, G. S. *The Books of Ruth and Tobit. Introduction and Commentary.* Collegeville: The Liturgical Press, 1968.

Wheeler, F. M. *Tobit, with Notes and Aids.* St. Paul: Bethel College & Seminary, 1956.

Zimmerman, F. *The Book of Tobit.* New York: Harper, 1958.

38. BARUCH

Burke, D. G. *The Poetry of Baruch.* Chico: Scholars, 1982.

Charles, R. H. *The Apocalypse of Baruch.* London: S.P.C.K.; New York: Macmillan, 1918.

Dancy, J. C. *The Shorter Books of the Apocrypha: Tobit, Judith, Rest of Esther, Baruch, Letter of Jeremiah, additions to Daniel and Prayer of Manasseh.* Cambridge: University Press, 1972.

Ellis, P. F. *Jeremiah, Baruch.* Collegeville: The Liturgical Press, 1986.

Fitzgerald, A. "Baruch." *The New Jerome Biblical Commentary.* Ed. by R. Brown et al. Englewood Cliffs: Prentice Hall, 1990. Pp. 563–567.

Kodell, J. *Lamentations, Haggai, Zechariah, Malachi, Obadiah, Joel, Second Zechariah, Baruch.* Wilmington: Michael Glazier, 1982.

Lindberg, C. "*The Book of Baruch.*" *The Middle English Bible.* New York: Columbia University Press, 1985.

Martin, R. A. *Syntactical and Critical Concordance to the Greek Text of Baruch and the Epistle of Jeremiah.* Wooster: Biblical Research Associates, 1977.

Moore, C. A. *I Baruch. Daniel, Esther, and Jeremiah: The Additions. The Anchor Bible* 44. Garden City: Doubleday, 1977.

Murphy, F. J. *The Structure and Meaning of Second Baruch.* Atlanta: Scholars, 1985.

Robertson, E. H. *Jeremiah, Lamentations, Baruch, Ezekiel, Isaiah 40–66.* London: Mowbray, 1970.

Sayler, G. B. *Have the Promises Failed?: A Literary Analysis of II Baruch.* Chico: Scholars, 1984.

Stuhlmueller, C. *The Books of Jeremiah and Baruch.* Collegeville: The Liturgical Press, 1971.

Tox, E. *The Book of Baruch. Also called I Baruch (Greek and Hebrew).* Missoula: Scholars, 1975.

39. I & II MACCABEES

Bartlett, J. R. *The First and Second Books of Maccabees.* Cambridge: Cambridge University Press, 1973.

Bickerman, E. J. *The God of The Maccabees.* Trans. by H. Moehring. Leiden: Brill, 1979.

Collins, J. J. *Daniel, First Maccabees, Second Maccabees.* Wilmington: Michael Glazier, 1981.

Dancy, J. C. *A Commentary on I Maccabees.* Oxford: Blackwells, 1954.

Doran, R. *Temple Propaganda: The Purpose and Character of II Maccabees.* Washington: Catholic Biblical Association, 1981.

Goldstein, J. A. *I Maccabees.* Garden City: Doubleday, 1976.

_____. *II Maccabees.* Garden City: Doubleday, 1983.

Harrington, D. J. *The Maccabean Revolt. Anatomy of a Biblical Revolution.* Wilmington: Michael Glazier, 1988.

Hengel, M. *Jews, Greeks and Barbarians.* Philadelphia: Fortress, 1980.

_____. *Judaism and Hellenism.* 2 vols. Trans. by J. Bowden. Philadelphia: Fortress, 1974.

Kampen, J. *The Hasideans and the Origin of Pharisaism. A Study in I and II Maccabees.* Atlanta: Scholars, 1988.

McEleney, N. J. "I–II Maccabees." *The New Jerome Biblical Commentary.* Ed. by R. Brown et al. Englewood Cliffs: Prentice Hall, 1990. Pp. 421–446.

Schalit, A., ed. *The Hellenistic Age.* New Brunswick: Rutgers University Press, 1972.

Tcherikover, V. *Hellenistic Civilization and the Jews.* Trans. by S. Applebaum. Philadelphia: Jewish Publication Society, 1966.

Tedesche, S. and S. Zeitlin. *The First Book of Maccabees.* New York: Harper, 1950.

_____. *The Second Book of Maccabees.* New York: Harper, 1954.

40. ECCLESIASTICUS (SIRACH)

Alonso-Schökel, L. "The Vision of Man in Sirach 16:24–17:14." *Israelite Wisdom.* J. Gammie et al., eds. Missoula: Scholars, 1978. Pp. 235–245.

Beavin, E. L. "Ecclesiasticus or the Wisdom of Jesus the Son of Sirach." C. M. Laymon, ed. *The Interpreter's One Volume Commentary on the Bible.* Nashville: Abingdon, 1971. Pp. 550–76.

Burkilll, T. A. "Ecclesiasticus." *The Interpreter's Dictionary of the Bible* 2. New York–Nashville: Abingdon, 1962. Pp. 13–21.

Crenshaw, J. L. *Old Testament Wisdom.* Atlanta: John Knox, 1981.

Di Lella, A. A. *"The Wisdom of Ben Sira: A New Translation with Notes."* Garden City: Doubleday, 1987.

_____. "Sirach." *The New Jerome Biblical Commentary.* Ed. by R. Brown et al. Englewood Cliffs: Prentice Hall, 1990. Pp. 396–509.

_____. "The Wisdom of Ben Sira." *The Bible Today* 101 (1979) 154–161.

Driver, G. R. "Hebrew on the Wisdom of Jesus Ben Sirach." *Journal of Biblical Literature* 53 (1934) 273–290.

Fearghail, F. O. "Sir. 50:5–21. Yom Kippur or the Daily Whole Offering?" *Biblica.* 59 (1978) 301–316.

Hartmann, L. "Sirach in Hebrew and Greek." *Catholic Biblical Quarterly* 23 (1961) 443–451.

Jacob, E. "Wisdom and Religion in Sirach." *Israelite Wisdom.* Missoula: Scholars, 1978. Pp. 247–60.

Kearns, C. "Ecclesiasticus, on the Wisdom of Jesus the Son of Sirach." *A New Catholic Commentary on Holy Scripture.* R. C. Fuller et al., eds. London: Nelson, 1969. Pp. 541–62.

Lee, T. R. *Studies in the form of Sirach 44–50.* Atlanta: Scholars, 1986.

Lussier, E. *The Book of Proverbs and the New Book of Sirach.* Collegeville: The Liturgical Press, 1965.

Mac Kenzie, R. A. "Ben Sira as Historian." *Trinification of the World: A Festschrift in Honor of F. E. Crowe.* T. A. Dunne and J. M. Laporte, eds. Toronto: Regis College, 1978. Pp. 313–27.

_____. *Sirach.* Collegeville: Michael Glazier, 1991.

Mack, B. L. *Wisdom and the Hebrew Epic.* Chicago: University of Chicago Press, 1985.

Nelson, M. D. *The Syriac Version of the Wisdom of Ben Sira Compared to the Greek and Hebrew Materials.* Atlanta: Scholars, 1988.

Norden, R. F. *Wisdom from the Apocrypha; Selections from Ecclesiasticus.* St. Louis: Concordia, 1973.

Oesterley, W. O. "Ecclesiasticus." *Apocrypha and Pseudepigrapha of the Old Testament.* Oxford: The University Press, 1913. Pp. 268–315.

_____. *The Wisdom of Ben Sira (Ecclesiasticus).* London: S.P.C.K., 1916.

_____. *The Wisdom of Jesus the Son of Sirach or Ecclesiasticus.* Cambridge: Cambridge University, 1912.

Power, A. D. *Ecclesiasticus, or The Wisdom of Jesus, the Son of Sira.* London: Hodder & Stoughton, 1939.

_____. *The Wisdom of Jesus Son of Sirach Commonly Called Ecclesiasticus.* London: Ashendene, 1932.

Roth, L. "Ecclesiasticus in the Synagogue Service." *Journal of Biblical Literature.* 1 (1952) 171–178.

Rybolt, J. E. *Sirach.* Collegeville: The Liturgical Press, 1986.

Sanders, J. *Ben Sira and Demotic Wisdom.* Chico: Scholars, 1983.

Schmidt, N. *Ecclesiasticus. The Temple Bible.* London: Dent, 1903.

Siebeneck, R. "May Their Bones Return to Life: Sirach's Praises of the Fathers." *Catholic Biblical Quarterly* 21 (1959) 411–28.

Skehan, P. W. and A. A. Di Lella. *The Wisdom of Ben Sira.* New York: Doubleday, 1987.

Snaith, J. G. *Ecclesiasticus, on the Wisdom of Jesus Son of Sirach.* London–New York: Cambridge University Press, 1974.

Taylor, A. F. *Meditations in Ecclesiasticus.* London: Clarke, 1928.

Trenchard, W. C. *Ben Sira's View of Women: A Literary Analysis.* Chico: Scholars, 1982.

Vawter, B. *The Book of Sirach with a Commentary.* New York: Paulist, 1962.

von Rad, G. *Wisdom in Israel.* Nashville: Abingdon, 1972.

Winter, M. M. "The Origins of Ben Sira in Syriac (Part-I)." *Vetus Testamentum* 27 (1977) 237–253, 494–507.

Yadin, Y. *The Ben Sira Scroll from Masada with Introduction, Emendations and Commentary.* Jerusalem: Israel Exploration Society, 1965.

41. WISDOM OF SOLOMON

Amir, Y. "The Figure of Death in the Book of Wisdom." *Journal of Jewish Studies* 30 (1979) 154–178.

Caird, G. B. "New Wine in Old Wineskins: I Wisdom." *The Expository Times* 84 (1973) 164–168.

Clarke, E. G. *The Wisdom of Solomon.* Cambridge: University Press, 1973.

Cragan, J. F. *Esther, Judith, Tobit, Jonah, Ruth.* Wilmington: Michael Glazier, 1982.

Geyer, J. *The Wisdom of Solomon.* London: SCM, 1963.

Gregg, J. A. *The Wisdom of Solomon.* Cambridge: University Press, 1909.

Heidt, W. G. *The Canticle of Canticles. The Book of Wisdom.* Collegeville: Human Life Center, 1979.

Kuntz, J. K. "Retribution Motif in Psalmic Wisdom." *Zeitschrift für die AlttesamentlicheWissenschaft* 89 (1977) 223–233.

Maly, E. H. "The Wisdom of Solomon." *The Bible Today* 18 (1980) 154–159.

Maly, E. *The Book of Wisdom.* New York: Paulist, 1961.

Oesterley, W. O. *The Wisdom of Solomon.* London: S.P.C.K.; New York: Macmillan, 1917.

Reese, J. M. *Hellenistic Influence on the Book of Wisdom and Its Consequences.* Rome: Pontifical Biblical Institute, 1970.

_____. *The Book of Wisdom, Song of Songs.* Collegeville: Michael Glazier, 1991.

Reider, J. *The Book of Wisdom.* New York: Harper, 1957.

Rybolt, J. E. *Wisdom.* Collegeville: The Liturgical Press, 1986.

Skehan, P. W. "Ecclesiasticus." *The Interpreter's Dictionary of the Bible.* Supplementary Volume. Nashville: Abingdon, 1976. Pp. 250–251.

Schoenbechler, R. *The Book of Wisdom: An Interpretative Version in Measured Rhythm.* Collegeville: The Liturgical Press, 1975.

Whedbee, J. W. *Isaiah and Wisdom.* Nashville: Abingdon, 1971.

Winston, D. *The Wisdom of Solomon.* Garden City: Doubleday, 1979.

Wright, A. G. "Wisdom." *The Jerome Biblical Commentary.* Ed. by R. Brown et al. Englewood Cliffs: Prentice-Hall, 1968. Pp. 556–558.

_____. "Wisdom." *The New Jerome Biblical Commentary.* Ed. by R. Brown et al. Englewood Cliffs: Prentice Hall, 1990. Pp. 510–522.

IX. OLD TESTAMENT THEOLOGY

42. OLD TESTAMENT THEOLOGY: GENERAL

Achtemeier, P. *The Old Testament Roots of Our Faith.* Philadelphia: Fortress, 1979.

Anderson, B. W. *Creation versus Chaos.* New York: Association, 1967; Philadelphia: Fortress, 1987.

_____. *The Old Testament and the Christian Faith.* New York: Harper & Row, 1963.

Anderson, G. W., ed. *Tradition and Interpretation.* Essays by Members of the Society for Old Testament Study. Oxford: Clarendon, 1979.

_____. "Israel: Amphictyony: `Am; Kâhâl; `Edah." *Translating and Understanding the Old Testament.* Ed. by H. T. Frank and W. L. Reed. New York: Abingdon, 1970. Pp. 135–151.

Barr, J. *Old and New Interpretation.* New York: Harper & Row, 1966.

_____. "Story and History in Biblical Theology." *Journal of Religion* 56 (1976) 1–17.

Barth, K. *Deliverance to the Captives.* San Francisco: Harper & Row, 1978.

Blenkinsopp, J. *Prophecy and Canon.* Notre Dame–London: University of Notre Dame Press, 1977.

Brueggemann, W. "Old Testament Theology as a Particular Conversation: Adjudication of Israel's Socio–Theological Alternatives." *Theology Digest* 32 (1985) 303–306.

_____. "Futures in Old Testament Theology." *Horizons in Biblical Theology* 6 (1984) 1–11.

_____. "A Shape for Old Testament Theology, I: Structure Legitimation." *Catholic Biblical Quarterly* 47 (1985) 28–46.

_____. "A Shape for Old Testament Theology, II: Embrace of Pain." *Catholic Biblical Quarterly* 47 (1987) 395–415.

_____. *In Man We Trust: The Neglected Side of Biblical Faith.* Richmond: John Knox, 1973.

Carroll, D. *A Pilgrim God for a Pilgrim People.* Dublin: Gill & Macmillan, 1988; Wilmington: Michael Glazier, 1989.

Childs, B. *Biblical Theology in Crisis.* Philadelphia: Westminster, 1970.

Childs, B. *Old Testament Theology in a Canonical Context.* Philadelphia: Fortress, 1990.

Clements, R. E. *Old Testament Theology: A Fresh Approach.* Atlanta: John Knox, 1978.

Dake, F. J., Sr. *God's Plan for Man.* Lawrenceville: Dake Bible Sales, 1949.

Dentan, R. C. *Preface to Old Testament Theology.* New Haven: Yale, 1950; New York: Seabury, 1963.

DeVries, S. J. *The Achievements of Biblical Religion: A Prolegomenon to Old Testament Theology.* Lanham: University Press of America, 1983.

Dyrness, W. A. *Themes in Old Testament Theology.* Downers Grove: Inter–Varsity, 1979.

Eichrodt, W. *Theology of the Old Testament.* 2 vols. Philadelphia: Westminster, 1961. Vol. II, 1967.

Frontain, R. J. and J. Wojcik, eds. *The David Myth in Western Literature.* West Lafayette: Purdue University Press, 1980.

Gaster, T. H. *Myth, Legend and Custom in the Old Testament.* 2 vols. New York: Harper & Row, 1975.

Gese, H. *Essays on Biblical Theology.* Minneapolis: Augsburg, 1981.

Hasel, G. F. *Old Testament Theology: Basic Issues in the Current Debate.* Grand Rapids: Eerdmans, 1972, rev. ed. 1975.

Hayes, J. H. and F. Prussner. *Old Testament Theology, Its History and Development.* Atlanta: John Knox, 1985.

Herberg, W. "Biblical Faith as Heilsgeschichte: The Meaning of Redemptive History in Human Existence." *Faith Enacted as History: Essays in Biblical Theology.* B. W. Anderson, ed. Philadelphia: Westminster, 1976. Pp. 32–42.

Hogenhaven, J. *Problems and Prospects of Old Testament Theology.* Sheffield: JSOT Press, 1987.

Hyatt, J. P., ed. *The Bible in Modern Scholarship.* Nashville: Abingdon, 1965.

Jacob, E. *Theology of the Old Testament.* New York: Harper, 1958.

Kelsey, D. H. *The Uses of Scripture in Recent Theology.* Philadelphia: Fortress, 1975.

Knight, D. *Tradition and Theology in the Old Testament.* Philadelphia: Fortress, 1977.

Knight, G. A. *A Christian Theology of the Old Testament.* Richmond: John Knox, 1959.

Kohler, L. H. *Old Testament Theology.* London: Lutterworth Press, 1957.

Laurin, R. B. *Contemporary Old Testament Theologians.* Valley Forge: Judson, 1970.

McKenzie, J. *Myths and Realities: Studies in Biblical Theology.* Milwaukee: Bruce, 1963.

_____. *The Two-Edged Sword: An Interpretation of the Old Testament.* Garden City: Doubleday, 1956.

Meyers, C. L. and M. O'Connor, eds. *The Word of the Lord Shall Go Forth.* Winona Lake: Eisenbrauns, 1983.

Niebuhr, H. R. *The Meaning of Revelation.* New York: Macmillan, 1941.

Otzen, B., et al. *Myths in the Old Testament.* London: SCM, 1980.

Rogerson, J. W. *Myth in Old Testament Interpretation.* BZAW 134. Berlin–New York: de Gruyter, 1974.

Rowley, H. H. *The Faith of Israel.* Philadelphia: Westminster, 1957.

Schmidt, W. H. *The Faith of the Old Testament.* Philadelphia: Westminster, 1983.

Sheehan, J. F. *The Threshing Floor.* New York: Paulist, 1972.

Snaith, N. H. *The Distinctive Ideas of the Old Testament.* London: Epworth, 1944.

Spriggs, D. G. *Two Old Testament Theologies.* Naperville: Allenson, 1974.

Stadelmann, L. I. *The Hebrew Conception of the World: A Philological and Literary Study.* Rome: Biblical Institute Press, 1970.

van Imschoot, P. *Theology of the Old Testament. Vol. I: God.* New York: Descleé, 1965.

Voegelin, E. *Israel and Revelation.* Baton Rouge: Louisiana State University Press, 1956.

von Rad, G. *God at Work in Israel.* Nashville: Abingdon, 1980.

_____. *Old Testament Theology.* 2 vols. New York: Harper & Row, 1962, 1965.

Vriezen, T. C. *An Outline of Old Testament Theology.* 2nd ed. rev. and enlarged Newton: Branford, 1970.

Westermann, C. *Elements of Old Testament Theology.* Atlanta: John Knox, 1982.

Wilson, R. R. *Sociological Approaches to the Old Testament.* Philadelphia: Fortress, 1984.

Wood, C. M. *The Formation of Christian Understanding.* Philadelphia: Westminster, 1981.

Wright, G. E. *"God Who Acts: Biblical Theology as Recital. Studies in Biblical Theology."* Vol. 8. London: SCM, 1952.

Wright, G. E. *The Old Testament and Theology.* New York: Harper & Row, 1969.

Zimmerli, W. *Old Testament Theology in Outline.* Atlanta: John Knox, 1978.

_____. *The Old Testament and the World.* Atlanta: John Knox, 1976.

43. THEOLOGIES OF THE OLD TESTAMENT

Anderson, B. W., ed. *Creation in the Old Testament.* Philadelphia: Fortress, 1984.

Becker, J. *Messianic Expectations in the Old Testament.* Philadelphia: Fortress, 1980.

Beier, U. *Origin of Life and Death.* London: Heinemann, 1966, 1982.

Bright, J. *The Kingdom of God.* Nashville: Abingdon-Cokesbury, 1953.

Bruce, F. F. *New Testament Development of Old Testament Themes.* Grand Rapids: Eerdmans, 1968.

Brueggemann, W. "A Convergence in Recent Old Testament Theologies." *Journal for the Study of the Old Testament* 18 (1980) 2–18.

Byrne, B. *"Sons of God"—Seed of Abraham."* Rome: Biblical Institute Press, 1979.

Coggins, R. J. *Samaritans and Jews.* Atlanta: John Knox, 1975.

Davidson, R. *The Courage to Doubt: Exploring an Old Testament Theme.* London: SCM, 1983.

Drane, J. W. *Old Testament Faith.* New York: Harper, 1986.

Eichrodt, W. *Theology of the Old Testament.* Eng. tr. *Old Testament Library.* Philadelphia: Westminster, Vol. I, 1961, Vol. II, 1967.

Goldberg, M. *Theology and Narrative. A Critical Introduction.* Nashville: Abingdon, 1982.

Gunnel, A. *Determining the Destiny, PQD in the Old Testament.* Lund: Gleerup, 1980.

Hals, R. *Grace and Faith in the Old Testament.* Minneapolis: Augsburg, 1980.

Hanson, P. D. *The Diversity of Scripture, A Theological Interpretation.* Philadelphia: Fortress, 1982.

Hasel, G. *Old Testament Theology: Basic Issues in the Current Debate.* Grand Rapids: Eerdmans, 1975.

Hendry, G. S. *Theology of Nature.* Philadelphia: Westminster, 1980.

Hinson, D. *Old Testament Introduction 3. Theology of the Old Testament.* Theological Education Fund Study Guides, 15. London: S.P.C.K., 1976.

Hogenhaven, J. *Problems and Prospects of Old Testament Theology.* Sheffield, England: JSOT Press, Sheffield Academic Press, 1987.

Hummel, H. D. *The Word Becoming Flesh. An Introduction to the Origin, Purpose, and Meaning of the Old Testament.* St. Louis: Concordia, 1979.

Humphreys, W. L. *The Tragic Vision and the Hebrew Tradition.* Philadelphia: Fortress, 1985.

Jacob, E. *Theology of the Old Testament.* Eng. tr. London: Hodder & Stoughton, 1958.

Kaiser, W. *Toward an Old Testament Theology.* Grand Rapids: Zondervan, 1978.

Levenson, J. D. *Creation and the Persistence of Evil.* San Francisco: Harper & Row, 1988.

Lohfink, N. *Great Themes from the Old Testament.* Chicago: Franciscan; Edinburgh: Clark, 1982.

McKenzie, J. *A Theology of the Old Testament.* Garden City: Doubleday, 1974.

McKim, D. *What Christians Believe About the Bible.* Nashville: Nelson, 1985.

Muilenberg, J. *The Way of Israel: Biblical Faith and Ethics.* San Francisco: Harper & Row, 1961.

Parker, T. H. *Calvin's Old Testament Commentaries.* Edinburgh: Clark, 1986.

Reventlow, H. G. *Problems of Old Testament Theology in the Twentieth Century.* Philadelphia: Fortress, 1985.

Ringgren, H. *The Messiah in the Old Testament.* London: SCM, 1956.

Robinson, H. W. *Religious Ideas of the Old Testament.* London: Duckworth; New York: Scribner, 1913.

Schneidau, H. N. *Sacred Discontent. The Bible and Western Tradition.* Berkeley: University of California Press, 1976.

Theissen, Gerd. *Biblical Faith: An Evolutionary Approach.* Philadelphia: Fortress, 1985.

van Imschoot, P. *Theology of the Old Testament* 2 vols. New York: Descleé, 1965.

Viviano, B. T. *The Kingdom of God in History.* Wilmington: Michael Glazier, 1988.

von Rad, G. *Old Testament Theology.* Eng. tr. Edinburgh–London: Oliver & Boyd; New York: Harper & Row, Vol. I, 1962; Vol. II, 1965.

Vriezen, T. C. *An Outline of Old Testament Theology.* 2nd Eng. ed. Wageningen: Veenman, 1970.

Wright, G. E. *The Old Testament Against Its Environment.* London: SCM, 1950.

_____. *The Old Testament and Theology.* Harper & Row, 1969.

44. ANTHROPOLOGY

Blumenthal, W. B. *The Creator and Man.* Lanham: University Press of America, 1980.

Boer, H. R. *An Ember Still Glowing: Humankind as the Image of God.* Grand Rapids: Eerdmans, 1989.

Clements, R. E. *The World of Ancient Israel: Sociological, Anthropological and Political Perspectives.* Cambridge: Cambridge University Press, 1989.

Cooper, J. W. *Body, Soul and Life Everlasting.* Grand Rapids: Eerdmans, 1989.

Culley, R. C. and T. W. Overholt, eds. *Anthropological Perspectives on Old Testament Prophecy. Semeia* 21. Chico: Scholars, 1982.

Engel, M. P. *John Calvin's Perspectival Anthropology.* Atlanta: Scholars, 1989.

Eslinger, L. and G. Taylor. *Ascribe to the Lord: Biblical & Other Studies in Memory of Peter C. Cragie.* Sheffield: JSOT Press, 1988.

Frankfurt, H., H. A. Frankfurt et al. *The Intellectual Adventure of Ancient Man.* Chicago: University of Chicago Press, 1946. Reprinted as *Before Philosophy.* New York: Penguin, 1949.

Gowan, D. E. *When Man Becomes God. Humanism and Hybris in the Old Testament.* Pittsburgh: Pickwick, 1975.

Jacobson, D. *The Social Background of the Old Testament.* Cincinnati: Hebrew Union College Press, 1942.

Janzen, W. *Still in the Image. Essays in Biblical Theology and Anthropology.* Newton: Faith and Life; Winnipeg: CMBC, 1982.

Lang, B. *Anthropological Approach to the Old Testament. Issues in Religion and Theology Series.* Philadelphia: Fortress, 1985.

Oden, R. A., Jr. *The Bible Without Theology. The Theological Tradition and Alternatives to It.* New York: Harper, 1987.

Rogerson, J. W. *Anthropology and the Old Testament.* London: Blackwell, 1978.

Steck, O. H. *World and Environment.* Nashville: Abingdon, 1980.

Wolff, H. W. *Anthropology of the Old Testament.* Philadelphia: Fortress, 1974, 1981.

45. FAMILY LIFE

Barrick, B. and J. R. Spencer. *In the Shelter of Elyon: Essays of Ancient Palestinian Life and Literature in Honor of G. W. Ahlstrom.* Sheffield: JSOT Press, 1984.

Brennan, R. *Man and Wife in Scripture.* New York: Herder, 1964.

Coleman, W. L. *Today's Handbook of Bible Times and Customs.* Minneapolis: Bethany, 1984.

Cross, E. B. *The Hebrew Family: A Study in Historical Sociology.* Chicago: The University of Chicago Press, 1927.

Deen, E. *The Family in the Bible.* San Francisco: Harper & Row, 1978.

Dulin, R. Z. *A Crown of Glory: A Biblical View of Aging.* Mahwah: Paulist, 1988.

Frick, F. S. *The City in Ancient Israel.* Missoula: Scholars, 1977.

Hanson, P. D. *The People Called. The Growth of Community in the Bible.* San Francisco: Harper & Row, 1987.

Harrington, W. J. *The Promise to Love; A Scriptural View of Marriage.* Staten Island: Alba, 1968.

Harris, J. G. *Biblical Perspective on Aging.* Philadelphia: Fortress, 1987.

Heaton, E. W. *Everyday Life in Old Testament Times.* Batsford: Scribner's, 1956, 1977.

Luck, W. F. *Divorce and Remarriage: Recovering the Biblical View.* 1st ed. San Francisco: Harper & Row, 1987.

Mace, D. R. *Hebrew Marriage. A Sociological Study.* New York: Philosophical Library, 1953.

Matthews, V. H. *Manners and Customs in the Bible.* Peabody: Hendrickson, 1988.

Patai, R. *Sex and Family in the Bible and the Middle East.* Garden City: Doubleday, 1959.

Porter, J. R. *The Extended Family in the Old Testament.* London: Edutext, 1967.

Schelke, K. H. *The Spirit and the Bride: Woman in the Bible.* Collegeville: The Liturgical Press, 1979.

Strange, M. R. *Couples of The Bible.* Notre Dame: Fides, 1963.

Vollegregt, G. N. *The Bible on Marriage.* London–Melbourne–New York: Sheed & Ward, 1965.

Wiseman, D. J., ed. *Peoples of the Old Testament Times.* London–New York: Oxford University Press, 1973.

46. POLITICS

Boecker, H. J. *Law and the Administration of Justice in the Old Testament.* Minneapolis: Augsburg, 1980.

Carpenter, S. C. *Politics and Society in the Old Testament.* London: Williams & Norgate, 1931.

Christensen, D. L. *Transformations of the War Oracle in Old Testament Prophecy.* Missoula: Scholars, 1978.

Coote, R. and M. Coote. *Power, Politics, and Making the Bible: An Introduction.* Philadelphia: Fortress, 1990.

Craigie, P. C. *The Problem of War in the Old Testament.* Grand Rapids: Eerdmans, 1978.

Frick, F. S. *The Formation of the State in Ancient Israel.* Decatur: Almond Press, 1985.

Gottwald, N. K. *The Bible and Liberation Political and Social Hermeneutics.* Maryknoll: Orbis, 1983.

Gray, J. *The Biblical Doctrine of the Reign of God.* Edinburgh: Clark, 1979.

Hobbs, T. R. *A Time for War. A Study of Warfare in the Old Testament.* Wilmington: Michael Glazier, 1988.

Mettinger, T. N. *King and Messiah. The Civil and Sacral Legislation of the Israelite Kings.* Lund: Gleerup, 1976.

Patrick, D., ed. *Thinking Biblical Law. Semeia* 45. Atlanta: Scholars, 1989.

Priest, J. E. *Governmental and Judicial Ethics in the Bible and Rabbinic Literature.* New York: Ktav, 1980.

Rosenberg, J. *King and Kin: Political Allegory in the Hebrew Bible.* Bloomington: Indiana University, 1986.

Smith, M. *Palestinian Parties and Politics that Shaped the Old Testament.* New York: Columbia University Press, 1971.

von Rad, G. *Holy War in Ancient Israel.* Grand Rapids: Eerdmans, 1990.

Walsh, J. P. *The Mighty From Their Thrones.* Philadelphia: Fortress, 1987.

————. *Ways Towards Oneness: A Study in the Unity of the People of God in the Old Testament.* London: S.P.C.K., 1966.

Whitelam, K. *The Just King: Monarchial Judicial Authority in Ancient Israel.* Sheffield: JSOT Press, 1979.

47. WOMEN/FEMINIST HERMENEUTICS

Aschkenasy, N. *Eve's Journey: Feminine Images in Hebraic Literary Tradition.* Philadelphia: University of Pennsylvania Press, 1986.

Bilezikian, G. *Beyond Sex Roles: A Guide for the Study of Female Roles in the Bible.* Grand Rapids: Baker, 1985.

Bloesch, D. G. *Is the Bible Sexist?: Beyond Feminism and Patriarchalism.* Westchester: Crossway, 1982.

Brenner, A. *The Israelite Woman: Social Role and Literary Type in Biblical Narrative.* Sheffield: JSOT Press, 1985.

Bushnell, K. C. *God's Word to Women: 100 Bible Studies on Woman's place in the Divine Economy* Reprinted. North Collins: Munson, 1976.

Buswell, S. *The Challenge of Old Testament Women: A Guide for Bible Study Groups.* Grand Rapids: Baker, 1986.

Cady, S., M. Ronan and H. Taussig. *Wisdom's Feast. Sophia in Study and Celebration.* San Francisco: Harper & Row, 1989.

Camp, C. V. *Wisdom and The Feminine in the Book of Proverbs.* Decatur: Almond Press, 1985.

Carlisle, T. J. *Eve and After: Old Testament Women in Portrait.* Grand Rapids: Eerdmans, 1984.

Carmody, D. L. *Biblical Woman: Feminist Reflections on Scriptural Texts.* New York: Crossroad, 1988.

_____. *Biblical Women: Contemporary Reflections on Scriptural Texts.* New York: Crossroads, 1988.

Carmichael, C. M. *Women, Law, and the Genesis Traditions.* Edinburgh: Edinburgh University Press, 1979.

Cox, J. N. *Fore-Mothers, Women of the Bible.* New York: Seabury, 1981.

Day, P. L. *Gender and Difference in Ancient Israel.* Philadelphia: Fortress, 1989.

Deen, E. *All of the Women of the Bible.* New York: Harper & Row, 1955.

_____. *The Bible's Legacy for Womanhood.* Garden City: Double-day, 1969, 1970.

_____. *Wisdom from Women in the Bible.* San Francisco: Harper & Row, 1978.

de Fraine, J. *Women of the Old Testament.* Trans. by F. L. Ingram. De Pere: St. Norbert Abbey, 1968.

Drimmer, F. *Daughters of Eve; Women in the Bible.* Norwalk: C. R. Gibson, 1975.

Elizondo, V. and N. Greinacher, eds. *Women in a Man's Church. Concilium* 134. New York: Seabury, 1980.

Emswiler, S. N. *The Ongoing Journey: Women and the Bible.* New York: Women's Division, Board of Global Ministries, United Methodist Church, 1977.

Evans, M. J. *Woman in the Bible.* Exeter–Paternoster, 1983.

_____. *Woman in the Bible: an Overview of All the Crucial Passages on Women's Roles.* Downers Grove: Inter–Varsity, 1983.

Fiorenza, E. S. *Bread Not Stone: The Challenge of Feminist Biblical Interpretation.* Boston: Beacon, 1984.

_____. "Feminist Theology as a Critical Theology of Liberation." *Theological Studies.* 36, 4 (1975) 605–26.

_____. *In Memory of Her: A Feminist Theological Reconstruction of Christian Origins.* New York: Crossroads, 1983.

Fontaine, C. R. *Traditional Sayings in the Old Testament: A Contextual Study.* Sheffield: Almond Press, 1982.

Gladson, J. A. "The Role of Women in the Old Testament Outside the Pentateuch." *Symposium on the Role of Women in the Church.* J. Neuffer. Plainfield: General Council of Seventh Day Adventists, 1984. Pp. 46–61.

Harris, K. *Sex, Ideology and Religion: The Representation of Women in the Bible.* Totowa: Barnes & Noble, 1984.

Hartsoe, C. I. *Dear Daughter, Letters from Eve and other Women of the Bible.* Wilton: Morehouse-Barlow, 1981.

Hayter, M. *The New Eve in Christ: The Use and Abuse of the Bible in the Debate about Women in the Church.* Grand Rapids: Eerdmans, 1987.

Ide, A. F. *Woman in Ancient Israel Under the Torah and Talmud: with a translation and Critical Commentary on Genesis 1–3.* Mesquite: Ide, 1982.

Jensen, M. E. *Bible Women Speak to Us Today.* Minneapolis: Augsburg, 1983.

Kirk, M. A. *Celebrations of Biblical Women's Stories: Tears, Milk and Honey.* Kansas City, MO: Sheed & Ward, 1987.

LaCocque, A. *The Feminine Unconventional: Four Subversive Figures in Israel's Tradition.* Philadelphia: Fortress, 1990.

Lesko, Barbara S., ed. *Woman's Earliest Records. From Ancient Egypt and Western Asia.* Atlanta: Scholars, 1989.

Lockyer, H. *All the Women of the Bible: The Life and Time of All the Women of the Bible.* Grand Rapids: Zondervan, 1978.

Malchow, B. " Postexilic Defense of Women." *The Bible Today* 23 (1985) 325–331.

Mickelson, A., ed. *Women, Authority & The Bible.* Downers Grove: Inter–Varsity, 1986.

Mollenkott, V. R. *Godding: Human Responsibility and the Bible.* New York: Crossroads, 1987.

————. *The Divine Feminine.* New York: Crossroads, 1983.

————. *Women, Men and the Bible.* Nashville: Abingdon, 1977.

Moloney, F. *Women, First among the Faithful.* Notre Dame: Ave Maria, 1986.

Mulliken, F. H. *Women of Destiny in the Bible.* Independence: Herald, 1978.

Musgrove, P. *Who's Who Among Bible Women.* Springfield: Gospel Publishing, 1981.

Myers, C. *Discovering Eve: Ancient Israelite Women in Context.* New York: Oxford University Press, 1988.

Otwell, J. H. *And Sarah Laughed. The Status of Women in the Old Testament*. Philadelphia: Westminster Press, 1977.

Pape, D. R. *God & Women*. London–Oxford: Mowbrays, 1976.

Pobee, J. S., and Barbel von Wartenberg-Potter. *New Eyes for Reading. Biblical and Theological Reflections by Women from the Third World*. Bloomington: Meyer Stone, 1989.

Roddy, L. *Intimate Portraits of Women in the Bible*. Chappaqua: Christian World Books, Christian Herald, 1980.

Ruether, R. R. *Religion and Sexism: Images of Women in the Jewish and Christian Traditions*. New York: Simon & Schuster, 1974.

_____. *Mary, the Feminine Face of the Church*. Philadelphia: Westminster, 1977.

_____. *New Woman/New Earth: Sexist Ideologies and Human Liberation*. New York: Seabury, 1975.

_____. *Sexism and God-Talk: Towards a Feminist Theology*. Boston: Beacon, 1983.

Russell, L. M., ed. *Feminist Interpretation of the Bible*. Philadelphia: Westminster, 1989.

Selvidge, M. J. *Daughters of Jerusalem*. Scottdale: Herald, 1987.

Sheffield, A. B. *The Israelite Woman: Social Role and Literary Type in Biblical Narrative*. Sheffield: JSOT Press, 1985.

Stanton, C. *The Woman's Bible*. New York: Arno, 1974.

Stendahl, K. *The Bible and the Role of Women: A Case Study in Hermeneutics*. Philadelphia: Fortress, 1966.

Swidler, L. J. *Biblical Affirmations of Woman*. Philadelphia: Westminster, 1979.

_____. *Women in Judaism: The Status of Women in Formative Judaism*. Metuchen: Scarecrow, 1976.

Terrien, S. *Till the Heart Sings: A Biblical Theology of Manhood and Womanhood*. Philadelphia: Fortress, 1985.

The Bible's Legacy for Womanhood. Garden City: Doubleday, 1969, 1970.

Tischler, N. M. *Legacy of Eve: Women of the Bible.* Atlanta: John Knox, 1977.

Tolbert, M. A. "Defining The Problem: The Bible and Feminist Hermeneutics," *Semeia* 28 (1983) 110–119.

Trible, P. *God and the Rhetoric of Sexuality.* Philadelphia: Fortress, 1978.

_____. *Texts of Terror. Literary-Feminist Readings of Biblical Narratives.* Philadelphia: Fortress, 1984.

Vine, K. L. "The Legal and Social Status of Women in the Pentateuch." *Symposium on the Role of Women in the Church.* J. Neuffer. Plainfield: General Council of Seventh Day Adventists, 1984. Pp. 28–45.

Williams, J. G. *Women Recounted: Narrative Thinking and the God of Israel.* Sheffield, England: Almond Press, 1982.

World Council of Churches. *Stories of Women Today and in the Bible.* Geneva, 1985.

Zylstra, H. *Women of the Old Testament; Fifty Meditations.* Grand Rapids: Zondervan, 1933.

48. WORSHIP/PRIESTHOOD

Anderson, G. A. *Sacrifices and Offerings in Ancient Israel: Studies in Their Social and Political Importance.* Atlanta: Scholars, 1987.

Andreasen, N. E. *The Old Testament Sabbath: A Tradition-Historical Investigation.* Missoula: Scholars, 1972.

Bloch, A. P. *The Biblical and Historical Background of Jewish Customs and Ceremonies.* New York: Ktav, 1980.

_____. *The Biblical and Historical Background of the Jewish Holy Days.* New York: Ktav, 1978.

Bourdillon, M. F. and M. Fortes. *Sacrifice.* Sheffield: Sheffield Academic Press, 1980.

Castelot, J. J. and A. Cody. "Religious Institutions of Israel." *The New Jerome Biblical Commentary.* Ed. by R. Brown et al. Englewood Cliffs: Prentice Hall, 1990. Pp. 1253–1283.

Cody, A. *A History of Old Testament Priesthood.* Rome: Biblical Institute Press, 1969.

_____. *Ezekiel* (with an excursus on Old Testament priesthood). Wilmington: Michael Glazier, 1984.

Cragan, J. F. *Love and Thunder: A Spirituality of the Old Testament.* Collegeville: The Liturgical Press, 1983.

Cumming, C. G. *The Assyrian and Hebrew Hymns of Praise.* New York: Columbia University Press, 1934.

Daly, R. J. *The Origins of the Christian Doctrine of Sacrifice.* Philadelphia: Fortress, 1978.

DeVaux, R. *Ancient Israel, Its Life and Institutions.* Trans. by J. McHugh. New York: McGraw Hill, 1961.

_____. *Studies in Old Testament Sacrifice.* Cardiff: University of Wales Press, 1964.

Eaton, J. H. *Vision in Worship. The Relation of Prophecy and Liturgy in the Old Testament.* London: S.P.C.K.; New York: Seabury, 1981.

Endres, J. *Temple, Monarchy & Word of God.* Wilmington: Michael Glazier, 1988.

Feldman, E. *Biblical and Post-Biblical Defilement and Mourning: Law as Theology.* New York: Ktav, 1977.

Fox, M. V., ed. *Temple in Society.* Winona Lake: Eisenbrauns, 1988.

Gammie, J. G. *Holiness In Israel.* Minneapolis: Fortress, 1989.

Gray, G. B. *Sacrifice in the Old Testament.* Oxford: Clarendon, 1925.

Greenberg, M. *Biblical Prose Prayer as a Window to the Popular Religion of Ancient Israel.* Berkeley: University of California Press, 1983.

Haldar, A. O. *Associations of Cult Prophets Among the Ancient Semites.* Uppsala: Almqvist & Wiksells, 1945.

Haran, M. *Temples and Temple-service in Ancient Israel: An Inquiry Into the Character of Cult Phenomena and the Historical Setting of the Priestly School.* Oxford: Clarendon, 1978.

Harrelson, W. J. *From Fertility Cult to Worship.* Garden City: Doubleday, 1970; Atlanta: Scholars, 1980.

Heschel, A. *The Sabbath: Its Meaning for Modern Man.* New York: Farrar, Strauss & Giroux, 1951, 1975.

Johnson, A. R. *Sacral Kingship in Ancient Israel.* Cardiff: University of Wales Press, 1967.

_____. *The Cultic Prophet and Israel's Psalmody.* Cardiff: University of Wales Press, 1979.

Kiuchi, N. *The Purificiation Offering in the Priestly Literature: Its Meaning and Function.* Sheffield: JSOT Press, Sheffield Academic Press, 1987.

Kraus, H. J. *Worship in Israel.* Trans. by G. Buswell. Richmond: John Knox, 1966.

Kurtz, J. H. *Sacrificial Worship of the Old Testament.* Grand Rapids: Baker, 1980.

Malchow, B. *"The Authority of the Priest as an Advisor." Schola* 1 (1978) 51–60.

Mitchell, C. W. *The Meaning of BRK "To Bless" in the Old Testament.* Atlanta: Scholars, 1987.

Ofslager, K. H. *The Relationship Between Priesthood and Prophecy in the Old Testament.* Philadelphia: Westminster, 1974.

Ollenburger, B. C. *Holiness in Israel.* Minneapolis: Fortress, 1989.

_____. *Zion, The City of the Great King: A Theological Investigation of Zion Symbolism in the Tradition of the Jerusalem Cult.* Ann Arbor: University Microfilms, 1983.

Otto, E. and T. Schramm. *Festival and Joy.* Nashville: Abingdon, 1980.

Otto, R. *The Idea of the Holy.* 2nd ed. London: Oxford University Press, 1950.

Pfeiffer, R. H. *Religion in the Old Testament.* New York: Harper & Row, 1961.

Ringgren, H. *Israelite Religion.* Philadelphia: Fortress, 1966.

Rowley, H. H. *Worship in Ancient Israel.* Philadelphia: Fortress, 1967.

Snaith, N. H. *The Jewish New Year Festival.* London: S.P.C.K., 1947.

Welch, A. C. *Prophet and Priest in Old Israel.* London: SCM, 1936; New York: Macmillan, 1953.

Westermann, C. *Blessing in the Bible and the Life of the Church.* Philadelphia: Fortress, 1978.

49. VARIOUS THEMES

a. God

Albrektson, B. *History and the Gods. An essay on the idea of historical events as divine manifestations in the ancient Near East and in Israel.* Lund: Gleerup, 1967.

Alt, A. "The God of the Fathers." *Essays on Old Testament History and Religion.* Garden City: Doubleday, 1967. Pp. 1–100.

Bahy, D. *God and History in the Old Testament.* San Francisco: Harper & Row, 1976.

Balentine, S. E. *The Hidden Good. The Hiding of the Face of God in the Old Testament.* Oxford: University Press, 1983.

Barthelemy, D. *God and His Image.* New York: Harper & Row, 1966.

Blumenthal, D. R. *God at the Center, Meditations on Jewish Spirituality.* San Francisco: Harper & Row, 1988.

Boyce, R. N. *The Cry to God in the Old Testament.* Atlanta: Scholars, 1988.

Brueggemann, W. "Israel's Social Criticism and Yahweh's Sexuality." *Journal of the American Academy of Religion* 45 (1977) 349.

Campbell, J. *The Masks of God.* New York: Viking, 1959.

Cassuto, U., ed. *The Goddess Anath: Canaanite Epics of the Patriarchal Age.* Jerusalem: Magnes, 1951.

Chestnut, J. S. *The Old Testament Understanding of God.* Philadelphia: Westminster, 1968.

Clements, R. E. *God and Temple.* Philadelphia: Fortress, 1965.

Clines, D. "Yahweh and the God of Christian Theology." *Theology* 83 (1980) 323–30.

Crenshaw, J. *A Whirlpool of Torment: Israelite Traditions of God As An Oppressive Presence.* Philadelphia: Fortress, 1984.

_____. *Theodicy in the Old Testament.* Philadelphia: Fortress; London: S.P.C.K., 1983.

_____. "Popular Questioning of the Justice of God in Ancient Israel." *Zeitschrift für die Alttestamentliche Wissenschaft* 82 (1970) 380–95.

Cross, F. M., W. E. Lemke and P. D. Miller, eds. *Magnalia Dei: The Mighty Acts of God.* Garden City: Doubleday, 1976.

Danell, G. A. *Studies in the Name Israel in the Old Testament.* Uppsala: Appelbergs, 1946.

Dentan, R. C. *The Knowledge of God in Ancient Israel.* New York: Seabury, 1968.

Engelsman, J. C. *The Feminine Dimension of the Divine.* Philadelphia: Westminster, 1979.

Fretheim, T. *The Suffering of God: An Old Testament Perspective.* Philadelphia: Fortress Press, 1984.

Gammie, J. G. *Holiness in Israel.* Minneapolis: Fortress, 1989.

Gelpi, D. *The Divine Mother: A Trinitarian Theology of the Holy Spirit.* Lantom: University Press of America, 1984.

Gimbutas, Marija. *The Goddesses and Gods of Old Europe.* Berkeley: University of California Press, 1982.

Giblet, J. *The God of Israel, the God of Christians.* New York: Paulist, 1964.

Gray, J. *The Biblical Doctrine of the Reign of God.* Edinburgh: Clark, 1979.

Heron, A. I. *The Holy Spirit.* Philadelphia: Westminster, 1983.

Huffmon, H. B., et al. *The Quest for the Kingdom of God.* Winona Lake: Eisenbrauns, 1984.

Ingram, K. J. "The Goddess: Can We Bring Her into the Church?" *Spirituality Today* 39 (1987) 39–55.

Johnson, A. R. *The One and the Many in the Israelite Conception of God.* Cardiff: University of Wales Press, 1942, 1961.

Lindstrom, F. *God and the Origin of Evil: A contextual analysis of alleged monistic evidence in the Old Testament.* Trans. by F. H. Cryer. Lund: Gleerup, 1983.

L' Heureux, C. "Searching For The Origins of God." *Traditions in Transformation.* B. Halpern & J. Levenson, eds. Winona Lake: Eisenbrauns, 1981. Pp. 33–58.

Martens, E. A. *God's Design: A Focus on Old Testament Theology.* Grand Rapids: Baker Book House, 1981.

Parke-Taylor, G. H. *Yahweh: The Divine Name in the Bible.* Waterloo: Wilfrid Laurier University Press, 1975, 1977.

Patai, R. *The Hebrew Goddess.* Philadelphia: Ktav, 1967.

Patrick, D. *The Rendering of God in the Old Testament.* Philadelphia: Fortress, 1981.

Roberts, J. J. "Does God Lie? Divine deceit as a Theological Problem in Israelite Prophetic Literature." *Congress Volume Jerusalem 1986*, ed. by J. A. Emerton. Leiden: 1988.

Saggs H. W. *The Encounter with the Divine in Mesopotamia and Israel.* (Jordan Lectures 1976). London: Athlone Press, University of London, 1978.

Sakenfeld, K. D. *Faithfulness in Action.* Philadelphia: Fortress, 1985.

Scott, R. L. *The Hiding God.* Grand Rapids: Baker, 1976.

Smith, M. *The Early History of God: Yahweh and the Other Deities in Ancient Israel.* San Francisco: Harper & Row, 1990.

_____. "God Male and Female in the Old Testament Yahweh and his Asherah." *Theological Studies* 48 (1987) 333–340.

Straumann-Schungel, H. "God as Mother in Hosea 11." *Theological Digest* 34 (1987) 3–8.

Terrien, S. *The Elusive Presence: Toward a New Biblical Theology.* San Francisco: Harper & Row, 1978.

Thompson, A. *Responsibility for Evil in the Theodicy of IV Ezra.* Missoula: Scholars 1977.

Thompson, A. *Who's Afraid of the Old Testament God?* Grand Rapids: Zondervan–Academic, 1989.

Vawter, B. "The God of the Hebrew Scriptures." *Biblical Theology Bulletin* 12 (1982) 3–7.

von Rad, G. *God at Work in Israel.* Nashville: Abingdon, 1980.

Waskow, A. I. *Godwrestling.* New York: Schoken, 1978.

Westermann, C. *What Does the Old Testament Say About God?* Atlanta: John Knox, 1979.

Wifall, W. "Models of God in the Old Testament." *Biblical Theology Bulletin* 9 (1979) 179–86.

Wright, G. E. *The God Who Acts.* London: SCM, 1952, 1962.

Zannoni, A. E. "Feminine Language For God In The Hebrew Scripture." *Dialog and Alliance* 2 (1988) 3–15.

Zimmerli, W. *I Am Yahweh.* Atlanta: John Knox, 1982.

b. Babylonian Exile

Ackroyd, P. R. *Exile and Restoration: a study of Hebrew thought of the sixth century B.C.* London: SCM, 1968; Philadelphia: Westminster, 1972.

_____. *Israel Under Babylon and Persia.* Oxford: Oxford University Press, 1970.

Cross, F. M. "A Reconstruction of the Judean Restoration." *Journal of Biblical Literature* 94 (1975) 4–18.

Kaufman, Y. *The Babylonian Captivity and Deutero-Isaiah.* New York: Union of American Hebrew Congregations, 1970.

Klein, R. W. *Israel in Exile.* Philadelphia: Fortress, 1979.

Klein, R. W., Walter Brueggemann, and John R. Donahue, trans. *Israel in Exile: A Theological Interpretation.* Philadelphia: Fortress, 1979.

Langdon, S. *Babylonian Wisdom.* London: Luzac, 1923.

Mayes, A. D. *The Story of Israel Between Settlement and Exile.* London: SCM, 1983.

Petersen, D. L. *Israelite Prophecy and Prophetic Traditions in the Exilic and Post-Exilic Periods.* Ann Arbor: University Microfilms, 1979.

Raitt, T. *A Theology of Exile.* Philadelphia: Fortress, 1977.

Saggs, H. W. *The Greatness that was Babylon.* London: Sidgwick & Jackson; New York: Hawthorn, 1962.

Smith, D. *The Religion of the Landless: The Social Context of the Babylonian Exile.* Bloomington: Meyer-Stone, 1989.

van Wyk, W. C., ed. *The Exilic Period. Aspects of Apocalypticism.* Pretoria: University of Pretoria, 1984.

Whitley, C. F. *The Exilic Age.* Philadelphia: Westminster, 1957.

c. Sin

Gelin, A. *Sin in the Bible. Old Testament.* Trans. by Charles Schaldenbrand. New York: Desclée, 1965.

Gentz, W. H. *A Study of the Hebrew Words for Sin and Their Contribution to the Old Testament Sin-Concept.* St. Paul: Luther Seminary, 1944.

Haag, H. *Is Original Sin in Scripture?* New York: Sheed & Ward, 1969.

Miller, P. D. *Sin and Judgment in the Prophets: A Stylistic and Theological Analysis.* Chico: Scholars, 1962.

Porubcan, S. *Sin in the Old Testament: A Soteriological Study.* Rome: Herder, 1963.

Van Der Toorin, K. *Sin and Sanction in Israel and Mesopotamia.* Assen–Maastricht: Van Gorcum, 1985.

Wahl, W. E. *A Study of Old Testament Words for Sin.* St. Paul: Luther Northwestern Theological Seminary, 1952.

d. Land

Brueggemann, W. *The Land: Place as Gift, Promise, and Challenge in Biblical Faith.* Philadelphia: Fortress, 1977.

_____. "Reflections on Biblical Understanding of Property." *International Review of Mission* 64 (1975) 354–361.

_____. "The Earth's is the Lord's: A Theology of Earth and Land." *Sojourners* 15 (1986) 28–32.

_____. "Hunger, Food and the Land in the Biblical Witness: The 1986 Zimmerman Lecture." *Lutheran Theological Seminary Bulletin* 66 (1986) 48–61.

_____. "On Land-Losing and Land Receiving." *Dialogue* 19 (1980) 166–173.

Chaikin, M. *Joshua in the Promised Land.* New York: Clarion, 1982.

Clark, W. M. *The Origin and Development of the Land of Promise Theme in the Old Testament.* Ann Arbor: University Microfilms, 1964.

Davies, W. D. *The Territorial Dimension of Judaism.* Englewood Cliffs: Prentice-Hall, 1981.

Evetts, B. T. *New Light on the Bible and the Holy Land, Being an Account of Some Recent Discoveries in the East.* London–Paris: Cassell, 1892.

Hamlin, E. J. *Inheriting the Land: A Commentary on the Book of Joshua.* Grand Rapids: Eerdmans, 1983.

Hoth, I. *The Promised Land: Exodus 20:1-1, Samuel 16:19.* Elgin: D. C. Cook, 1973.

Kaiser, W. C. "The Promise Land: a Biblical Historical View." *Bibliotheca Sacra* 138 (1981) 302–12.

Martens, E. "The Promise of the Land to Israel." *Direction* 5 (1976) 8–13.

Miller, P. " The Gift of God: the Deuteronomic Theology of the Land." *Interpretation* 23 (1969) 451–65.

Vair, R. J. *The Old Testament Promise of the Land as Reinterpreted in 1st and 2nd Century Christian Literature*. Ann Arbor: University Microfilms, 1975.

Wright, C. *God's People in God's Land*. Grand Rapids: Eerdmans, 1991.

Zindle, K. E. *The Theology of the Land in the Prophets*. Philadelphia: Lutheran Theological Seminary, 1975.

e. Covenant

Anderson, B. W. "The New Covenant and the Old." *The Old Testament and Christian Faith*. New York: Herder, 1969. Pp. 225–242.

Angel, M. "Covenant: A Jewish View." *A Dictionary of the Jewish Christian Dialogue*. New York: Paulist, 1984. Pp. 35–37.

Baltzer, K. *The Covenant Formulary in Old Testament, Jewish and Early Christian Writings*. Philadelphia: Fortress, 1971.

Barrett, L. *Doing What is Right. What the Bible Says About Covenant and Justice*. Scottdale: Herald, 1989.

Becker, O. "Covenant, Guarantee, Mediator." *The New International Dictionary of New Testament Theology*. Vol. 1. Grand Rapids: Zondervan, 1975. Pp. 365–376.

Beckwith, R. T. "The Unity and Diversity of God's Covenants." *Tyndale Bulletin* 38 (1987) 93–118.

Berrigan, D. *The Bow in the Clouds; Man's Covenant with God*. New York: Coward-McCann, 1961.

Birch, B. C. "The Covenant at Sinai: Response to God's Freedom." *Social Themes of the Christian Year*. Philadelphia: Geneva, 1983. Pp. 142–148.

Bishop, J. *The Covenant: A Reading*. Springfield: Templegate, 1983.

Bouwmeester, W. *The Bible on the Covenant*. DePere: St. Norbert Abbey, 1966.

Bright, J. *Covenant and Promise*. Philadelphia: Westminster, 1976.

Brueggemann, W. "Covenant as a Subversive Paradigm: the move God has made in heaven opened up for us a new agenda: what is possible on earth." *The Christian Century* 97 (1980) 1094–1099.

_____. "Covenanting as Human Vocation: A Discussion of the Relation of Bible and Pastoral Care." *Interpretation* 33 (1979) 115–129.

Buchanan, G. W. *The Consequences of the Covenant.* Leiden: Brill, 1970.

Buck, H. M. *People of the Lord.* New York: Macmillan, 1965.

Bunn, J. T. "The Covenant with Abraham." *Biblical Illustrator* Fall 14 (1987) 10–13.

Clements, R. E. *Prophecy and Covenant.* Naperville: Allenson, 1965.

Croner, H. and L. Klenicki, eds. *Issues in the Jewish Christian Dialogue: Jewish Perspectives on Covenant Mission and Witness.* New York: Paulist, 1979.

Cross, F. M. "A Brief Excursus on Berit Covenant." *Canaanite Myth and Hebrew Epic: Essays in the History of Religion of Israel.* Cambridge: Harvard University Press, 1973. Pp. 265–73.

Damrosch, D. *The Narrative Covenant: Transformation of Genre in the Growth of Biblical Literature.* New York–San Francisco: Harper & Row, 1987.

Dumbrell, W. J. *Covenant and Creation: An Old Testament Covenantal Theology.* Nashville–New York: Nelson, 1984.

_____. "Creation Covenant and Work." *Evangelical Review of Theology* 13 (1989) 137–156.

Fischer, J. "Covenant Fulfillment and Judaism in Hebrews." *Evangelical Review of Theology* 13 (1989) 175–187.

Fisher, E. "Covenant Theology and Jewish–Christian Dialogue." *American Journal of Theology and Philosophy* 9 (1988) 5–39.

Flanders, H. S., R. W. Crappo, and D. A. Smith. *People of the Covenant.* New York: Oxford, 1988.

Ford, J. M. *Bonded with the Immortal.* Wilmington: Michael Glazier, 1987.

Hartman, D. *Living Covenant.* New York: Free Press, 1985.

Hillers, D. R. *Covenant: The History of A Biblical Idea.* Baltimore: Johns Hopkins Press, 1969.

_____. *Treaty Curses and Old Testament Prophets.* Rome: Pontifical Biblical Institute, 1964.

Ishida, T. *Studies in the Period of David and Solomon.* Winona Lakes: Eisenbrauns, 1982.

Jocz, J. *The Covenant.* Grand Rapids: Eerdmans. 1968.

Kalluveettil, P. *Declaration and Covenant. A Comprehensive Review of Covenant Formulae from the Old Testament and the Ancient Near East.* Rome: Biblical Institute Press, 1982.

Kapelrud, A. S. "The Covenant As Agreement." *Scandinavian Journal of the Old Testament* 1 (1988) 30–38.

Keller, J. "The Covenant of Understanding." *St. Luke's Journal of Theology* 31(1988) 283–294.

Kline, M. G. *By Oath Consigned: A Reinterpretation of the Covenant Signs of Circumcision and Baptism.* Grand Rapids: Eerdmans, 1968.

_____. *Treaty of the King: the Covenant Structure of Deuteronomy.* Grand Rapids: Eerdmans, 1963.

Kline, R. W. "Call, Covenant and Community: The Story of Abraham and Sarah." *Currents in Theology and Mission* 15 (1988) 120–27.

Lacocque, A. "Covenant: A Christian View." *A Dictionary of Jewish Christian Dialogue.* New York: Paulist, 1984. Pp. 35–40.

Levenson, J. D. *Sinai and Zion.* Minneapolis: Winston, 1985.

Malatesta, E. *Interiority and Covenant.* Rome: Pontifical Biblical Institute, 1978.

McCarthy, D. J. *Old Testament Covenant.* Atlanta: John Knox; Oxford: Blackwell, 1972.

_____. "Compact and Kingship: Stimuli for Hebrew Covenant Thinking (1 Sam. 9:16; 10:1; 16:1-13; 10:25; 8:11-17)." *Studies in the Period of David and Solomon.* Winona Lakes: Eisenbrauns, 1982.

_____. "Covenant in Narratives from Late Old Testament Times." *The Quest for the Kingdom of God.* Winona Lake: Eisenbrauns, 1983.

_____. *Institution and Narrative: Collected Essays.* Rome: Biblical Institute Press, 1985.

_____. *Treaty and Covenant: A Study in Form in the Ancient Oriental Documents and in the Old Testament.* Rome: Pontifical Biblical Institute, 1978.

McComiskey, T. E. *The Covenants of Promise: A Theology of the Old Testament Covenants.* Grand Rapids: Baker, 1985.

Mendenhall, G. E. "Covenant Forms in Israelite Tradition." *Biblical Archaeologist* 17 (1954) 50–76.

_____. "Covenant." *The Interpreter's Dictionary of the Bible.* New York–Nashville: Abingdon, 1962.

_____. *Law and Covenant in Israel and the Ancient Near East.* Pittsburgh: The Biblical Colloquium, 1955.

_____. *The Tenth Generation.* Baltimore: Johns Hopkins University Press, 1973.

Merrill, A. L. and T. W. Overholt, eds. *Scripture in History and Theology: essays in Honor of J. Coert Rylaarsdam.* Pittsburgh: Pickwick, 1977.

Murray, J. *The Covenant of Grace: a Biblio-Theological Study.* London: Tyndale, 1953.

Newman, M. L., Jr. *The People of the Covenant: A Study of Israel from Moses to the Monarchy.* New York: Abingdon, 1962.

Nicholson, E. W. *God and His People: Covenant and Theology in the Old Testament.* Oxford: Clarendon, 1986.

Plastaras, J. *Creation and Covenant.* Milwaukee: Bruce, 1968.

Rendtorff, R. "'Covenant' as a Structuring Concept in Genesis and Exodus." *Journal of Biblical Literature* 108 (1989) 385–93.

Riemann, P. A. "Covenant Mosaic." *The Interpreter's Dictionary of the Bible.* Supplementary volume. Nashville: Abingdon, 1976. Pp. 192–197.

Robertson, O. P. *The Christ of the Covenants.* Grand Rapids: Baker, 1980.

Roehrs, W. R. "Divine Covenants: Their Structure and Function." *Concordia Journal* 14 (1988) 7–27.

Ruether, R. R. *"Dimensions of Covenant: Particular, Universal and Messianic." Social Themes of the Christian Year.* Philadelphia: Geneva, 1983.

Rylaarsdam, J. C. "Jewish–Christian Relationship: The Two Covenants and the Dilemmas of Christology." *Journal of Ecumenical Studies* 9 (1972) 249–270.

Sakenfeld, K. D. *Faithfulness in Action.* Philadelphia: Fortress, 1985.

Sperling, S. D. "Rethinking Covenant in Late Biblical Books." *Biblica* 70 (1989) 50–73.

Stamm, J. J. and M. E. Andrew. *The Ten Commandments in Recent Research.* London: SCM, 1967.

Vogels, W. *God's Universal Covenant: A Biblical Study.* Ottawa: University of Ottawa Press, 1979.

Weinfield, M. "Berith" (covenant). *Theological Dictionary of the Old Testament.* Vol. 2. Grand Rapids: Eerdmans, 1975. Pp. 253–279.

_____. "Covenant, Davidic." *The Interpreter's Dictionary of the Bible.* Supplementary Volume. Nashville: Abingdon, 1976. Pp. 188–92.

_____. "Covenant." *Encyclopedia Judaica.* New York: Macmillan, 1971. V, cols. 1011–22.

Wilda, W. M. "The Covenant with Noah." *Biblical Illustrator* 14 (1987) 59–61.

Wilson, R. R. "Enforcing the Covenant: The Mechanisms of Judicial Authority in Early Israel." in *The Quest for the Kingdom of God.* Winona Lakes: Eisenbrauns, 1983.

f. Social Justice

Adamiak, R. *Justice and History in the Old Testament.* Cleveland: Zubal, 1982.

Barrett, L. *Doing What is Right. What the Bible Says About Covenant and Justice.* Scottdale: Herald, 1989.

Birch, B. and L. L. Rasmussen. *Bible and Ethics in the Christian Life.* Minneapolis: Augsburg, 1976.

Birch, B. C. *What Does the Lord Require?: The Old Testament Call to Social Witness.* 1st ed. Philadelphia: Westminster, 1985.

Boecker, H. J. *Law and the Administration of Justice in the Old Testament and Ancient East.* Trans. by Jeremy Moiser. Minneapolis: Augsburg, 1980.

Brueggemann, W. *To Act Justly, Love Tenderly, Walk Humbly: An Agenda for Ministers.* New York: Paulist, 1986.

_____. *Living Toward a Vision: Biblical Reflections on Shalom.* 2nd. ed. New York: United Church, 1982.

Crenshaw, J. L. and J. T. Willis, eds. *Essays in Old Testament Ethics.* New York: Ktav, 1974.

Epztein, L. *Social Justice in the Ancient Near East and the People of the Bible.* London: SCM, 1986.

Harrelson, W. J. *The Ten Commandments and Human Rights.* Philadelphia: Fortress Press, 1980.

Hendrickx, H. *Peace, Anyone? Biblical Reflections on Peace and Violence.* Philippines: Claretian; Bloomington: Meyer Stone, 1989.

_____. *Social Justice in the Bible.* Philippines: A Claretian Book; Bloomington: Meyer Stone, 1989.

Hoppe, L. J. *Being Poor: A Biblical Study.* Wilmington: Michael Glazier, 1987.

Malchow, B. "Social Justice in the Israelite Law Codes." *Word & World* 4 (1984) 299–306.

Mays, J. L. "Justice." *Interpretation* 37 (1983) 5–17.

Phillips, A. *Ancient Israel's Criminal Law.* London: Blackwell, 1970.

Spohn, W. C. *What Are They Saying About Scripture and Ethics?* New York: Paulist, 1984.

Wright, C. J. *Living as the People of God.* Leicester: Inter-Varsity, 1983.

Yoder, P. B. *Shalom: The Bible's Word for Salvation, Justice and Peace.* Newton: Faith and Life, 1987.

g. Preaching

Achtemeier, E. *Preaching From The Old Testament.* Louisville: West-minster–John Knox, 1989.

Barrett, C. K. *Biblical Problems and Biblical Preaching.* Philadelphia: Fortress, 1964.

Birch, B. and L. Rasmussen. *Bible and Ethics in Christian Life.* Minneapolis: Augsburg, 1989.

Bright, J. *The Authority of The Old Testament.* Nashville: Abingdon, 1967.

Carroll, T. K. *Preaching the Word.* Wilmington: Michael Glazier, 1984.

Cox, J. W. *A Guide to Biblical Preaching.* Nashville: Abingdon, 1976.

Craddock, F. B. *Preaching.* Nashville: Abingdon, 1985.

Flannery, A. *The Saving Word. Church Documents.* Wilmington: Michael Glazier, 1986.

Fuller, R. H. *The Use of the Bible In Preaching.* Philadelphia–London: Fortress–Bible Reading Fellowship, 1981.

Greidanus, S. *The Modern Preacher and the Ancient Text. Interpreting and Preaching Biblical Literature.* Grand Rapids: Eerdmans, 1986.

Halton, T. and M. Krupa. *The Saving Word. Patristic Readings.* Wilmington: Michael Glazier, 1986.

Harrington, W. *The Saving Word. Scriptural Commentary.* Wilmington: Michael Glazier, 1986.

Hellwig, M. K. *Gladness Their Escort. Homiletic Reflections for Sundays and Feastdays Years A, B, C.* Wilmington: Michael Glazier, 1987.

Kaiser, W. C. *The Old Testament In Contemporary Preaching.* Grand Rapids: Baker, 1973.

Keck, L. E. *The Bible In The Pulpit: The Renewal of Biblical Preaching.* Nashville: Abingdon, 1978.

Mc Curley, F. *Proclaiming the Promise, Christian Preaching from the Old Testament.* Phildelphia: Fortress, 1974.

Mezzer, M. "Preparation For Preaching–The Route from Exegesis to Proclamation." *Journal For Theology and the Church.* 2 (1965) 159–79.

Sanders, J. A. *God Has a Story Too: Sermons in Context.* Philadelphia: Fortress, 1979.

Sloyan, G. S. *Rejoice and Take it Away. Sunday Preaching from the Scriptures (Years A, B, C).* Wilmington: Michael Glazier, 1984.

Thompson, W. D. *Preaching Biblically: Exegesis and Interpretation.* Nashville: Abingdon, 1981.

Vogels, W. *Reading and Preaching the Bible. A New Approach.* Wilmington: Michael Glazier, 1986.

von Rad, G. *Biblical Interpretations in Preaching.* Nashville: Abingdon, 1977.

Yates, K. M. *Preaching From the Prophets.* Nashville: Broadman, 1942.

X. THE WORLD OF THE OLD TESTAMENT

50. ANTHOLOGIES

Baily, L. *Biblical Perspective on Death.* Philadelphia: Fortress, 1979.

Barr, J. *Biblical Words for Time.* 2nd rev. ed. London: SCM, 1969.

Bickerman, E. J. *Chronology of the Ancient World.* London: Thames & Hudson; Ithaca: Cornell University Press, 1968.

Blaiklock, E. M. *Today's Handbook of Bible Characters.* Minneapolis: Bethany, 1979.

Butler, J. T., E. W. Conrad and B. C. Ollenburger, eds. *Understanding the Word: Essays in Honor of Bernhard W. Anderson.* Sheffield: JSOT Press, 1985.

Childs, B. S. *Myth and Reality in the Old Testament.* London: SCM, 1960.

Davies, W. D. *The Territorial Dimension of Judaism.* Berkeley: University of California Press, 1982.

DeGeus, C. H. *The Tribes of Israel: An Investigation into Some of the Presuppositions of Martin Noth's Amphictyony Hypothesis.* Assen–Amsterdam: Van Gorcum, 1976.

Dyer, G. J. *The Pastoral Guide to the Bible.* Mundelein: Civitas Dei, 1978.

Ellison, H. L. *From Babylon to Bethlehem: The Jewish People from the Exile to the Messiah.* Exeter: Paternoster, 1976.

Edersheim, A. *Old Testament Bible History.* Grand Rapids: Eerdmans, 1972.

Eslinger, L. and G. Taylor, eds. *A Scribe to the Lord. Biblical and Other Studies in Memory of Peter C. Craigie.* Sheffield: JSOT Press, 1988.

Finegan, J. *Handbook of Biblical Chronology: Principles of Time Reckoning in the Ancient World and Problems of Chronology in the Bible.* Princeton: Princeton University Press, 1964.

Gelin, A. *The Key Concepts of the Old Testament.* New York: Sheed & Ward, 1955.

Hanson, P. D. *The People Called: The Growth of Community in the Bible.* San Francisco: Harper & Row, 1986.

Harrison, R. K. *Old Testament Times.* Grand Rapids: Eerdmans; Leicester: Inter–Varsity, 1970, 1972.

Huffmon, H. B., et al., eds. *The Quest for the Kingdom of God. Studies in Honor of George E. Mendenhall.* Winona Lake: Eisenbrauns, 1983.

Kaiser, W. *Hard Sayings of the Old Testament.* Downers Grove: Inter–Varsity, 1988.

Lindsell, H. *The Battle for the Bible.* Grand Rapids: Zondervan, 1976.

Livingstone, E. Z., ed. *Studia Biblica 1978, I –: Sixth International Congress on Biblical Studies.* Oxford: April 3–7, 1978.

Loader, J. A. and J. H. Le Roux, eds. *Old Testament Essays,* Vol. 2. Pretoria: UNISA, 1984.

Martin–Achard, R. *From Death to Life, A Study of the Development of the Doctrine of the Resurrection in the Old Testament.* Edinburgh: Oliver & Boyd, 1960.

Martin, J. D. and P. R. Davies, eds. *A Word in Season: Essays in Honour of William McKane.* Sheffield: JSOT Press, 1986.

Myers, J. M. *Grace and Torah.* Philadelphia: Fortress, 1975.

McKenzie, J. L. "Aspects of Old Testament Thought." *The New Jerome Biblical Commentary.* Ed. by R. Brown et al. Englewood Cliffs: Prentice Hall, 1990. Pp. 1284–1315.

Mendelsohn, A. *Philo's Jewish Identity.* Atlanta: Scholars, 1989.

Meyers, C. L. and M. O'Connor, eds. *The Word of the Lord Shall Go Forth. Essays in Honor of David Noel Freedman in Celebration of His Sixtieth Birthday.* Winona Lake: Eisenbrauns, 1983.

Muilenburg, J. *The Way of Israel.* New York: Harper & Row, 1961.

Noth, M. *The Old Testament World.* Philadelphia: Fortress, 1966.

Pritchard, J., ed. *Ancient Near Eastern Texts Relating to the Old Testament.* 3rd ed. Princeton: Princeton University Press, 1969.

Propp, W. H. *Water in the Wilderness. A Biblical Motif and Its Mythological Background.* Atlanta: Scholars, 1989.

Rowley, H. H. *The Rediscovery of the Old Testament.* Philadelphia: Westminster, 1946.

Smart, J. D. *The Strange Silence of the Bible in the Church.* Philadelphia: Westminster, 1977.

Snaith, N. H. *The Distinctive Ideas of the Old Testament.* London: Epworth, 1950.

Stuhlmueller, C. *New Paths Through the Old Testament.* New York: Paulist, 1989.

Sundberg, A. *The Old Testament of the Early Church. Harvard Theological Studies*, Vol. 20. Cambridge: Harvard University Press, 1964.

Thomas, D. W., ed. *Documents from Old Testament Times.* London–New York: T. Nelson, 1958; New York: Harper, 1961.

Tresmontant, C. *A Study of Hebrew Thought.* New York: Descleé, 1960.

Tromp, N. J. *Primitive Conception of Death and the Nether World in the Old Testament.* Rome: Biblical Institute Press, 1969.

Tuttle, G. A., ed. *Biblical and Near Eastern Studies.* Essays in Honor of William Sanford La Sor. Grand Rapids: Eerdmans, 1978.

Van der Woude, A. S., gen. ed. *The World of the Bible.* Grand Rapids: Eerdmans, 1986, 1988.

_____. *The World of the Old Testament.* Grand Rapids: Erdmans, 1986.

Wilson, R. R. *Sociological Approaches to the Old Testament.* Philadelphia: Fortress, 1984.

Zimmerli, W. *Man and His Hope in the Old Testament.* Naperville: Allenson, 1971.

51. ANCIENT NEAR EASTERN WORLD

Aharoni, Y. *Arad Inscriptions.* Jerusalem: I. E. S., 1981.

Al-khalesi, Y. M. *The Court of the Palms: A Functional Interpretation of the Mari Palace.* Malibu: Undena, 1978.

Albrektson, B. *History and The Gods: An Essay on the Idea of Historical Events as Divine Manifestations in the Ancient Near East and in Israel.* Lund, Sweden: Gleerup, 1967.

Albright, W. F. *The Biblical Period from Abraham to Ezra.* Rev. ed. New York: Harper, 1963.

_____. *The Role of the Canaanites in the History of Civilization.* Rev. ed. Menahsha: reprinted from *Studies in the History of Culture*, February, 1942. Pp. 328–362.

Albright, W. F. *Yahweh and Gods of Canaan.* The Athlone Press, University of London; New York: Doubleday, 1968.

Aling, C. F. *Egypt and Bible History.* Grand Rapids: Baker, 1981.

Amir, D. *Gods and Heroes: Canaanite Epics from Ugarit.* Kibbutz Dan: Beth Ussishkin, 1987.

Anati, E. *Palestine Before the Hebrews.* London: Cape, 1963.

Armstrong, A. H., ed. *Classical Mediterranean Spirituality. Egyptian, Greek, Roman.* New York: Crossroad, 1986.

Attridge, H. W. and R. A. Oden, Jr. *Philo of Byblos: The Phoenician History, Introduction, Critical Text, Translation, Notes.* Washington: Catholic Biblical Association, 1981.

Avishur, Y. and J. Blau. *Studies in Bible and Ancient Near East.* Jerusalem: Rubinstein's, 1978.

Bakonoff, I. M., ed. *Ancient Mesopotamia: Socio Economic History.* Moscow: Nauka, 1969.

Bamberger, B. J. *Essays on Ancient Near Eastern Literature.* Philadelphia: Jewish Publication Society of America, 1981.

Barrick, W. B. and J. R. Spencer, eds. *In the Shelter of Elyon: Essays on Ancient Palestinian Literature in Honor of G. W. Ahlstrom.* Sheffield: JSOT Press, 1984.

Barstone, W., ed. *The Other Bible: Ancient Esoteric Texts from the Pseudepigrapha, the Dead Sea Scrolls, the Nag Hammadi Library, and Other Sources.* San Francisco: Harper and Row, 1984.

Beyerlin, W., ed. *Near Eastern Religious Texts Relating to the Old Testament.* Philadelphia: Westminster, 1978.

Bottéro, J., E. Cassin and J. Vercoutter, eds. *The Near East: The Early Civilizations.* Eng. tr. London: Weidenfeld & Nicholson, 1967.

Cassuto, V. *Biblical and Oriental Studies. Bible and Ancient Oriental Texts, 2.* Trans. by I. Abrahams. Jerusalem: Magnes, The Hebrew University, 1975.

Charles, R. H. *Apocrypha and Pseudepigrapha of the Old Testament.* 2 Vols. Oxford: Clarendon, 1912.

Charlesworth, J. H. *The Old Testament Pseudepigrapha.* 2 vols. Garden City: Doubleday; London: Darton, Longman & Todd, 1983–1985.

Cohen, M. E. *Sumerian Hymnology: The Ersemma.* New York: Ktav, 1981.

Contenau, G. *Everyday Life in Babylon and Assyria.* London: Arnold, 1954.

Coogan, M. *Stories from Ancient Canaan.* Philadelphia: Westminster, 1978.

Cross, F. M., Jr. *Canaanite Myth and Hebrew Epic.* Cambridge: Harvard University Press, 1973.

————, ed. *Symposia Celebrating the Seventy-fifth Anniversary of the Founding of the American Schools of Oriental Research (1900–1975).* (Zion Research Foundation Occasional Publications, 1–2). Cambridge: American Schools of Oriental Research, 1979.

Dalley, S. *Myths From Mesopotamia: Creation, The Flood, Gilgamesh and Others.* New York: Oxford University Press, 1989.

de Vaux, R. *The Bible and the Ancient Near East.* Garden City: Doubleday, 1971.

Dentan, R. C. *The Idea of History in the Ancient Near East.* New Haven: Yale University Press, 1955.

Dever, W. G. "The Peoples of Palestine in the Middle Bronze I Period." *Harvard Theological Review* 64 (1971) 197–226.

Dothan, T. *The Philistines and their Material Culture.* New Haven: Yale University Press, 1982.

Driver, G. R. *Canaanite Myths and Legends.* Edinburgh: Clark, 1956.

Edwards, I. E., C. J. Gadd and N. G. Hammond, eds. *The Cambridge Ancient History.* 3rd ed. Cambridge University Press, 1970.

Eliade, M. *The Sacred and the Profane: The Nature of Religion.* New York: Harper, 1961.

Escobar, J. *Tecoa.* Jerusalem: Franciscan, 1976.

Finegan, J. *Light from the Ancient Past; the Archaeological Background of Judaism and Christianity.* 2nd ed. Princeton: Princeton University Press, 1959.

Finkel, A. and L. Frizzell, eds. *Standing Before God. Studies in Prayer in Scriptures and in Tradition with Essays in Honor of John M. Oesterreicher.* New York: Ktav, 1981.

Fisher, L., ed. *Ras Shamra Parallels: The Texts from Ugarit and the Hebrew Bible.* 2 vols. *Analecta Orientalia* 49, 50. Rome: Pontifical Biblical Institute, 1972, 1976.

Frankfort, H. *Ancient Egyptian Religion.* New York: Columbia University Press, 1948; San Francisco: Harper & Row, 1961.

_____, et al. *The Intellectual Adventure of Ancient Man: An Essay on Speculative Thought In the Ancient Near East.* Chicago: The University of Chicago Press, 1946.

Gardiner, A. *Egypt of the Pharaohs.* Oxford: Oxford University Press, 1966.

Gaster, T. H. *Thespis: Ritual, Myth and Drama in the Ancient Near East.* New York: Schuman, 1950; Doubleday, 2nd ed., 1961.

Gese, H. "The Idea of History in the Ancient Near East and the Old Testament." *Journal for Theology and Church* 1 (1965) 49–64.

Gibson, J. C. *Canaanite Myths and Legends.* Edinburgh: Clark, 1978.

Gordon, C. H. *Before the Bible.* New York: Harper & Row, 1962.

Gray, J. *The Canaanites*. London: Thames & Hudson, 1964.

_____. *The Legacy of Canaan*. 2nd ed. Leiden: Brill, 1965.

Grayson, A. K. *Assyrian and Babylonian Chronicles*. Locust Valley: Augustin, 1975.

Greene, J. T. *The Role of the Messenger and Message in the Ancient Near East*. Atlanta: Scholars, 1989.

Greunwald, I. *Apocalyptic and Merkavah Mysticism*. Leiden–Köln: Brill, 1980.

Gruber, M. I. *Aspects of Nonverbal Communication in the Ancient Near East*. Rome: Biblical Institute Press, 1980.

Gurney, O. R. *Some Aspects of Hittite Religion*. The Schweich Lectures of the British Academy, 1976. Oxford University Press, 1977.

_____. *The Hittites*. Melbourne: Penguin, 1952, 1954; Baltimore: Pelican, 1964.

Hackett, J. A. *The Balaam Text from Deir `Alla*. Chico: Scholars, 1984.

Hallo, W. W. and W. K. Simpson. *The Ancient Near East – A History*. New York: Harcourt, Brace, Jovanovich, 1971.

Hanson, P. D. *The People Called: The Growth of Community in the Bible*. San Francisco: Harper & Row, 1986.

Harper, R. F. *Assyrian and Babylonian Letters*. 14 vols. Chicago: University of Chicago Press, 1892–1914.

Heider, G. C. *The Cult of Molek: A Reassessment*. Sheffield: JSOT Press, 1985.

Hitti, P. K. *History of Syria, including Lebanon and Palestine*. New York: Macmillan, 1951.

Hooke, S. H. *Middle Eastern Mythology*. Baltimore: Penguin, 1963.

Hopkins, D. *The Highlands of Canaan: Agricultural Life in the Early Iron Age*. Sheffield: Almond, 1985.

Irvin, D. *Mytharian. The Comparison of Tales from the Old Testament and the Ancient Near East*. Kevalaer: Butzon and Bercker–Neukirchen-Vluyn: Neukirchener, 1978.

Kenyon, K. M. *Digging Up Jericho.* New York: Praeger, 1957.

Kitchen, K. A. *Ancient Orient and Old Testament.* Leicester–Downers Grove: Inter–Varsity, 1966, 1975.

Kramer, S. N. *History Begins at Sumer.* Garden City: Doubleday, 1959.

_____, ed. *Mythologies of the Ancient World.* Chicago: Quadrangle; Garden City: Doubleday, 1961.

_____. *The Sumerians.* Chicago: The University of Chicago Press, 1963.

Lamsa, G. M. *Old Testament Light. The Indispensable Guide to the Customs, Manners, and Idioms of Biblical Times.* New York: Harper, 1985.

Lichthiem, M. *Ancient Egyptian Literature, I-II.* Berkeley: University of California Press, 1973–76.

Macqueen. J. G. *The Hittites and Their Contemporaries.* New York: Thames & Hudson, 1986.

Malamat, A. "Twilight of Judah: in the Egyptian-Babylonian Maelstrom." *Supplements to Vetus Testamentum* 28 (1975) 123–145.

Mallowan, M. E. *Early Mesopotamia and Iran.* London: Thames & Hudson, 1965.

Margalit, B. *A Matter of 'Life' and 'Death.' A Study of the Baal-Mot Epic.* Neukirchen-Vluyn: Neukirchener, 1980.

Martinez, E. R. *Hebrew-Ugaritic Index II with an Eblaite Index to the Writings of Mitchell J. Danhood.* Rome: Biblical Institute Press, 1981.

Matthews, V. H. *Manners and Customs in the Bible.* Peabody: Hendrickson, 1988.

_____ and D. Benjamin. *Old Testament Parallels: Documents from the Ancient Near East.* Mahwah: Paulist, 1991.

McCurley, F. R. *Ancient Myths and Biblical Faith.* Philadelphia: Fortress, 1983.

Meier, S. A. *The Messenger in the Ancient Semitic World.* Atlanta: Scholars, 1989.

Mellaart, J. *Earliest Civilizations of the Near East.* London: Thames & Hudson; New York: McGraw-Hill, 1965.

Mendenhall, G. E. *Law and Covenant in Israel and the Ancient Near East.* Pittsburgh: Biblical Colloquium, 1955.

Mikasa, T., ed. *Monarchies and Socio-Religious Traditions in the Ancient Near East.* Weisbaden: Harrassowitz, 1985.

Morenz, S. *Egyptian Religion.* Ithaca: Cornell University Press, 1973.

Moscati, S. *Ancient Semitic Civilizations.* Eng. tr. London: Elek, 1957.

_____. *The Face of the Ancient Orient.* Garden City: Doubleday, 1967.

_____. *The World of the Phoenicians.* Eng. tr. London: Weidenfeld & Nicolson, 1968.

Noth, M. *The Old Testament World.* Philadelphia: Fortress, 1966.

O'Brien, J. and W. Major. *In the Beginning: Creation Myths from Ancient Mesopotamia, Israel and Greece.* Chico: Scholars, 1982.

Olmstead, A. T. *The History of the Persian Empire.* The University of Chicago Press, 1948.

Olyan, S. M. *Asherah and The Cult of Yahweh in Israel.* Atlanta: Scholars, 1989.

Oppenheim, A. L. *Ancient Mesopotamia.* Chicago: University of Chicago Press, 1964, 1976.

Parker, S. B. *The Pre-Biblical Narrative Tradition.* Atlanta: Scholars, 1989.

Pitard, W. T. *Ancient Damascus.* Winona Lake: Eisenbrauns, 1987.

Pritchard, J. B. *Ancient Near Eastern Texts Relating to the Old Testament.* 3rd ed. Princeton: Princeton University Press, 1969.

_____. *The Ancient Near East in Pictures Relating to the Old Testament.* Princeton: Princeton University Press, 1954, 1958, 1969, 1975.

_____. *The Ancient Near East: An Anthology of Texts and Pictures.* Princeton: Princeton University Press, 1965.

_____, ed. *The Ancient Near East: Supplementary Texts and Pictures Relating to the Old Testament.* Princeton University Press, 1969.

Ringgren, H. *Religions of the Ancient Near East.* Philadelphia: Westminster, 1973.

Roberts, J. J. "The Ancient Near Eastern Environment." *The Hebrew Bible and Its Modern Interpreters.* D. A. Knight, ed. Chico: Scholars, 1985. Pp. 75–121.

Robinson, J. M., ed. *The Nag Hammadi Library in English.* San Francisco: Harper & Row, 1977.

Rogerson, J. and P. Davies. *The Old Testament World.* Englewood Cliffs: Prentice-Hall, 1989.

Saggs, H. W. *The Greatness That Was Babylon.* New York: Hawthorne, 1962.

Sasson, J. M. *Dated Texts from Mari: A Tabulation.* Malibu: Undena, 1980.

_____. *The Military Establishments at Mari.* Rome: Biblical Institute Press, 1969.

Schwartes, S. *A Short History of the Ancient Near East.* Grand Rapids: Baker, 1975.

Snell, D. C. *A Workbook of Cuneiform Signs.* Malibu: Undena , 1979.

Soggin, J. A. *Old Testament and Oriental Studies. Biblica et Orientalia* 29. Rome: Biblical Institute Press, 1975.

Sonsino, R. *Motive Clauses in Hebrew Law: Biblical Forms and Near Eastern Parallels.* (Society of Biblical Literature Dissertation Series, 45). Chico: Scholars, 1980.

Sparks, H. F., ed. *The Apocryphal Old Testament.* London–New York: Oxford University Press, 1984.

Steindorff, G. and K. C. Seele. *When Egypt Ruled the East.* Chicago: The University of Chicago Press, 1947.

Teixidor, J. *The Pagan God. Popular Religion in the Greco–Roman Near East.* Princeton: Princeton University Press, 1977.

Thomas, D. W. *Documents From Old Testament Times*. New York: Harper & Row, 1961.

Unger, M. F. *Israel and the Arameans of Damascus*. London: Clarke, 1957.

Van der Leeuw, G. *Religion in Essence and Manifestation*. London: Allen & Unwin, 1938; New York: Harper, 2nd ed., 1963.

Walton, J. H. *Ancient Israelite Literature In Its Cultural Content: A Survey of Parables Between Biblical and Ancient Near Eastern Literature*. Grand Rapids: Zondervan, 1989.

Wilson, J. A. *The Burden of Egypt*. Chicago: The University of Chicago Press, 1951.

Wiseman, D. J. *Peoples of Old Testament Times*. Oxford: Clarendon, 1973.

Wright, G. E., ed. *The Bible and the Ancient Near East*. Garden City: Doubleday, 1961.

Yadin, Y. *The Art of Warfare in Biblical Lands*. 2 vols. New York: McGraw-Hill, 1963.

Yamauchi, E. M. *Persia and The Bible*. Grand Rapids: Baker, 1990.

Young, G. D., ed. *Ugarit in Retrospect: Fifty Years of Ugarit and Ugaritic*. Winona Lake: Eisenbrauns, 1981.

52. "HISTORIES" OF ISRAEL

Ahlström, G. W. *Who Were the Israelites?* Winona Lake: Eisenbrauns, 1986.

Albright, W. F. *The Biblical Period from Abraham to Ezra*. New York: Harper, 1963, 1965.

Alt, A. *Essays on Old Testament History and Religion*. London: Blackwell, 1966.

Anderson, G. W. *The History and Religion of Israel. The New Clarendon Bible*. London: Oxford University Press, 1966.

Barr, J. "Story and History in Biblical Theology." *Journal of Religion* 56 (1980) 1–17.

Ben-Sasson, H. H. *A History of the Jewish People.* Cambridge: Harvard University Press, 1976.

Blenkinsopp, J. *A History of Prophecy in Israel from the Settlement in the Land to the Hellenistic Period.* Philadelphia: Westminster, 1983.

Bright, J. *A History of Israel.* 3rd ed. Philadelphia: Westminster, 1981.

_____. *Early Israel in Recent History Writing.* SBT. London: SCM, 1956.

Bruce, F. F. *Israel and the Nations.* Grand Rapids: Eerdmans, 1969.

Buber, M. "Saga and History." *The Writings of Martin Buber.* Ed. by W. Herberg. New York: Meridian, 1956. Pp. 149–56.

Cambridge Ancient History. London: Cambridge University Press, 1975. (Constantly updated.)

Castel, F. *The History of Israel and Judah in Old Testament Times.* Mahwah: Paulist, 1983.

Coote, R. B. and K. W. Whitelam. *The Emergence of Israel in Historical Perspective.* Sheffield: Almond Press, 1987.

Cross, F. M. *Canaanite Myth and Hebrew Epic: Essays in the History of the Religion of Israel.* Cambridge: Harvard University Press, 1973.

Davies, W. D. and L. Finkelstein, eds. *The Cambridge History of Judaism.* Multivolume. Cambridge–New York: Cambridge University Press, 1984.

de Vaux, R. *Ancient Israel.* Eng. tr. London: Darton, Longman & Todd; New York: McGraw-Hill, 1961.

_____. "Method in the Study of Early Hebrew History." *The Bible in Modern Scholarship.* New York: Abingdon, 1963. Pp. 15–29.

_____. *The Early History of Israel.* Vol. 1. Philadelphia: Westminster; London: Darton, Longman & Todd, 1978.

_____. *Ancient Israel: Its Life and Institutions.* New York: Darton, Longman & Todd, 1961.

Eakin, F. E., Jr. *The Religion and Culture of Israel.* Boston: Allyn & Bacon, 1971.

Ehrlich, E. L. *A Concise History of Israel from the Earliest Time to the Destruction of the Temple in A.D. 70.* Eng. tr. London: Darton, Longman & Todd, 1962.

Elliott-Binns, L. E. *From Moses to Elisha; Israel to the End of the Ninth century B. C.* Oxford: Clarendon, 1929.

Flanagan, J. W. *David's Social Drama: A Hologram of Israel's Early Iron Age.* Sheffield: Almond Press, 1988.

Fohrer, G. *History of Israelite Religion.* Nashville: Abingdon, 1972.

Freedman, D. N. and D. F. Graf, eds. *Palestine in Transition: The Emergence of Ancient Israel.* Sheffield: Almond Press, 1983.

Guignebert, C. A. *The Jewish World in the Time of Jesus.* London: Routledge & Kegan Paul, 1939, 1951.

Halpern, B. *The Emergence of Israel in Canaan.* Chico: Scholars, 1983.

_____. *The First Historians: The Hebrew Bible and History.* New York: Harper & Row, 1988.

Harrelson, W. "The Religion of Ancient Israel." *Listening: Journal of Religion and Culture* 19 (1984) 19-29.

Hayes, J. H. and J. M. Miller, eds. *A History of Ancient Israel and Judah.* Philadelphia: Westminster, 1986.

_____, eds. *Israelite and Judaean History.* Philadelphia: Westminster, 1977.

Herrmann, S. *A History of Israel in Old Testament Times.* Philadelphia: Fortress, 1981.

Hinson, D. F. *History of Israel.* London: S.P.C.K., 1973.

Horsley, R. A. and J. S. Hanson. *Bandits, Prophets, and Messiahs: Popular Movements in the Time of Jesus.* Minneapolis: Winston, 1985.

Jagersma, H. *A History of Israel in the Old Testament Period.* Philadelphia: Fortress, 1983.

Johnson, P. *A History of the Jews.* New York: Harper, 1987.

Kaufmann, Y. *The Religion of Israel, from Its Beginnings to the Babylonian Exile.* Chicago: University of Chicago Press, 1960; Schoken, 1972.

_____. *History of the Religion of Israel: From the Babylonian Captivity to the End of Prophecy.* Vol. 4. New York: Ktav, 1977.

_____. *The Religion of Israel.* Chicago: University of Chicago Press, 1966.

Lamsa, G. M. *Old Testament Light. The Indispensable Guide to the Customs, Manners, & Idioms of Biblical Times.* New York: Harper, 1985.

Leaney, A. R. *The Jewish and Christian World 200 B.C. to A.D. 200.* New York: Cambridge University Press, 1984.

Lemche, N. P. *Ancient Israel: A New History of Israelite Society.* Sheffield: JSOT Press, 1988.

Lindblom, J. *Prophecy in Ancient Israel.* Philadelphia: Fortress, 1962.

McCullough, W. S. *The History and Literature of the Palestinian Jews from Cyrus to Herod, 550 B.C. to 4 B.C.* Toronto: University of Toronto Press, 1975.

McCurley, F. R. *Ancient Myths and Biblical Faith: Scriptural Transformations.* Philadelphia: Fortress, 1983.

Meek, T. J. *Hebrew Origins.* Rev. ed. New York: Harper & Row, 1950; Harper, 1960.

Merrill, E. H. *Kingdom of Priests: A History of Old Testament Israel.* Grand Rapids: Baker, 1987.

Miller, J. M. and J. H. Hayes. *A History of Ancient Israel and Judah.* Philadelphia: Westminster; London: SCM, 1986.

Miller, P. D., Jr., P. D. Hanson and S. D. McBride, eds. *Ancient Israelite Religion: Essays in Honor of Frank Moore Cross.* Philadelphia: Fortress, 1987.

Noth, M. *The History of Israel.* London: Black, 1958, 1960; New York: Harper, 1980.

Orlinsky, H. M. *Ancient Israel.* Ithaca: Cornell University Press, 1954.

Payne, D. F. *Kingdoms of the Lord.* Grand Rapids: Paternoster–Eerdmans, 1981.

Pedersen, J. *Israel: Its Life and Culture.* 4 vols. Copenhagen: Povl Branner, 1946–47; London: Oxford University Press, 1953–54.

Ramsey, G. W. *The Quest for the Historical Israel.* Atlanta: John Knox, 1981.

Ringgren, H. *Israelite Religion.* Eng. tr. London: S.P.C.K., 1966; Philadelphia: Fortress, 1966.

Robinson, H. W. *The History of Israel.* London: Duckworth, 1938, 1957, 1963.

Robinson, T. H. *The Decline and Fall of the Hebrew Kingdoms.* Oxford: Clarendon, 1926.

Schmidt, W. *The Faith of the Old Testament.* Philadelphia: Westminster, 1983.

Schürer, E. *The History of the Jewish People in the Age of Jesus Christ.* Vol. I. Rev. ed. by G. Vermes and F. Millar. Edinburgh: Clark, 1973.

Soggin, J. A. *A History of Ancient Israel: From the Beginnings to the Bar Kochba Revolt, A.D. 135.* Philadelphia: Westminster, 1985.

Simpson, C. A. *The Early Traditions of Israel.* Oxford: Blackwell, 1948.

Smith, W. R. *Lectures on the Religion of the Semites: The Fundamental Institutions.* New York: Ktav, 1972.

Snaith, N. H. *The Jews from Cyrus to Herod.* Wallington: Religious Education, 1949.

Talmon, S. *King, Cult and Calendar in Ancient Israel: Collected Essays.* Jerusalem: Magnes, 1986.

Tcherikover, V. *Hellenistic Civilization and the Jews.* Philadelphia: Jewish Publication Society of America, 1959; New York: Atheneum, 1970.

Thompson, T. L. *The Historicity of the Patriarchal Narratives: The Quest for the Historical Abraham.* Berlin–New York: de Gruyter, 1974.

Vriezen, T. C. *The Religion of Ancient Israel* Eng. tr. London: Lutterworth; Philadelphia: Westminster, 1967.

Weippert, M. *The Settlement of the Israelite Tribes in Palestine.* Naperville: Allenson; London: SCM, 1971.

Welch, A. C. *Post-Exilic Judaism.* Edinburgh: Blackwood, 1935.

Wellhausen, J. *Prolegomena to the History of Israel.* Edinburgh: Black, 1957.

Wiseman, D. J., ed. *Peoples of Old Testament Times.* Oxford: Clarendon, 1973.

World History of the Jewish People: Ancient Times. Tel Aviv–Jerusalem: Massada, 1964.

Wright, G. E. *The Old Testament Against Environment.* London: SCM; Chicago: Regnery, 1950.

Wright, A. G., R. E. Murphy and J. A. Fitzmyer "A History of Israel." *The New Jerome Biblical Commentary.* Ed. by R. Brown, et al. Englewood Cliffs: Prentice Hall, 1990. Pp. 1219–1252.

XI. MISCELLANEOUS

53. GENERAL

Adar, Z. *The Biblical Narrative*. Jerusalem: Word Zionist Organization, 1959.

Alexander, G. M. *The Handbook of Biblical Personalities*. New York: Seabury, 1981.

Altmann, A., ed. *Biblical Motifs*. Cambridge: Harvard University Press, 1966.

Bar-Efrat, S. *Narrative Art in the Bible*. Sheffield: Sheffield Academic Press, 1989.

Barker, M. *The Older Testament*. London: S.P.C.K., 1987.

Bartlett, J. R. *Edom and the Edomites*. Sheffield: JSOT Press, 1989.

Bornkamm, H. *Luther and the Old Testament*. Philadelphia: Fortress, 1969.

Bruce, F. F. *The New Testament Development of Old Testament Themes*. Grand Rapids: Eerdmans, 1969.

Brueggemann, W. "Passion and Perspective: Two Dimensions of Education in the Bible." *Theology Today* 42 (1985) 172–180.

_____. "Theodicy in a Social Dimension." *Journal for the Study of the Old Testament* 33 (1985) 3–25.

_____. "Weariness, Exile, and Chaos; A Motif in Royal Theology." *Catholic Biblical Quarterly* 34 (1972) 19–38.

_____. "The Bible and Mission: Some Interdisciplinary Implications for Teaching." *An International Review* (1982) 397–412.

Caird, G. B. *The Language and Imagery of the Bible*. London: Duckworth, 1980.

Charlesworth, J. H. *The Odes of Solomon*. Missoula: Scholars, 1978.

Chouraqui, A. *The People and the Faith of the Bible.* Amherst: University of Massachusetts Press, 1975.

Clements, R. E. *One Hundred Years of Old Testament Interpretation.* Philadelphia: Westminster, 1976.

Collins, J. J. and J. D. Crossan, eds. *The Biblical Heritage in Modern Catholic Scholarship.* Wilmington: Michael Glazier, 1986.

Dannell, G. A. *Studies in the Name Israel.* Uppsala: Appelburgs, 1946.

Davidson, R. F. *The Courage to Doubt: Exploring an Old Testament Theme.* London: SCM, 1983.

Dotan, A. *Ben Asher's Creed. A Study of the History of the Controversy.* Missoula: Scholars, 1977.

Dumm, D. *Flowers in the Desert.* New York: Paulist, 1987.

Durham, J. I. and J. R. Porter, eds. *Proclamation and Presence.* Richmond: John Knox, 1970.

Fogerty, G. P. *American Catholic Biblical Scholarship. A History from the Early Republic to Vatican II.* San Francisco: Harper & Row, 1989.

Fowler, J. D. *Theophoric Personal Names in Ancient Hebrew: A Comparative Study.* Sheffield: JSOT Press, Sheffield Academic Press, 1988.

Freehof, S. B. *Preface to Scripture.* Cincinnati: Union of American Hebrew Congregations, 1950.

Frerichs, E. S., ed. *The Bible and Bibles in America.* Atlanta: Scholars, 1988.

Gaster, T. H. *The Dead Sea Scriptures: In English Translation with Introduction and Notes.* 3rd ed. rev. Garden City: Doubleday, 1976.

Good, E. M. *Irony in the Old Testament.* Sheffield: Almond Press, 1981.

Greenberg, M. *The Hab/piru.* New Haven: American Oriental Society, 1955.

Greenspah, F. E. *Hapax Legomena in Biblical Hebrew.* Chico: Scholars, 1984.

Halpern, B. and J. D. Levenson. *Traditions in Transformation: Turning Points in Biblical Faith.* Winona Lake: Eisenbrauns, 1981.

Harrington, W. *A Cloud of Witnesses: Creative People of the Bible.* Wilmington: Michael Glazier, 1989.

Harvey, V. A. *The Historian and the Believer.* New York: Macmillan, 1966.

Heirs, R. H. *Reading the Bible Book by Book.* Philadelphia: Fortress, 1988.

Herzog, C. and M. Gichon. *Battles of the Bible.* New York: Random, 1978.

Horgan, M. P. *Pesharim: Qumran Interpretation of Biblical Forms.* Washington: Catholic Biblical Association, 1979.

Johnson, A. R. *The Vitality of the Individual in the Thought of Ancient Israel.* Cardiff: University of Wales Press, 1949.

Kaiser, W. C., Jr. *A Biblical Approach to Personal Suffering.* Chicago: Moody, 1982.

Katsh, A. I. *The Biblical Heritage of American Democracy.* New York: Ktav, 1977.

Kaye, B. and G. Wenham, eds. *Law, Mortality, and the Bible: A Symposium.* Downers Grove: Inter–Varsity, 1977.

Knight, D. A. and G. M. Tucher, eds. *The Hebrew Bible and Its Modern Interpreters.* Philadelphia: Fortress, 1985.

Kraeling, E. G. *The Old Testament Since the Reformation.* London: Lutterworth, 1955.

Kushner, L. *When Bad Things Happen to Good People.* New York: Schocken, 1981.

L'Heureux, C. E. *Life Journey and the Old Testament.* New York: Paulist, 1986.

Levenson, J. D. *Creation and the Persistence of Evil.* San Francisco: Harper & Row, 1988.

Levison, J. R. *Portraits of Adam in Early Judaism: From Sirach to 2 Baruch.* Sheffield: JSOT Press, 1988.

Long, B. O. *Images of Man and God: Old Testament Short Stories in Literary Focus*. Sheffield: Almond Press, 1981.

Lund, S. and J. Foster. *Variant Versions of Targumic Traditions Within Codex Neofiti 1*. Missoula: Scholars, 1977.

Malchow, B. "Contrasting Views of Nature in the Hebrew Bible." *Dialog* 26 (1987) 40–43.

McAlpine, T. H. *Sleep, Divine and Human, in the Old Testament*. Sheffield: JSOT Press, 1987.

McCarthy, C. and W. Riley. *The Old Testament Short Story: Exploration into Narrative Spirituality*. Wilmington: Michael Glazier, 1986.

McFarland, D. *Who & What & Where in the Bible*. Atlanta: John Knox, 1973.

McNamara, M. *Intertestamental Literature*. Wilmington: Michael Glazier, 1983.

Mettinger, T. N. *The Dethronement of Sabaoth. Studies in the Shem and Kabod Theologies*. Lund: Gleerup, 1982.

Morris, L. *Testaments of Love. A Study of Love in the Bible*. Grand Rapids: Eerdmans, 1981.

Muilenburg, J. *The Way of Israel: Biblical Faith and Ethics*. New York: Harper, 1961.

Neusner, J. *Christian Faith and the Bible of Judaism*. Grand Rapids: Eerdmans, 1987.

_____. *The* Tosefta *Translated from the Hebrew Sixth Divinisin,* Tohorot *(The Order of Purities)*. New York: Ktav, 1977.

Niditch, S. *Underdogs and Tricksters, A Prelude to Biblical Folklore*. San Francisco: Harper & Row, 1987.

Nigosian, S. A. *Occultism in the Old Testament*. Philadelphia: Dorrance, 1978.

O'Connor, M. P. and D. N. Freedman, eds. *Background for the Bible*. Winona Lake: Eisenbrauns, 1987.

Orlinsky, H. M., ed. *The Library of Biblical Studies*. Cincinatti: Hebrew Union College Press, 1969.

Phipps, W. E. *Recovering Biblical Sensuousness.* Philadelphia: Westminster, 1975.

Rendtorf, R. *Men of the Old Testament.* Philadelphia: Fortress, 1968.

Robinson, H. W. *Corporate Personality in Ancient Israel.* Philadelphia: Fortress, 1980.

Robinson, J. J., ed. *The Nag Hammadi Library.* San Francisco: Harper & Row, 1978.

Rogerson, J. W. *Myth in Old Testament Interpretation.* Berlin–New York: de Gruyter, 1974.

_____ and B. Lindars. *The Study and Use of the Bible.* Grand Rapids: Eerdmans, 1988.

Rosner, F. *Medicine in the Bible and the Talmud.* New York: Ktav, 1977.

Rost, L. *Judaism Outside the Hebrew Canon.* Nashville: Abingdon, 1976.

Scott, R. W. *A New Look at Biblical Crime.* Chicago: Nelson Hall, 1979.

Seale, M. S. *The Desert Bible: Nomadic Tribal Culture and Old Testament Interpretation.* New York: St Martin's, 1974.

Sheehan, J. F. *Let the People Cry Amen.* New York: Paulist, 1977.

Silverman, M. H. *Religious Values in the Jewish Proper Names at Elephantine.* Neukirchen–Vluyn: Neukirchner; Kevelaer: Butzon & Bercker, 1985.

Smally, B. *The Study of the Bible in the Middle Ages.* Notre Dame: University of Notre Dame Press, 1964, 1978.

Sundberg, A. C. *The Old Testament of the Early Church.* Cambridge: Harvard University Press, 1964.

Tamez, E. *Bible of the Oppressed.* Maryknoll: Orbis, 1982.

The Bible and People Who Lived and Wrote It: A Layman's Discovery of the Fascination of the Old Testament and of Its Influence on the New. 1st ed. New York: Exposition, 1955.

Trump, D. *Primitive Conceptions of Death and the Nether World in the Old Testament.* Rome: Biblical Institute Press, 1969.

Tsevat, M. *The Meaning of the Book and Other Biblical Studies: Essays on the Literature and Religion of the Hebrew Bible.* New York: Ktav, 1980.

Vanderkam, J. C. *Textual and Historical Studies in the Book of Jubilees.* Missoula: Scholars, 1977.

Van Ruler, A. A. *The Christian Church and the Old Testament.* Grand Rapids: Eerdmans, 1971.

Vermes, G. and M. D. Goodman, eds. *The Essenes According to the Classical Sources.* Sheffield: JSOT Press, 1989.

Walher, W. O., ed. *Harper's Biblical Pronunciation Guide.* San Francisco: Harper & Row, 1989.

Weber, H. R. *Experiments with Bible Study.* Philadelphia: Westminster, 1981.

Westermann, C. *The Old Testament and Jesus Christ.* Minneapolis: Augsburg, 1970.

Wilson, M. R. *Our Father Abraham. Jewish Roots of the Christian Faith.* Grand Rapids: Eerdmans, 1989.

Wink, W. *The Bible in Human Transformation: Towards a New Paradigm for Biblical Study.* Philadelphia: Fortress, 1973.

54. SEMANTICS AND LINGUISTICS

Barr, J. *Comparative Philology and the Text of the Old Testament.* London–New York: Oxford University Press, 1968.

_____. *The Semantics of Biblical Language.* London–New York: Oxford University Press, 1961.

Caird, G. B. *The Language and Imagery of the Bible.* London: Duckworth; Philadelphia: Westminster, 1980.

Calloud, J. "A Few Comments on Structural Semiotics: A Brief Explanation of a Method and Some Explanation of Procedures." *Semeia* 15 (1979) 51–83.

Gibson, A. *Biblical Semantic Logic: A Preliminary Analysis.* Oxford: Blackwell; New York: St. Martin's, 1981.

Cotterell, P. and M. M. Turner. *Linguistics and Biblical Interpretation.* Downers Grove: Inter-Varsity, 1989.

Louw, J. P. *Semantics of the New Testament Greek.* Chico: Scholars; Philadelphia: Fortress, 1982.

Nickelsburg, G. W. *Jewish Literature Between the Bible and the Mishnah. A Historical   and Literary Introduction.* Philadelphia: Fortress, 1981.

Nida, E. A. and C. R. Taber. *The Theory and Practice of Translation.* 2nd edition. Leiden: Brill, 1982.

Sawyers, J. F. *Semantics in Biblical Research.* London: SCM, 1972.

Taber, C. R. "Semantics." *The Interpreter's Dictionary of the Bible.* Supplementary Volume. Pp. 800–807.

55. THE OLD TESTAMENT IN THE NEW TESTAMENT

Archer, G. L. and G. Chirichigno. *Old Testament Quotations in the New Testament.* Chicago: Moody, 1983.

Black, M. "The Christological Use of the Old Testament in the New Testament." *New Testament Studies* 18 (1971) 1–14.

Bratcher, R. G. *Old Testament Quotations in the New Testament.* London–New York–Stuttgart: United Bible Studies, 1984.

Chilton, B. D. *A Galilean Rabbi and His Bible. Jesus' Use of the Interpreted Scripture of His Time.* Wilmington: Michael Glazier, 1984.

Dodd, C. H. *According to the Scriptures. The Sub-Structure of New Testament Theology.* London: Collings, 1965.

Doeve, J. W. *Jewish Hermeneutics in the Synoptic Gospels and Acts.* Assen: Van Gorcum, 1954.

Fitzmyer, J. A. "The Use of Explicit Old Testament Quotations in Qumran Literature and in the New Testament." *New Testament Studies* 7 (1961) 297–333.

France, R. T. *Jesus and the Old Testament. His Application of Old Testament Passages to Himself and His Mission.* Grand Rapids: Baker, 1982.

Goppelt, L. *Typos. The Typological Interpretation of the Old Testament in the New.* Grand Rapids: Eerdmans, 1982.

Hanson, A. T. *The Living Utterance of God. The New Testament Exegesis of the Old.* London: Darton, Longman and Todd, 1983.

Josipovici, G. *The Book of God: A Response to the Bible.* New Haven: Yale, 1988.

_____. *The New Testament Interpretation of Scripture.* London: S.P.C.K., 1980.

Lindars, B. *New Testament Apologetic. The Doctrinal Significance of Old Testament Quotations.* Philadelphia: Westminster, 1961.

_____ and P. Borgan. "The Place of the Old Testament in the Formation of the New Testament Theology. Prolegomena and Response." *New Testament Studies* 23 (1976) 59–75.

Shires, H. M. *Finding the Old Testament in the New.* Philadelphia: Westminster, 1974.

56. PERIODICALS

Note: The following list of technical and non-technical journals in the field of biblical studies has been selected on the basis of their usage of the English language and their accessibility in the United States of America. The list is *not* intended to be exhaustive or encyclopedic but rather functional. It is provided for the reader to help him/her keep abreast of recent developments in the area of biblical research.

American Journal of Archaeology
Anglican Theological Review
Annual of the Swedish Theological Institute
Archaeology
Bible Review
Bible Today
Bible Translator
Biblica
Biblical Archaeologist
Biblical Archaeology Review
Biblical Illustrator
Biblical Reports

Biblical Research
Biblical Theology Bulletin
Bibliotheca Sacra
Bulletin of Biblical Studies
Bulletin of the American Schools of Oriental Research
Catholic Biblical Quarterly
Chicago Studies
Downside Review
Evangelical Review of Theology
Expository Times
Harvard Theological Review
Hebrew Union College Annual
Horizons in Biblical Literature
Interpretation
Journal for the Study of the Old Testament
Journal of Biblical Literature
Journal of Near Eastern Studies
Journal of the Ancient Near Eastern Society
New Blackfriars
Old Testament Abstracts
Old Testament Essays
Review and Expositor
Scandinavian Journal of the Old Testament
Scottish Journal of Theology
Scripture Bulletin
Semeia
Shofar
Southwestern Journal of Theology
Studia Biblica et Theologia
The Evangelical Quarterly
The Furrow
The Journal of the Ancient Near Eastern Society
Tyndale Bulletin
Union Seminary Quarterly
Vetus Testamentum
Word and Spirit
Zeitschrift für die Alttestamentliche Wissenschaft

XII. EXCURSUS: BIBLICAL FUNDAMENTALISM

Ammerman, N. T. *Bible Believers: Fundamentalists in the Modern World.* New Brunswick: Rutgers University Press, 1987.

Averill, L. J. *Religious Right, Religious Wrong. A Critique of the Fundamentalist Phenomenon.* New York: Paulist, 1989.

Barr, J. *Beyond Fundamentalism.* Philadelphia: Westminster, 1984.

_____. *Fundamentalism.* Philadelphia: Westminster, 1978.

Boone, K. C. *The Bible Tells Them So: The Discourse of Protestant Fundamentalism.* Albany: State University of New York Press, 1989.

Caplan, L. *Studies in Religious Fundamentalism.* Albany: State University of New York Press, 1987.

Cole, S. G. *The History of Fundamentalism.* New York: R. R. Smith, 1931.

Daschbach, E. *Interpreting Scripture: A Catholic Response To Fundamentalism.* Dubuque: Religious Education Division, W. C. Brown, 1985.

Gasper, L. *The Fundamentalist Movement.* The Hague: Mouton, 1963.

Gilles, A. *Fundamentalism, What Every Catholic Needs to Know.* Cincinnati: St. Anthony Messenger, 1984.

Girdleston, R. G. *Synonyms of the Old Testament: Their Bearing on Christian Doctrine.* Grand Rapids: Eerdmans, 1987.

Hamann, H. P. *The Bible Between Fundamentalism and Philosophy.* Minneapolis: Augsburg, 1980.

Hebert, G. *Fundamentalism and the Church of God.* London: SCM, 1957.

Keating, K. *Catholicism and Fundamentalism: The Attack on "Romanism" by "Bible Christians."* San Francisco: Ignatius, 1988.

Marrow, S. B. *The Words of Jesus In Our Gospels: A Catholic Response to Fundamentalism.* New York: Paulist, 1979.

Marsden, G. M. *Fundamentalism and American Culture: The Shaping of Twentieth Century Evangelism, 1870–1925.* New York: Oxford University Press, 1980.

Neuhaus, R. J. and M. Cromartie, eds. *Piety and Politics: Evangelicals and Fundamentalists Confront the Word.* Washington, D.C.: Ethics and Public Policy Center; Lanham: University Press of America, 1987.

Neuhaus, R. J. *What the Fundamentalists Want.* Washington, D.C.: Ethics and Public Policy Center, 1985.

Noll, M. A. *Between Faith and Criticism: Evangelicals, Scholarship, and the Bible in America.* San Francisco: Harper & Row, 1986.

O' Meara, T. F. *Fundamentalism: A Catholic Perspective.* Mahwah: Paulist, 1990.

Packer, J. I. *'Fundamentalism' and the Word of God.* Grand Rapids: Eerdmans, 1958.

Petersen, P. D. *Evangelicalism and Fundamentalism: A Bibliography Selected from the ATLA Religion Database.* Chicago: American Theological Library Association, 1983.

Sandeen, E. R. *The Origins of Fundamentalism: Toward a Historical Interpretation.* Philadelphia: Fortress Press, 1968.

_____. *The Roots of Fundamentalism.* Chicago: Chicago University Press, 1970; Grand Rapids: Baker, 1970.

Selvidge, M. J. *Fundamentalism Today: What Makes it so Attractive!* Elgin: Brethren, 1984.

Valbracht, L. H. *The Follies of Fundamentalism.* Lima: C. S. S., 1974.

INDEX OF NAMES

Winter, M. M., 195
Winter, R. D., 195
Winton, T. D., 65
Winward, S., 152
Wiseman, D. J., 205, 238, 243
Wiseman, P. J., 81
Wolf, H. M., 155
Wolff, H. W., 27, 42, 81, 152, 170,
    172, 174, 175, 176, 178, 182, 204
Wonneberger, R., 7
Wood, C. M., 200
Wood, J., 56, 120
Wood, J. D., 120
Wood, L. J., 152
Woodbridge, J. D., 243
Woods, R. R., 122
Worden, T., 130
Woudstra, M. H., 97
Wright, A. G., 138, 140, 196, 243
Wright, C., 220, 225
Wright, G. E., 2, 31, 65, 67, 81, 87,
    94, 97, 155, 200, 203, 217, 238,
    243
Wright, J. S., 110, 140
Wright, R. A., 243
Wuellner, W., 47
Wurthwein, E., 7, 39

Yadin, Y., 65, 195, 238
Yahuda, A. S., 72
Yamauchi, E. M., 238
Yates, K. M., 12, 227
Yee, G. A., 171
Yoder, P., 27
Yoder, P. B., 36, 225
Yohannan, J. D., 81
Young, E. J., 27, 155
Young, G. D., 9, 238
Young, N., 81
Young, R., 16
Young, W. A., 81

Zannoni, A. E., 91, 113, 120, 130,
    217
Zeitlin, S., 211
Zerafa, P. P., 135
Zevit, Z., 87
Zimmerli, W., 120, 152, 158, 160,
    200, 217, 230
Zimmermann, F., 15, 140, 191
Zindle, K. E., 220
Zlotowitz, B. M., 165
Zylstra, H., 211